A SCOTTISH MURDER

*Rewriting the
Madeleine Smith
Story*

About the Author

Jimmy Powdrell Campbell is an historian and composer. He has researched several areas of Scottish history and has scripted and participated in many BBC Radio and TV documentaries. His research into the Madeleine Smith case began in 1991 for a stage production in the Edinburgh Fringe Festival and, in the 2003 Fringe, he produced the full musical. His review of the case is also to form the basis of a screenplay. He lives in Stirlingshire.

A SCOTTISH MURDER

Rewriting the Madeleine Smith Story

JIMMY POWDRELL CAMPBELL

TEMPUS

Front cover: Picture of Madeleine Smith by courtesy of the
Mitchell Library, Cultural & Leisure Services, Glasgow City
Council; letter from Madeleine Smith to Pierre Emile L'Angelier
and envelope by courtesy of the National Archives of Scotland.

Back cover: The scene in Court by courtesy of David Warrilow.

First published 2007

Tempus Publishing
Cirencester Road, Chalford
Stroud, Gloucestershire, GL6 8PE
www.tempus-publishing.com

Tempus Publishing is an imprint of NPI Media Group

British Library Cataloguing in Publication Data.
A catalogue record for this book is available from the British Library.

ISBN 978 07524 4008 8

Typesetting and origination by Tempus Publishing Limited
Printed in Great Britain

Contents

To the memory of Maryann

List of Illustrations

Acknowledgements

Grateful thanks to:

David Warrilow, artist, the owner of the 1857 *London Illustrated* artist's drawing of the trial, for his permission to use the image and also for taking the trouble to take the photographs; Corinthian Restaurant, Ingram St, Glasgow, owners of the painting of David Hamilton (Hamilton was the architect of the bank that is now the Corinthian); Graham Hopner, Dumbarton Library; William Morris Society; Society for the Protection of Ancient Buildings; Linda Parry (previously at the V&A); Victoria and Albert Museum ; the late Nick Salmon; many staff, past and present, in the Mitchell Library, Glasgow; Mr A. Aitken – 'The David Hamilton Collection' (Mitchell Library); Rosalind Prince, Leek Library, Leek, Staffs.; Maclay, Murray & Spens, solicitors and notaries, Glasgow; the Earl of Crawford and Balcarres K T; John Allan, L.L.B., Callander; Falkirk Library; Falkirk County Buildings; Alloa Library; Perth Library; the Scottish National Archives; Hunterian Museum, Glasgow University; Societe Jersaise (Jersey Archives); Miss C. Easterbrook, Jersey; Martha & Steven Boyd; Ron and Alice Milne, Jersey; Mrs Newall, Rhu; Mrs Woods, Rhu.

Chapter One

Thursday, 9 July 1857 – The atmosphere outside the High Court in Edinburgh was charged to fever pitch as the crowd awaited the verdict at the end of the most sensational trial of the century. Hanging in the balance was the life of Madeleine Smith, attractive twenty-two-year-old daughter of a prosperous Glasgow architect. Over the last few days, revelations of Madeleine's secret romance had been making headlines in London, Paris and New York. By the end of the trial, in spite of widespread belief in her guilt, sympathy had swung towards Madeleine and the crowds cheered when news of the Not Proven verdict reached the street. Madeleine was free to leave the court but never was she free from suspicion.

The *New York Herald* announced:

> We devote this morning half our available space to the trial of Madeleine Smith, the young Scotch lady who was accused of murdering her lover by poison. Our readers will probably find it the most thrilling narrative of crime, passion and judicial inquiry that has ever fallen under their notice. No case, in any volume of celebrated causes, can compare with it for vividness of interest, intense passion and dramatic effect.

At twenty-two years of age, Madeleine Smith, eldest daughter of Glasgow architect, James Smith, had become public property. Her story

– the murder of Emile L'Angelier – had all the ingredients: sex, ambition, blackmail, poison and, of course, mystery. Her remarkable composure throughout the trial only added fuel to the fire; it was as shocking to some as it was admirable to others. She 'stepped up into the dock with all the buoyancy with which she might have entered the box of a theatre … ' Even so, her place in history was not assured until the foreman of the jury rose and slowly and distinctly read out the verdict. The *New York Herald* journalist reported that, 'when the last Not Proven is reached, loud cheers and hurrahs and hand-clappings rend the rafters, and are raised again and again, deafening the angry judges who strive in vain to still the tumult.' This reaction was yet another feature that sets the case apart. Many of Madeleine Smith's supporters believed that she may, indeed, have committed murder, such was their contempt for the deceased. At the extremes, some asserted that the only tragedy was that she had had to do it herself when, had they known the circumstances, so many would have been willing to dispatch L'Angelier on her behalf.

Madeleine's hope, expressed after the trial, that 'God Almighty may yet unveil the mystery', was never realised in her lifetime. One hundred and fifty years on, and the case continues to be rediscovered with tedious regularity. Madeleine's supposedly enigmatic character has been explored in films, plays, newspaper articles and an endless succession of books. The path is deep and wide with footsteps leading to the same anti-climactic conclusion that the jury arrived at in 1857. I suppose it's the mystery that holds our interest but there remains another story to be told, and it deals with one simple question that, incredibly, has remained unanswered for all that time: what really happened?

The traditional version, which has put food on the table for many an author, can be told very simply. Spoiled society belle, Madeleine Smith, meets rather interesting French packing clerk, Pierre Emile L'Angelier. Her father forbids the relationship but she continues to see L'Angelier secretly. They write literally hundreds of letters to each other. They meet whenever they can, even if only at her basement-bedroom window. They fall in love. They make love. They plan to marry in secret (although Emile would prefer to have the blessing of Madeleine's parents).

But time passes and Madeleine meets another man, William Minnoch, a friend of the Smith family. Minnoch proposes. Madeleine accepts and she writes to L'Angelier to end the affair. Emile, however, can't live without her. He's willing to do anything to get her back. He reminds her of all the letters she's written, letters in which she expresses her feelings very candidly, rather too explicitly. If her father saw those letters …

Madeleine can't marry Minnoch while L'Angelier is around. She can see only one way out. She calmly walks into the local chemist and buys arsenic. When L'Angelier next comes for their usual assignation at the basement-bedroom window, she passes a cup of cocoa through the stanchions. The first attempt merely makes him ill so she repeats the procedure and, on the third occasion, she succeeds. On the morning of Monday 23 March 1857, L'Angelier dies of arsenic poisoning.

It's a passably entertaining story as evidenced by the number of times it has been told but it is a work of utter fiction and no less so for all the repetition. The principal players are caricatures, figments of the imagination and that, perhaps, has been an obstacle for students of the case since 1857. Without an understanding of the real Madeleine Smith, the real Emile L'Angelier, the riddle of L'Angelier's death would almost certainly, as Tennyson Jesse confidently predicted, have remained unsolved.

The public response to the evidence, as printed, almost verbatim, in every major newspaper was overwhelmingly supportive of the accused. As soon as the trial was over, however, began the analysis, the speculation, and the humbug about declining moral standards. This was Victorian Scotland and the Presbyterian hypocrisy of the time was still in full vigour. Here was a lesson to us all. A girl from a thoroughly respectable family, with every benefit of a sound upbringing and education … a family who respected the Sabbath and met for prayers every Sunday evening. Which of us could say their own house was in better order? The explicit sexual references in her letters were shocking but, in themselves, it was not they that were criminal. This girl had given herself to L'Angelier and, under Scots Law, she was his wife. It was her treachery that condemned her. She was not born evil but she had chosen evil, and her descent into depravity had begun as soon as she entered into a clandestine relationship. That foul murder should be the conclusion of this spiral of degeneracy must come as no surprise.

Before long, like Richard III, even Madeleine's features and demeanour became unattractive. Her composure was now a defiance; her smile became a smirk; she grew a 'hawkish nose, a steely eye and a determined jaw.' Phrenologists were enlisted to examine the bumps on Madeleine's head; graphologists, psychologists and criminologists were likewise recruited to lend weight to the latest author's pronunciations. Who can argue with an 'ology'?

A few years ago, Madeleine's great-granddaughter was contacted by a writer who was working on the case. A meeting was arranged and the writer's wife came along too. At one point, Madeleine's great-granddaughter, conscious of being scrutinised, said, 'if you're thinking I look anything like Madeleine, I don't. I take after my mother's side of the family.' The writer's wife said, 'oh no, it's just that he likes to study the criminal mind.'

The case certainly affords an unique insight into the workings of an extremely unhealthy and criminal mind but that writer, like so many before him, was looking in entirely the wrong direction. It's human nature. We form an impression about a person based upon what we have observed or what we have been told. From that point on, it's next to impossible to see that person, or their context, in any other way. It might be complete and utter nonsense but, once established, it's very hard to rid our minds of that first impression. Who was Madeleine Smith? Oh, she was that Glasgow girl who murdered her French boyfriend … arsenic, wasn't it?

It is the connotations that do the most damage, the adjectives that immediately spring to mind: cold, callous, heartless … well, she must have been, to do what she did. With the best will in the world, we can't un-create the Madeleine that has now been established in the minds of so many. This, however, is the story of an altogether different girl of the same name.

This Madeleine Smith was the granddaughter of the architect David Hamilton. Born 11 May 1768, Hamilton grew up in a Glasgow which gave little indication of the grandeur that was to visit the 'Second City of the Empire' over the next hundred years. Glasgow's Queen Street was then a muddy track called Cow Loan, along which cattle were driven to pasture in the 'Cowcaddens'. They would pass by the area now occupied by George Square, then a large hollow filled with green water, on the banks of which dead horses were being skinned. Only a short distance away in the Trongate, the Tobacco Lords, with their scarlet cloaks, cocked hats and huge wigs could be seen 'pacing the plain stanes'. The combination of industry and trade with the colonies was now beginning to bring prosperity and, more than ever before, the city was in need of builders to reflect its increasing status.

David Hamilton had progressed from stonemason to architect by the age of twenty-two and, four years later, he married sixteen-year-old Magdalene Marshall, daughter of a Glasgow wine merchant. They had twelve children over the next twenty years and, during that period, a succession of civic, domestic and ecclesiastic works was to take him to the top of the profession in the West of Scotland. Hamilton is remembered with respect and affection as a man almost devoid of self-interest, and one whose qualities seemed always to inspire admiration without envy. The only criticism that can be found to have been levelled against him was to the effect that he had a tendency to forget the passage of time when enjoying good company. Thomas Gildard, a pupil of Hamilton's, left us these recollections of the Father of Glasgow Architecture:

In December 1838, I was apprenticed for five years with Messrs David & James Hamilton, whose office was at the head of Buchanan Street, on the site now occupied by the Langham Hotel. The house was a self-contained one of three stories, the first a few steps above the street. On the street floor, the office was to the right of the entrance lobby and Mr Hamilton's room to the left, and behind were kitchens, servants' quarters etc. Up one stair was a very handsome room which served the purpose of both dining-room and drawing-room, and a library of a somewhat unique plan which could be connected with it. Behind, and in the floor above were bedrooms.

Mr Hamilton was in about his seventieth year, and was a man of most impressive presence, frank and kindly in manner, and with a bearing of easy dignity. He was what is commonly or conventionally called somewhat 'aristocratic' in appearance, and in social intercourse was distinguished by much grace and courtesy. He was a man eminently to be looked up to. James, his son, who had not much more than attained his majority, was tall and remarkably handsome, his fine features somewhat of an Italian cast, and his long, glossy black hair rolling in ringlets.

When I entered the office the late Mr Rochead had been in it six months a draughtsman and my friend, Mr Baird, a year or two. As the house and office were together, the lads, as we were called, were occasionally favoured by a visit from Mrs Hamilton and her daughters; indeed, Mrs Hamilton looked in almost every morning, took a seat, and had a kindly chat with us for half-an-hour or so. It seemed almost as if we were living 'in family' and although it is a long time since, there remains with me a pleasant impression of the homely, hearty kindness that I experienced from all the Hamiltons under the old-fashioned arrangement of house and office together. Occasionally we dined in state with the family and sometimes we were favoured with a Saturday excursion to some important work in progress in the country.

Mr Hamilton had formed an excellent library of not only great books on architecture but of books illustrative of painting and sculpture. He had also many choice line engravings and other things that might be expected in the house of a family all of inborn and suave and highly cultivated taste. He was the recognised head of the profession. His position was unique and as his fame had gone beyond, he had, I might almost say, frequent visits from men of eminence in the arts, bearing letters of introduction.

I remember seeing Kemp, the architect of the Scott Monument, and Mr Hamilton bringing him down stairs to see the office.

Mr James (Hamilton), Mr Rochead and Mr Baird were alike assiduous in the instructing of the apprentices; if there was a fault at all, it was in the apprentices being dealt with too much like pupils instead of being made immediately useful.

The office hours were from nine till seven, the hour between four and five being the interval for dinner. On Saturdays the office closed at four. There was no gas in the office and, in the winter evenings we wrought by candlelight.

Of all of David Hamilton's works, perhaps the most familiar to Glaswegians is the Royal Exchange (now the Gallery of Modern Art) in Queen Street. When the foundation stone was laid in 1827, work was nearing completion on the new Royal Bank building which stands to the rear of the Exchange, and the builders who had secured the lucrative bank contract were the company of John Smith & Son, from Alloa. By a happy coincidence, the then head of the Royal Bank in Glasgow was another Alloa man, John Thomson, son of Thomas Thomson, a well-known Alloa merchant and maltster. Here, evidently, was a bank manager who believed in supporting family businesses. John Smith was his brother-in-law.

In contrast to the innate integrity and selflessness of David Hamilton, the Smiths, both father and son, were businessmen, first and foremost. They were amiable and social gentlemen, but it wouldn't do either of them justice to portray them as paragons of virtue. There was always the feeling that, on occasion, they may over-enthusiastically embrace the prevailing economic theory that risk returns profit. Smith's firm was contracted for the building of the Royal Exchange and worked also on the surrounding proper-ties of Royal Exchange Square. James Smith, at twenty years of age, could see that industry (and networking) did not go unrewarded.

Six years later, he and David Hamilton's daughter Janet were mar-ried. Their first daughter, Magdalene (Madeleine) Hamilton Smith, was born on 29 March 1835. Betsy, John, James and Janet were to follow. It might seem, at that time, that the Smith's business interests went from strength to strength but, in reality, there had been many setbacks and reverses. The most serious occurred in 1843 when the Glasgow Marine, one of several insurance companies in which the Smiths held directorships, declared that it had lost its entire paid-up capital. Within weeks, both John and James Smith were bankrupt.

John Smith's estate Birkenshaw (now Rouken Glen public park, Renfrewshire), the fruit of many years of work, was sold to pay creditors but another, much less important property, was to become the subject of some controversy. A Glasgow solicitor, Alexander Manson, tried for several years to bring John Smith to justice, claiming that Smith had backdated the sale of one of his commercial properties in Glasgow, subsequent to the publication of his sequestration. Manson's accusations, which led to a series of libel cases, alleged the complicity of several well-known Glasgow figures, including the Lord Provost and the Procurator Fiscal.

Hopefully, their descendants will forgive me for, thus far, having presented the Smith family in a less than favourable light. The fact is that their assiduity and industry was endless, their contribution to the city of Glasgow was inestimable and, if a man's character can, in any degree, be inferred from his associations, his popularity, or from the loyalty his friendship engenders, both John and James Smith can only be judged considerable men. On 5 December of that same year, David Hamilton died. Few of his contemporaries would have believed that, in the years to come, his fame would be surpassed by the notoriety of his granddaughter.

Prosperity returned and by the 1850s James Smith was right back at the hub of Glasgow society. Madeleine was sent to a Clapton finishing school, Miss Gorton's, where she made a best friend of another Scottish girl, Mary Buchanan. Mary, born only a fortnight before Madeleine, was the daughter of Dumbarton surgeon, banker and magistrate, Dr Robert Buchanan and Mary Dixon of the Dumbarton Glassworks family. The two girls promised each other that whichever should marry first, the other would be bridesmaid. Madeleine had grown into a very desirable young woman; confident, vivacious, and just naïve enough to become involved with a man from a world she didn't even know existed.

James Smith had been one of several Glaswegians involved in the erection of a statue of the Duke of Wellington, commemorating the British victory at Waterloo, never thinking that he would, one day, pay a personal price for the insecurity and disharmony that ensued amongst the French populace in the aftermath of the allied victory. Rumours of the atrocities of the 'White Terror' had spread quickly and many of those who had supported Napoleon's return had reason to feel somewhat uneasy.

Two brothers, both nurserymen, Francoise and Rene L'Angelier evidently decided that enough was enough and left their home in Normandy to start a new life in the Channel Islands. Francoise later married Melanie de la Croix, also from Normandy, and the first of their five children, Emile, was born on 30 April 1823. Melanie, it should perhaps be mentioned, was very proud of sharing the surname of the marquises and dukes of Castries. This was possibly not unconnected with the fact that, in the course of Emile's upbringing, he was to acquire something approaching a sense of entitlement and inborn importance that, while sitting somewhat incongruously with the reality of his circumstances, would nevertheless influence both his manners and his aspirations throughout his life.

When he was sixteen, Emile was apprenticed for five years to another nurseryman, Bernard Saunders, but in 1842, after three years of his apprenticeship had been served, Emile's father died and shortly after that a customer at the Saunders nursery, Sir Francis Mackenzie of Gairloch, was somehow persuaded to take Emile to Scotland. One of the many myths that have become attached to this story is that Emile, under the guidance of Sir Francis, was set to become a trainee in estate management and it may well be that both Emile and his mother entertained some such belief in his prospects, provided he could continue to raise himself in the esteem of this seemingly wealthy Scottish laird.

Sir Francis Mackenzie was certainly a good-hearted and generous man. During the famine of 1836–37 he put his own finances at risk by sending cargoes of food to his tenants on the Gairloch estate. This, and similar acts of magnanimity, had eventually put him in debt. He found Emile a position with an Edinburgh seed merchant, Dickson & Co. in Waterloo Place (fate has a sense of humour). The story goes that 'Sir Francis had taken a great liking to Emile' and before taking him to his estates in the north Sir Francis intended to 'inure Emile by degrees' to the harsh climate of Scotland. However, the notion that Edinburgh was warmer than the Gairloch estate could not have come from Sir Francis, but only from someone who didn't know Scotland at all. The Gairloch estate has the mildest climate in Scotland. The youngest son of Sir Francis MacKenzie was the founder of the famous Inverewe Gardens whose unique position with respect to the Gulf Stream permits the growth of plants that would normally survive only in a sub-tropical climate. If Sir Francis had had any desire to employ Emile on his estate, in any capacity, it certainly wouldn't have been the climate that prevented him from doing so.

From 1842 until at least 1846, Emile worked with Dicksons. He spent some time on the continent in the late 1840s but by 1851 we find him back in Edinburgh, staying at the Rainbow Tavern. The owner's nephew Robert Baker, who shared a room with Emile, recalled:

He lived in the Rainbow between six and nine months, as far as I recollect. L'Angelier's circumstances were very bad; he was living on Mr Baker's bounty, waiting there till he got a situation. I thought him a quiet sort of person but he was very easily excited, at times subject to low spirits. I have often seen him crying at night. Latterly, before he went to Dundee, he told me he was tired of his existence and wished himself out of the world. I remember on one occasion he got out of bed and went to the window and threw it up. I rose out of bed and went to him, and he said that if I had not disturbed him he would have thrown himself out. The windows of the Rainbow are about six stories from the ground, the height of the North Bridge. He was in the habit, very often, of getting up at night and walking up and down the room in an excited state, weeping. He had met with a disappointment in love. It was about some lady in Fife. He was in distress about not having a situation in order to enable him to keep to his engagement with her.

Emile's distress was real enough but his predicament could never have been resolved by his having a situation. This girl came from a well-known Fifeshire family with titled connections. The lady may have succumbed to his Gallic charm but, job or no job, as far as her parents were concerned the idea of her marriage to Emile was not just unthinkable, it was the stuff of nightmares. They saw him off, *toute de suite*.

Dublin merchant, Edward Volkes MacKay, was in the habit of staying at the Rainbow when he came to Edinburgh. 'I had several meetings and conversations with L'Angelier,' MacKay said.

I saw quite enough of him to enable me to form an opinion of his character and disposition and formed anything but a good opinion of him. I considered him a vain, lying fellow. He was very boastful of his personal appearance, and parties admiring him, ladies particularly. He boasted of his high acquaintances repeatedly, and the high society he had moved in. He mentioned several titled people whom he had known but, not believing anything he was saying at the time, I did not store up in my mind any of their titles.

Shortly before he went to Dundee I came on him one evening in Princes Street Gardens. He was sitting by himself with his head in his handkerchief. I put my hand on him and said, 'L'Angelier.' He held up his head, and I could see he had been crying. He mentioned that a lady in Fifeshire had slighted him, but I made light of the matter. He made a long complaint about her family.

It might have seemed to MacKay that Emile's tears were for a lost love but it will later become clear that a lost fortune would be a more apt description. He was a planner and a manipulator with a grandiose sense of his rightful place in society. Like an infant, his relationship with the world was almost entirely passive. He had not the slightest aversion to soliciting sympathy but lacked any natural empathy with others, and viewed the rest of humanity only in terms of how their actions impacted upon him, what they were doing to him, what they could do for him. Incapable of seeing beyond his own desires, he genuinely had no understanding of why her family should find him unacceptable.

In January 1852, Emile started work with Dundee seed merchant William Laird. Emile impressed his new employer as being,

> a very sober young man, and very kind and obliging; rather excitable and changeable in his temper, sometimes very melancholy and sometimes very lively. It was maybe a fortnight or a month after he came, that he told me that he had been crossed in love. He told me it was reported that the girl was to be married to another but that he could scarcely believe it, because he did not think she could take another. I understood that that was because she was pledged to him. He told me who she was.

Laird had evidently discussed this unlikely relationship with his brother who later sent him a letter asking if Emile had seen the notice of the girl's marriage in the *Scotsman* newspaper. He had.

> One of the apprentices told me something which led me to speak to L'Angelier. I told him I was sorry to see him so melancholy and sad, and that I was still more so to hear that he had taken up a knife to stab himself. He said he was truly miserable, and that he wished he was out of the world, or words to that effect. After this, he was gloomy and moody, hardly speaking to anyone.

His distress over the lady in Fife was evidently less acute by the time he told nurseryman William Anderson that he was on 'very intimate' terms with two girls in Dundee, 'both very beautiful girls, and worth a considerable sum of money.' Anderson also remembered Emile making a strange comment on the subject of being jilted. 'He said something to the effect that he would have revenge on them in some shape or other if they did jilt him.'

Emile's time in Dundee also revealed an unusual piece of information about his predilections which, like his views on the propriety of revenge, would in time acquire a crucial significance. William Ogilvie, a teller in the Dundee Bank, recalled that Emile had entertained him with an account of his time in France. It seems he had been travelling with 'with some person of distinction' and had charge of all their luggage, carriages, and horses. Finding the horses exhausted, Emile had apparently given them some arsenic. He explained that it refreshed them sufficiently for them to complete the journey. Asked if he was not afraid of poisoning them, he went on to say that he was quite sure there was no danger; he'd taken it himself. He mentioned that it improved the complexion. Ogilvie also remembered seeing him, on more than one occasion, eat handfuls of poppy-seeds in the shop. Emile admitted to him that, when he was with Dickson's, he had 'taken poppy-seeds in such quantities that he had got quite giddy with them.'

David Hill, another employee at Laird's, spoke of having found a small parcel that he believed to contain arsenic. He later mentioned this to Emile and was told, 'that's nothing strange; I use it regularly.'

The practice of using arsenic as a drug was not at all unknown in the nineteenth century, and particularly on the Continent. In Britain, its effects were being discussed in magazine and newspaper articles. The 'arsenic-eaters' might be expected to have bright eyes, a rosy complexion and a general feeling of well-being ... if they survived.

On 9 September 1852, Madeleine's father submitted plans for a major development in Glasgow's Sauchiehall Street. He and Glasgow businessman and art collector, Archibald McLellan, were banking on Sauchiehall Street's continued increase in popularity as a fashionable shopping centre. The entire block was to be taken over for the building of a multi-purpose complex, fronted by up-market stores with housing above, an exhibition centre and, central to the theme, a conference centre and art galleries extending to the rear.

Only a few days earlier, Emile L'Angelier had arrived in Glasgow to take up a new post as a packing clerk with W.B. Huggins and Co., one of the city's mercantile houses. His prospects there might have seemed limited but that was not really important; Emile's ambitions had little to do with advancement in the workplace. At that time, Glasgow was a hive of industry, and commerce. His optimism was restored by the sheer potential of it. His landlady, Mrs Elizabeth Wallace, knew him only as a well-conducted, cheerful young man, who kept good hours and no company. He played the guitar at night and sung occasionally. She understood that he had been a lieutenant in the navy but that he had been out of work for some time.

Not long after his arrival, Emile became acquainted with the chancellor to the French Consul at Glasgow, Auguste De Mean. He told De Mean that he had once been 'jilted by an English lady, a rich person,' and he admitted that on account of that disappointment he was 'almost mad for a fortnight, and ran about, getting food from a farmer in the country.' According to De Mean, Emile was 'easily excited and very much affected when he had any cause of grief.' He also remembered Emile speaking to him about arsenic. 'I don't remember how the conversation arose,' he said. 'It lasted about half an hour. Its purport was how much arsenic a person could take without being injured by it. He maintained that it was possible to do it by taking small quantities.'

The consequences, however, of taking arsenic in any quantity could, now and then, be quite unpleasant. Emile, it might be said, appeared to be a martyr to his digestive system and several acquaintances were to be treated to the delights of his company on the occasions of his violent stomach upsets and cholera-like symptoms. On a visit to De Mean's lodgings, Emile was late in coming to dinner. De Mean called on him, complaining that he was being kept from his meal, and Emile replied weakly that he would be along immediately. Emile still not appearing, De Mean went out and found him quite unwell and vomiting down the staircase.

Emile had become a regular member of the congregation at St Jude's church and sat in the same pew as forty-two-year-old, Irish-born merchant, William D'Esterre Roberts. Roberts, who also held the somewhat precarious appointment of Consul for Haïti, was married to Christina McCall Brown, granddaughter of George McCall, one of Glasgow's esteemed tobacco lords. Being naturally drawn to the company of the well-heeled, Emile became acquainted with Roberts and managed an invitation to dinner on Christmas Day 1853. Roberts remembered that:

> there were a few friends at dinner. When the ladies retired L'Angelier became very ill, and wished to leave the room. I went with him, and came back to the dining-room, and remained some time. I wondered why he did not come. I opened the dining-room door, and heard a groan as of some person vomiting. I found him very ill – vomiting and purging. A good many gentlemen came out of the room and saw him. I sent for cholera mixture, and gave him a good deal of it. He nearly emptied the bottle. I got very much frightened, as cholera had been in the town shortly before. After a time, one of the gentlemen took him in a cab to his lodgings. He called on me the next day, or day after that, to apologise for his illness. He was nearly two hours, ill in my house.

Obviously, any number of things might have occasioned these illnesses but it does no harm at this point simply to bear in mind that Emile was no stranger to these symptoms.

Another member of the St Jude's congregation was Miss Mary Perry, sister of a Glasgow drysalter who lived in comfortable circumstances at 144 Renfrew Street. She first met Emile in 1853 but it was not until the spring of 1855 when, distressed at the news of his brother's death, he found a sympathetic friend in Miss Perry. She was then almost thirty-eight years old, exactly six years older than Emile. They found they had much in common and he became a frequent visitor, occasionally dining with her.

While it might seem absurd to speculate as to what they discussed, there was one subject that could not fail to arise. By the spring of

1855, Miss Perry's front windows, on the north side of Renfrew Street, commanded an expansive vista of the dull, plain, red sandstone rear wall of the beautiful new McLellan Galleries. Designed by architect, James Smith, the soon-to-be-opened and much-publicised galleries were a topic of conversation throughout the town. If that was not enough, Miss Perry's house at 144 Renfrew Street was also situated between the architect's workshops at number 100, and the architect's home for the last two years, 100 paces away, at number 164. The Smith family had only recently moved away. She didn't actually know them personally but what she knew about them, and their eldest unmarried daughter, was of more than passing interest to Emile. He would discover that the Smiths were wealthy, respected and one of the most influential families in the city, exactly what Emile wanted for himself. Perhaps he didn't quite possess Smith's talent, drive or acumen but he was confident of one asset that he did have: he was attractive to women.

He had to go no further than his place of work to find someone who did know the Smiths. A colleague at Huggins was in a position to have introduced L'Angelier to Madeleine Smith but the direct approach doesn't appear to have been an option. He first became acquainted with the man's nephew, Charles Baird and then with Charles's seventeen-year-old brother, Robert. The younger brother proved to be easier to manipulate. He asked Robert, repeatedly, if he could arrange an introduction to Madeleine. Robert thought it would be better to come from his uncle who, of course, knew Emile from Huggins, but his uncle refused. Emile persisted and Robert next asked his mother if she would invite Madeleine to their house some evening that he might invite Emile. She too refused. In the end, Emile persuaded Robert to help him contrive an introduction in the street.

Soon to celebrate her twentieth birthday, Madeleine Smith was described by a contemporary as being 'strikingly attractive, stylish, confident, with dark hair and the most entrancing grey eyes … Her appearance in any of Glasgow's public promenades or in its social circles was always marked with an admiring welcome and a flattering sensation.' She was accompanied by her sister Bessie when Robert Baird and Emile 'chanced' upon them in Bath Street. Robert told Madeleine that his friend wished to be introduced to her. Madeleine jokingly replied that she presumed he 'would not introduce her to any improper person.' Presumably, regardless of the subtext, etiquette was observed on that first occasion but Emile subsequently way-laid Bessie and gave her a note to pass on to her older sister. Bessie, according to her own statement, seems to have taken an immediate dislike to him. She told Madeleine that she was 'averse to recognize him,' and she was later to explain that she refused to notice him since she 'did not think he was a respectable person.' Madeleine, however, accepted the invitation to meet him in Sauchiehall Street.

There was never the remotest possibility of Emile being accepted by Mr and Mrs Smith as suitable company for their daughter but the inevitable clandestine nature of the affair, as it progressed from pleasant conversation to a passionate intimacy, only served to increase the already uncontrollable attraction and the thrill of this *liaison dangereux*.

My dear Emile, I do not feel as if I were writing to you for the first time. Though our intercourse has been very short, yet we have become as familiar friends. May we long continue so. And ere long, may you be a friend of papa's is my most earnest desire. We feel it rather dull here in Rhu after the excitement of a town's life. But then we have much more time to devote to study and improvement. I often wish you were near us. We could take such charming walks. One enjoys walking with a pleasant companion and where could we find one equal to yourself?

I am trying to break myself off all my very bad habits. It is you I have to thank for this for which I do sincerely from my heart ... We'll be in town next week. We are going to the ball on the 20th, so we'll be several times in Glasgow before that. Papa and Mama are not going to town next Sunday. So, of course you do not come to Rhu. We shall not expect you. Bessie desires me to remember her to you. Write on

Wednesday or Thursday. I must now say adieu. With kind love, believe me, yours very sincerely, Madeleine.

The ball, on 20 April 1855, was the opening ball of the McLellan Galleries. Written at Rowaleyn, the Smith's country house at Rhu near Helensburgh, this was the first of a series of letters that Madeleine would write to Emile over the next two years. His lodgings were now in Glasgow's West End with Mr Clark, the curator of the Botanic Gardens.

My Dear Emile, Many thanks for your last kind epistle. We are to be in town tomorrow (Wednesday). Bessie said I was not to let you know. But I must tell you why! Well, some friend was kind enough to tell Papa that you were in the habit of walking with us. Papa was very angry with me for walking with a gentleman unknown to him. I told him he had been introduced, and I saw no harm in it. Bessie joins with Papa and blames me for the whole affair. She does not know I am writing to you so don't mention it.

We are to call at our old quarters in the Square on Wednesday about quarter past 12 o'c. So if you could be in Mr McCall's lodgings – see us come out of Mrs Ramsay's – come after us – say you are astonished to see us in Town without letting you know – and we shall see how Bessie acts.

… Rest assured that I shall not mention to anyone that you have written me. I know, from experience, that the world is not lenient in its observations. But I don't care for the world's remarks so long as my own heart tells me I am doing nothing wrong. Only if the day is fine, expect us tomorrow. Not a word of this letter. Adieu till we meet. Believe me, yours most sincerely, Madeleine.

Miss Perry, who, almost certainly unwittingly, had brought Madeleine to Emile's attention, now helped the course of this far-from-true love by occasionally providing a respectable venue for their secret meetings. By July 1855 Madeleine and Emile were talking of marriage but this also brought a brief interruption of the relationship with Madeleine informing Emile that her father would not give his consent. The inference that she had actually spoken to her father isn't quite plausible. Madeleine had never entertained any serious belief that her parents would even consider Emile as husband material; her father had made his feelings abundantly clear. The reality, the hopelessness of the situation seems to have finally registered and, in a moment of sanity, she writes to finish with him.

Hardly surprisingly, none of Emile's original letters to Madeleine have survived. This, however, was not just a difficult moment in an otherwise normal relationship. Emile had planned this relationship from the start and he wasn't about to let Madeleine spoil everything. He had to think ahead. He had to be mindful that this correspondence, and his conduct at this moment, may have to stand up to future scrutiny. He, the injured party, had to be seen to be beyond reproach. Like a cautious litigant, he kept a draft copy of his reply.

In the first place, I did not deserve to be treated as you have done. How you astonish me by writing such a note without condescending to explain the reasons why your father refuses his consent. He must have reasons, and I am not allowed to clear myself of accusations. I should have written you before, but I preferred awaiting until I got over the surprise your last letter caused me, and also to be able to write you in a calm and a collected manner, free from any animosity whatever.

Never, dear Madeleine, could I have believed you were capable of such conduct. I thought and believed you unfit for such a step. I believed you true to your word and to your honour. I will put questions to you which answer to yourself. What would you think if even one of your servants had played with anyone's affections as you have done, or what would you say to hear that any lady friends had done what you have – or what am I to think of you now? What is your opinion of your own self after those solemn vows you uttered and wrote to me. Show my letters to any one, Madeleine, I don't care who, and if any find that I mislead you I will free you from all blame. I warned you repeatedly not to be rash in your engagement and vows to me, but you persisted in that false and deceitful flirtation, playing with affections which you know to be pure and undivided, and knowing at the same time that at a word from your father you would break all your engagement.

You have deceived your father as you have deceived me. You never told him how solemnly you bound yourself to me, or if you had, for the honour of his daughter he could not have asked to break of an engagement as ours. Madeleine, you have truly acted wrong. May this be a lesson to you never to trifle with any again. I wish you every happiness. I shall be truly happy to hear that you are happy with another. You desire and now you are at liberty to recognise me or cut me just as you wish – but I give you my word of honour I shall act always as a Gentleman, towards you. …Think what your father would say if I sent him your letters for a perusal. Do you think he could sanction your breaking your promises. No, Madeleine, I leave your conscience to speak for itself. I flatter myself he can only accuse me of a want of fortune. But he must remember he too had to begin the world with dark clouds round him. I cannot put it into my mind that yet you are at the bottom of all this.

The veiled threat was probably unnecessary. Madeleine was more than a willing partner in her own destruction although, to be fair, she had no idea of what kind of man she was dealing with.

In keeping with the fashionable conceits of the day, a pretension to a love of virtue and an aspiration to self-improvement were common topics in their correspondence. Neither Emile nor Madeleine would be vaguely conscious of their own insincerity as they strove to impress in terms that might be most appreciated by the other. Each existed only as a creation of the other's imagination. The entire relationship was a fantasy or rather, two very different fantasies. Emile's dream lay almost entirely in the future: his destiny, he believed, was to be respected and admired as a man of distinction. At twenty years old, Madeleine's experience of the world was so much more limited than a modern mind might imagine. She had been blessed with a real, flesh and blood, secret French lover. Surely most girls of her age could only dream of such passion, such romance. Above all, for

Madeleine, this was a thing of the present. She was the wealthy young girl who would be spirited away by her handsome but impoverished hero. She now signed her letters to Emile, 'Mimi L'Angelier.'

> My own darling husband, I did not expect the pleasure of, seeing you last evening, of being fondled by you, dear, dear, Emile. I trust ere long to have a long, long interview with you, sweet one of my soul, my love, my all, my own best beloved. I hope you slept well last evening, and find yourself better to-day. … Is it not horrid cold weather? I did, my love, so pity you standing in the cold last night, but I could not get Janet to sleep – little stupid thing. … My own sweet beloved, I can say nothing as to our marriage. … I fear the Banns in Glasgow, there are so many people know me. If I had any other name but Madeleine it might pass – but it is not a very common one. … Sweet love, I adore you with my heart and soul. I must have a letter from you soon. … Much much love kisses tender long embraces kisses love. I am thy own thy ever fond, thy own dear loving wife, thy Mimi L'Angelier.

During the winter of 1855/6, when the family were in Glasgow, they lived in India Street and for a time there Madeleine had an arrangement with the Smiths' maid Christina Haggart, by which Emile would address his letters to Christina. There was a mutual understanding since Christina's future husband, Duncan McKenzie, was a regular caller at the back door of the house in India Street, but it was short-lived. It was discovered by Mrs Smith, and Christina was left in no doubt that the deception must never be repeated. Mrs Smith confronted Madeleine and insisted upon her giving her word never again to see or write to L'Angelier. Mrs Smith believed that was an end to the matter and it seems Mr Smith was not told about it. Madeleine, nevertheless, continued to see Emile and to write to him. She also continued to count on Christina's help. Occasionally, she would ask Christina to open the back gate for Emile, which facilitated the odd half hour of privacy in the laundry room.

It's easy to forget that outside of this disastrous career of passion and romance, Madeleine's natural, normal family life continued as before. Even among the lines of the fateful correspondence, there is a glimpse here and there of another story that reaches out precisely because it is so unremarkable, so precious, so fragile. From Rowaleyn, she writes, 'I have got a new employment – the hen yard. I go there every morning. You can fancy me every morning at 10 o'clock seeing the hens are fed and feeding my donkey. I don't get on very fast with it – I fear it has little affection – do for it what I shall, it only appears to know me and come to me when I call.'

In June 1856, in the grounds of Rowaleyn, they made love for the first time. Once again, Emile keeps a draft copy of his letter to Madeleine:

> My dearest and beloved Wife Mimi, since I saw you I have been wretchedly sad. Would to God we had not met that night – I would have been happier. I am sad at what we did, I regret it very much. Why, Mimi, did you give way after your promises? My pet, it is a pity. Think of the consequences if I were never to marry you. What reproaches I should have, Mimi. I never shall be happy again. If ever I meet you again, love, it must be as at first. …
> Truly, dearest, I am in such a state of mind I do not care if I were dead. We did wrong. God forgive us for it. Mimi, we have loved blindly. It is your parents' fault if shame is the result; they are to blame for it all.
>
> I got home quite safe after leaving you, but I think it did my cold no good. I was fearfully excited the whole night. I was truly happy with you, my pet; too much so, for I am now too sad. I wish from the bottom of my heart we had never parted. Though we have sinned, ask earnestly God's forgiveness and blessings that all the obstacles in our way may be removed from us. I was disappointed, my love, at the little you had to say, but I can understand why. You are not stupid, Mimi, and if you disappoint me in information, and I have cause to reproach you of it, you will have no one to blame but yourself, as I have given you warning long enough to improve yourself. Sometimes I do think you take no notice of my wishes and my desires, but say yes for mere matter of form.
>
> Mimi, unless Huggins helps me I cannot see how I shall be able to marry you for years. What misery to have such a future in one's mind.

Do speak to your brother, open your heart to him, and try and win his friendship. Tell him if he loves you to take your part. And besides, my dear, if once you can trust, how pleasant it would be for you and me to meet. I could come over to Helensburgh when you would be riding or driving, or of a Sunday. I could join you in a walk of a Sunday afternoon. Mimi, dearest, you must take a bold step to be my wife. I entreat you, pet, by the love you have for me, Mimi, do speak to your mother – tell her it is the last time you ever shall speak of me to her. You are right, Mimi, you cannot be the wife of any one else than me. I shall ever blame myself for what has taken place. I never never can be happy until you are my own, my dear fond wife. Oh! Mimi, be bold for once, do not fear them – tell them you are my wife before God. Do not let them leave you without being married, for I cannot answer what would happen. My conscience reproaches me of a sin that marriage can only efface.

I can assure you it will be many days before I meet such nice people as the Seaverights, especially the daughter. I longed so much to have introduced you to her, to see the perfect lady in her, and such an accomplished young person. My evenings, as you say, are very long and dreary. We must not be separated all next winter, for I know, Mimi, you will be as giddy as last. You will be going to public balls, and that I cannot endure. On my honour, dearest, sooner than see you or hear of you running about as you did last, I would leave Glasgow myself. Though I have truly forgiven you, I do not forget the misery I endured for your sake. You know yourself how ill it made me, if not, Mary can tell you, my pet.

... I do not understand, my pet, your not bleeding, for every woman having her virginity must bleed. You must have done so some other time. Try to remember if you never hurt yourself in washing, &c. I am sorry you felt pain. I hope, pet, you are better. I trust, dearest, you will not be with child. Be sure and tell me immediately you are ill next time, and if at your regular period. I was not angry at your allowing me, Mimi, but I am sad it happened. You had no resolution. We should indeed have waited till we were married, Mimi. It was very bad indeed. I shall look with regret on that night. No, nothing except our Marriage will efface it from my memory. Mimi, only fancy if it was known. My dear, my pet, you would be dishonoured, and that by me! Oh! why was I born, my pet? I dread lest some great obstacle prevents our marriage. If Mary did know it, what should you be in her eyes?

… I cannot help doubting your word about flirting. You promised me the same thing before you left for Edinburgh, and you did nothing else during your stay there. You cared more for your friends than for me. I do trust you will give me no cause to find fault again with you on that score, but I doubt very much the sincerity of your promise. Mimi, the least thing I hear of you doing, that day shall be the last of our tie, that I swear. You are my wife, and I have the right to expect from you the behaviour of a married woman or else you have no honour in you; and more, you have no right to go any where but where a women could go with her husband. Oh! Mimi, let your conduct make me happy. Remember when you are good how truly happy it makes Emile – but remember this, and if you love me you will do nothing wrong.

Dearest, your letter to Mary was very pretty and good. I thought a great deal of it, and I like its seriousness. Fancy how happy I was when Mary told me the other day how Mimi was improving fast; she could tell it by her letters.

For God's sake burn this, Mimi, for fear any thing happening to you, do dearest.

It's true; love conquers all: judgement, common sense, instinct and natural revulsion. So, it was all her fault; 'she had no resolution.' Somehow, the relationship survived this horrendous epistle but the event did mark a turning point. Once they had made love, and he was able to talk in terms of his right to expect the behaviour of a wife, there was, for the first time, a very real ambivalence. For all the talk of marriage, Madeleine had not the slightest inclination to give up her independence, nor did she feel that, just by having sex with Emile, she had lost any more than her virginity. She was now in real danger of her repressed feelings about Emile finding a route to surface, and this was no mythical Victorian sexual repression; this was the natural unconscious distaste that any woman would have for what, in reality, amounted to a very weak man. For the time being, it would remain unconscious. Her love for Emile continued to be expressed passionately and extravagantly in line after line, with only the odd hint at rebellion:

> My own, my darling husband, to-morrow night by this time I shall be in possession of your dear letter. I shall kiss it and press it to my bosom. Hearing from you is my greatest pleasure, it is next to seeing you, my sweet love. My fond Emile, are you well, darling of my soul? This weather is enough to make one ill, is it not? We have had most dull, wet days – but I have had time to read and practise, which is a comfort to me. I am well. I am longing so to see you, sweet pet – to kiss and pet you. Oh! for the day when I could do so at any time. I fear we shall spoil each other when we are married, we shall be so loving and kind. We shall be so happy, happy in our own little room – no one to annoy us, to disturb us. All to ourselves, we shall so enjoy that life. The thought of these days makes me feel happy. If it were not for these thoughts I should be sad, miserable, and weary of this cold, unfeeling, thoughtless world. Wealth is the ruling passion. Love is a second consideration, when it should be the first, the most important.
>
> … True and constant shall I prove. Don't fear me. I shall be thine. Don't give ear to any reports you may hear. There are several I hear going about regarding me going to get married. Regard them not. A kiss dear love from thy devote and loving, much attached wife, thine own Mimi.

Emile had to be disabused of the notion that he possessed her completely and irrevocably. There were, of course, no rumours at this time but a little insecurity, a little jealousy, she felt wouldn't do him any harm at all. There was, however, a basis in fact for this invention. The real life of Madeleine Smith was about to come into conflict with her fantasy world of intrigue, lust and imagination. Thirty-five-year-old William Minnoch, a director of Houldsworth and Company, and a friend of James Smith, had become a regular visitor at the Smith home. Minnoch lived directly above the Smith's new town house at 7 Blythswood Square. Ironically, Madeleine was teasing Emile by making reference to the man who, in only a few months, would become her fiancé:

> Minnoch was here to-day again (Monday). Only left on Saturday and back to-day again. He was here for four hours. He brought a fellow Weymiss with him. I think he might have a little better feeling than come so soon knowing that every one down here has heard the report regarding myself and him. Papa and Mama were much displeased at him – they said nothing, but Mama said it was enough to make people think there was something in the report. Say nothing to him in passing – it will only make him rude if you say anything.

The truth was that Papa and Mama were very pleased with Billy Minnoch and they intended to continue to invite him for as long as it took. At this point, Emile's assessment of the situation was probably more accurate than Madeleine's. His alarm, however, did not translate into the insecurity that Madeleine desired. His experience with the girl in Fife had taught him a lesson. He had no intention of allowing history to repeat itself. This time, he would have proof of their intimacy. This time, the family would be in no position to send him packing. Emile had kept almost every letter she had written and, throughout the correspondence, he had encouraged Madeleine to write ever more passionately, ever more explicitly. He had complained whenever a letter was 'too cool' and Madeleine had been more than happy to oblige, in the most un-Victorian terms. In almost every letter, Madeleine is humouring him, pandering to his insecurities, or bolstering his ego, and still he asks for more passion. Here are two consecutive letters, the first transcribed in full:

> My own dear Emile, I must bid you adieu in this note. May you enjoy your trip, be happy with your friends and may you again return in health, safety, and happiness to Glasgow. I hope and trust the change may do you good, that you shall put in a stock of health for the winter months.

I hope you feel well and strong. I am better though still cold. When I get into a breeze I cough but I shall be all well soon. Adieu, my dear love. May you escape all danger – be careful of yourself for my sake. We have a lot of friends to dinner to night. I do wonder if you are in Helensburgh to-night. I fancy no – something says you are not. I had an invitation yesterday from some friends in London to go and pay them a visit (not Bessie), but M. would not allow me – so I have declined, for which I am very sorry. We are to have friends from Ireland next week, among the number a very nice young fellow with large moustache.

If you wish to cut all the hair off your face, why then do it, but I am sure it wont improve your appearance in the least. Now be a dear good little husband mine, and excuse me writing you a longer note – it is so late. A fond dear embrace, much love and lots of kisses. Adieu my sweet love, take care of yourself. A kiss, a fond embrace from thy ever true and ever devoted dear Mimi L'Angelier. I shall write to you to Badgemore the end of the week, about Thursday. Adieu sweet love ever and ever yours, Mimi L.

Her next letter begins: 'My dearest Emile, I was sorry you found my last letter so cool. I was not aware it had been so … ' It would be an exaggeration to say that the tone of the letters can be seen to travel, by increments, from the demure to the depraved, but certainly Madeleine's natural inhibition and sense of propriety can be seen to deteriorate as the correspondence progresses, her personality 'on paper' being moulded to better please the recipient. There was, perhaps, one detail that had been overlooked: it was not absolutely clear from the letters that Madeleine Smith and Mimi L'Angelier were one and the same person. She now writes, 'if I did not sign my name, it was for no reason. Unless it is to stranger, I never do put Smith – only Madeleine.' A subsequent letter is signed 'Madeleine Smith, alias Mimi L'Angelier.'

By July 1856 Emile had moved from the Botanic Gardens and had taken lodgings with Mrs Jenkins at 11 Franklin Place (11 Great Western Road), but he and his landlady at the Gardens had remained good friends. His interest in botany, along with his interest in arsenic – at that time, it was used in the Botanic Gardens as a weed killer and pesticide – made him a regular visitor.

Slowly but surely, the relationship deteriorates. October 1856:

… Our meeting last night was peculiar. Emile you are not reasonable. I do not wonder at your not loving me as you once did. Emile I am not worthy of you. You deserve a better wife than I. I see misery before me this winter. I would to God we were not to be so near to Mr M. You shall hear all stories and believe them. You will say I am indifferent because I shall not be able to see you much. … Yes, you must think me cool – but it is my nature. I never did love any one till I loved you, and I shall never love another. Love, Emile, my sweet Darling, causes unhappiness in more ways than one. I know you will, I feel sure you will quarrel with me this winter. I know it well, sweet love – but God only knows, dearest, that I have no desire ever to be parted from you, so, Emile, my own sweet Emile, if we should ever part it will be on your side, not mine.

I sometimes fancy you are disappointed with me. I am not what you once thought I was. I am too much of a child to please you. I am too fond of amusement to suit your fancy. I am too indifferent, and I do not mind what the world says, not in the least – I never did. I promised to marry you knowing I would never have my father's consent. I would be obliged to marry you in a clandestine way. I knew you were poor. All these I did not mind. I knew the world would condemn me for it but I did not mind. I trust we have days of happiness before us, but God knows we have days of misery too.

Emile, my own, my ever dear husband, I have suffered much on your account from my family. They have laughed at my love for you – they taunted me regarding you. I was watched all last winter. I was not allowed out by myself for fear I should meet you – but if I can I shall cheat them this winter. I shall avoid you at first, and that may cause them to allow me out by myself. I shall write you as often as I can, but it cannot be three times a week as it has been.

Billy Minnoch, clearly, was proving to be good company and Madeleine was discovering that a normal relationship had its advantages. With Billy, she could be seen at the theatre or at any social event. They could walk together, dine or dance together while attracting nothing but admiration. Emile, on the other hand, was accustomed to coming late at night to her bedroom window in order to exchange letters. If the family were asleep, he would stay to talk with her. Occasionally when, for instance, her father was away from home, Emile might be let into the house by the area door, for a more tangible expression of their affection. She was still, on occasion, capable of feeling passion for Emile, but some part of the chemistry had gone forever.

Emile, my beloved, you have just left me. At this moment my heart and soul burns with love for you. What would I not give to be your fond wife. My night dress was on when you saw me. Would to God you were in the same attire. We would be happy. I never felt so unhappy as I have done for sometime past. I would do anything to keep sad thoughts from my mind, but in whatever place, some things make me feel sad.

A dark spot is in the future. What can it be? Oh God keep it from us. I weep now, Emile, to think of our fate. If we could only get married, all would be well, but alas, I see no chance, no chance of happiness for me. I must speak with you.

Chapter Two

By the end January 1857 it was all over. On the 28th Billy Minnoch proposed and Madeleine accepted. He bought a house in Woodside Crescent, in anticipation of their marriage. The next letter that Madeleine sent to Emile was not well-received; he returned it to her, and this seemed to offer a long-awaited opportunity to finish with him:

I felt truly astonished to have my last letter returned to me. But it will be the last you shall have the opportunity of returning. When you are not pleased with the letters I send you, then our correspondence shall be at an end, and, as there is a coolness on both sides, our engagement had better be broken. This may astonish you, but you have, more than once, returned me my letters, and my mind was made up that I should not stand the same thing again. Altogether I think, owing to coolness and indifference (nothing else), that we had better, for the future, consider ourselves as strangers. I trust to your honour as a gentleman that you will not reveal anything that may have passed between us. I shall feel obliged by your bringing me my letters and likeness on Thursday evening at 7. Be at the area gate, and Christina Haggart will take the parcel from you. On Friday night, I shall send you all your letters and likeness etc. I trust you may yet be happy, and get one more worthy of you than I.

You may be astonished at this sudden change, but, for some time back, you must have noticed a coolness in my notes. My love for you has ceased and that is why I was cool. I did once love you truly, fondly but, for some time back, I have lost much of that love. There is no other reason for my conduct, and I think it but fair to let you know this. I might have gone on and become your wife but I could not have loved you as I ought. My conduct, you will condemn but I did, at one time, love you with heart and soul. It has cost me much to tell you this – sleepless nights – but it is necessary you should know.

If you remain in Glasgow or go away, I hope you succeed in all your endeavours. I know you will never injure the character of one you so fondly loved. No, Emile, I know you have honour and are a gentleman. What has passed, you will not mention. I know, when I ask you that, you will comply. Adieu.

She had postponed this day for so long and with good reason, but it seemed to Madeleine that her logic was sound: if Emile wished to maintain his pretensions to being a gentleman, he would have no choice but to return her letters and remain forever silent about their affair.

Thomas Kennedy, Emile's friend and colleague at Huggins, later recalled,

he came to me one morning in February, with tears in his eyes, and said that he had received a letter from Miss Smith, demanding back all her letters and wishing the correspondence to cease. I advised him strongly to give back the letters, but he said, 'No, I won't. She shall never marry another man as long as I live.' I said it was very foolish. He said he knew it was, that it was an infatuation. He said, 'Tom, she will be the death of me.'

By the morning of Monday 9 February, Emile still hadn't replied. Madeleine's previously-unconscious antipathy to Emile's weakness now begins to surface. She writes,

I attribute it to your having a cold that I had no answer to my last note. On Thursday evening you were, I suppose, afraid of the night air. I fear your cold is not better. I again appoint Thursday night first, same place, Street Gate, 7 o'c. If you can not send me or bring me the parcel on Thursday, please write a note saying when you shall bring it, and address it to Christina Haggart. Send it by post.

If her discretion was lacking, her timing was worse. Emile had, in fact, responded. His letter, however, would not arrive until later that day. The two notes had effectively crossed in the post. When Emile's letter did arrive, Madeleine was totally unprepared for its content. The thought of what he was about to do, of the consequences for herself and for her family, presented a prospect that, in the first shock of it, she felt she couldn't bear to live through. She came out of her bedroom and called for the houseboy Billy Murray. The note she gave him read, 'A small phial of prussic acid.' She told him she wanted it for her hands and then she warned him to be careful because it is poison. Billy took the note to the apothecary, but was sent back empty-handed. Madeleine, in the meantime, had recovered just enough composure to put pen to paper.

Monday night – Emile, I have just had your note. Emile, for the love you once had for me do nothing till I see you – for God's sake do not bring your once loved Mimi to an open shame. Emile, I have deceived you. I have deceived my Mother. God knows she did not boast of any thing I had said of you – for she, poor woman, thought I had broken off with you last winter. I deceived you by telling you she still knew of our engagement. She did not. This I now confess – and as for wishing for any engagement with another, I do not fancy she ever thought of it. Emile, write to no one, to Papa or any other. Oh, do not till I see you on Wednesday night. Be at the Hamiltons' at 12, and I shall open my shutter, and then you come to the area gate, and I shall see you. It would break my mother's heart. Oh, Emile be not harsh to me. I am the most guilty, miserable wretch on the face of the Earth. Emile, do not drive me to death. When I ceased to love you, believe me, it was not to love another. I am free from all engagements at present.

Emile, for God's sake do not send my letters to Papa. It will be an open rupture. I will leave the house. I will die. Emile, do nothing till I see you. One word to-morrow night at my window to tell me or I shall go mad. Emile, you did love me. I did fondly, truly love you too. Oh, dear Emile, be not so harsh to me. Will you not – but I cannot ask forgiveness, I am too guilty for that. I have deceived – it was love for you at the time made me say Mama knew of our engagement. To-morrow one word – and on Wednesday we meet. I would not again ask you to love me, for I know you could not. But oh, Emile, do not make me go mad. I will tell you that only myself and Christina Haggart knew of my engagement to you. Mama did not know since last winter. Pray for me for a guilty wretch, but do nothing. Oh, Emile, do nothing. 10 o'clock to-morrow night, one line, for the love of God.

I am ill. God knows what I have suffered. My punishment is more than I can bear. Do nothing till I see you, for the love of heaven do nothing. I am mad, I am ill.

Emile received this on the afternoon of Tuesday 10 February but the first letter he received from her that day was her abrupt note in which she felt bold enough to show her disdain for his hypochondria. Late that night, Madeleine received his reply. Once again, she writes to him:

Tuesday evening, 12 o'c – Emile, I have this night received your note. Oh, it is kind of you to write to me. Emile, no one can know the intense agony of mind I have suffered last night and today. Emile, my father's wrath would kill me; you little know his temper. Emile, for the love you once had for me do not denounce me to my Papa. Emile, if he should read my letters to you – he will put me from him, he will hate me as a guilty wretch. I loved you, and wrote to you in my first ardent love. It was with my deepest love I loved you. It was for your love I adored you. I put on paper what I should not. I was free, because I loved you with my heart. If he or any other one saw those fond letters to you, what would not be said of me. On my bended knees I write you, and ask you as you hope for mercy at the Judgement Day, do not inform on me; do not make me a public shame.

Emile, my life has been one of bitter disappointment. You and you only can make the rest of my life peaceful. My own conscience will be a punishment that I shall carry to my grave. I have deceived the best of men. You, may forgive me, but God never will. For God's love, forgive me, and betray me not. For the love you once had to me do not bring down my father's wrath on me. It will kill my mother (who is not well). It will for ever cause me bitter unhappiness. I am humble before you and crave your mercy. You can give me forgiveness and you, oh, you only can make me happy for the rest of my life. I would not ask you to love me or ever make me your wife. I am too guilty for that. I have deceived and told you too many falsehoods for you ever to respect me. But oh, will you not keep my secret from the world? Oh, will you not, for Christ's sake, denounce me? I shall be undone. I shall be ruined. Who would trust me. Shame would be my lot. Despise me, hate me, but make me not the public scandal. Forget me for ever. Blot out all remembrance of me. I have treated you ill. I did love you, and it was my soul's ambition to be your wife. I asked you to tell me my faults. You did so, and it made me cool towards you gradually. When you have found fault with me, I have cooled; it was not love for another, for there is no one I love. My love has all been given to you. My heart is empty, cold. I am unloved. I am despised.

I told you I had ceased to love you. It was true. I did not love you as I did but oh, till within the time of our coming to town I loved you fondly. I longed to be your wife. I had fixed February. I longed for it. The time I could not leave my father's house I grew discontented, then I ceased to love you. Oh, Emile, this is indeed the true statement. Now you can know my state of mind. Emile, I have suffered much for you. I lost much of my father's confidence since that September, and my mother has never been the same to me. No, she has never given me the same kind look. For the sake of my mother, her who gave me life, spare me from shame.

Oh, Emile, will you in God's name hear my prayer. I ask God to forgive me. I have prayed that he might put it in your heart yet to spare me from shame. Never, never while I live can I be happy. No, no, I shall always have the thought I deceived you. I am guilty. It will be a punishment I shall bear till the day of my death. I am humbled thus to crave your pardon. But I care not. While I have breath I shall ever think of you as my best friend, if you will only keep this between ourselves. I blush to ask you. Yet, Emile, will you not grant me this, my last favour. If you will never reveal what has passed. Oh, for God's sake, for the love of heaven, hear me. I grow mad. I have been ill, very ill, all day. I have had what has given me a false spirit. I had to resort to what I should not have taken, but my brain is on fire. I feel as if death would indeed be sweet. Denounce me not, Emile. Emile, think of our once happy days.

Pardon me if you can, pray for me as the most wretched, guilty, miserable creature on the earth. I could stand anything but my father's hot displeasure. Emile, you will not cause me death. If he is to get your letters, I can not see him any more. And my poor mother. I will never more kiss her – it would be a shame to them all. Emile, will you not spare me this? Hate me, despise me, but do not expose me. I cannot write more. I am too ill to-night. M.

P.S. – I cannot get to the back stair. ... I will take you within the door. The area gate will be open. I shall see you from my window, 12 o'c. I will wait till 1 o'c.

The following day, Wednesday 11 February 1857, came and went like any other for the people of Glasgow. Robert Dalglish, the Independent Radical candidate, was preparing for the General Election coming up at the end of March. Even more than usual, his election agent and friend, James Smith, was pre-occupied with the competing demands of business and politics. James Smith's daughter had never been more completely alone. It wasn't in her nature to betray any sign of her torment but, if she had done, it's unlikely anyone would have noticed.

At 11 Franklin Place, Emile's landlady Mrs Jenkins went about her business as usual. Behind the closed door of an upstairs room – the vortex of self-pity and fury that was Emile L'Angelier had undergone a cathartic transformation, the ramifications of which would last for generations. With each line of Madeleine's letter he had studied, he had felt his hopes and dreams slipping from his grasp. ' … my father's wrath would kill me; you little know his temper.' ' … if he should read my letters to you – he will put me from him.' This was not at all according to plan.

Mr Smith was supposed to accept that his daughter now belonged to Emile and, albeit reluctantly, accept the situation as a *fait accompli*. Emile had absolutely no use for a disowned Madeleine Smith and even less inclination to learn about the extent of her father's temper. She had ruined everything. She had robbed him of more than she could ever know; she had robbed his mother and his sisters of their future security. She had no idea what she had done. The pain had been more than he could bear, but that was past. He was now relaxed as he searched around his room for a diary that he hadn't yet used: a small, dark-red, soft-covered memorandum book.

That evening he kept an appointment for dinner at a friend's house. When he left he made his way to Blythswood Square. Police Constable Thomas Kavan was on his beat that night. Around eleven o'clock he saw L'Angelier standing near a lamp-post at the end of the lane behind the Smiths' house. As the constable approached him, Emile said 'Cold night, policeman. Do you smoke?' The policeman said 'yes, sir.' Emile put his hand in his breast-pocket, gave him two cigars and passed on. PC Kavan would be unlikely to forget a stranger who gave him not one but two cigars at the corner of Blythswood Square.

It was midnight before Emile saw Madeleine. He was taken into Christina Haggart's room. Madeleine took the only course that seemed to be open to her: she explained, she pleaded, she made her profuse apologies and, to her great relief, a semblance of a relationship was restored, or so she thought. Emile returned home and made the first entry in his diary: – 'Dined at Mr Mitchell's; Saw M. at 12pm in CH Room.'

Madeleine had absolutely no idea what she was going to do about the situation but, as always, her focus was very much in the present. She couldn't let herself dwell upon what might lie ahead. She had survived the day. She knew she was in serious trouble but, like Scarlett O'Hara, she would think about that tomorrow. Emile, true to his type, was once again thinking ahead and thoroughly future-motivated. His long-standing *raison d'etre*, his goal of marrying into the Smith family, had been taken from him but the vacuum had now been filled, and by the only object that could satisfy the unimaginable depth of his disappointment, resentment and hatred. She had to suffer for what she had done to him and to his mother and sisters, and she would pay in full measure. He lived for that day.

The idea had possibly come to him as early as July 1856. At the time, it may only have been an amusing thought and he would not then have guessed that he would ever have the opportunity or the desire to put it into practice. He was in the habit of reading *Chambers* magazine. In July they had featured an article on the arsenic-eaters in the Austrian province of Styria. Various experts had been debating the effects of arsenic, how much can be taken with safety, how the dose can be varied on a monthly basis, etc. One sentence stands out: 'Lastly, let me urge upon all who adopt the Styrian system, to make some written memorandum that they have done so, lest, in case of accident, some of their friends may be hanged in mistake.'

On Friday 13th, Emile's memorandum book records: 'Saw Mr Phillpot, saw Mimi, dined at 144 Renfrew St.' Saturday 14th: 'A letter from M.' Monday 16th: 'Wrote M. Saw Mr Phillpots.' Thus far, the purpose of his making these memoranda might seem somewhat obscure. It is clearly not a diary of future appointments; every entry is in the past tense. At first sight, it appears to be a simple retrospective record of events but there we have another problem because his criteria for inclusion of these presumably noteworthy events, is even more obscure. It is started on 11 February and yet it makes no mention of the crisis of the previous day. The most traumatic incident that had occurred in his life since the lady in Fife jilted him all those years ago does not even rate a mention. Already, this is a most unusual diary.

Emile next dined with Mary Perry at 144 Renfrew Street on Tuesday 17th. He told her that he would be seeing Madeleine on Thursday. From that day onwards, the diary entries become much more interesting. For Thursday 19th, he writes: 'Saw Mimi a few moments. Was very ill during the night.' Friday 20th: 'Passed two pleasant hour with M. in the Drawing Room.' Saturday 21st: 'Don't feel well.' Sunday 22nd: 'Saw Mimi in Drawing Room. Promised me French Bible. Taken very ill.'

On three occasions, Emile records an illness subsequent to a meeting with Madeleine. To understand the purpose of this diary, we have to consider firstly the powerful inference of its content i.e. that Madeleine is responsible for these illnesses. We then have to ask what preoccupied his thoughts on 11 February when he started making these entries, and what was his state of mind on that day? It is hard to imagine a person seething with more malevolence than he had felt for her in these hours. From the moment of putting pen to paper, these memoranda had only one purpose, as did Emile.

On 2 March he again visited Mary Perry. He was looking very ill. He said, 'Well, I never expected to have seen you again, I was so ill.' He told her he had fallen on the floor, and been unable to ring the bell for his landlady. A week later he paid Mary Perry another visit. On this occasion, he told her of having had a cup of chocolate from Madeleine which had made him ill. The ground having been prepared, the seed could now be planted. He said, 'I can't think why I was so unwell after getting that coffee and chocolate from her.' It seems, however, that this was still just a bit too subtle for Miss Perry; he would have to spell it out. He told her, 'it is a perfect fascination my attachment to that girl; if she were to poison me I would forgive her.'

Mary Perry had no great liking for Madeleine Smith. She disapproved of her wearing the crinoline and she took a very dim view of Miss Smith's flighty behaviour but this was just a bit beyond the pale. Slightly taken aback, she replied, 'you ought not to allow such thoughts to pass through your mind; what motive could she have for giving you anything to hurt you?' Emile replied, 'I don't know that. Perhaps she might not be sorry to be rid of me.'

On 16 March he visited a Mr and Mrs Towers in Portobello, Mrs Towers being Miss Perry's sister. According to Mrs Towers, 'he talked almost the whole time about his health. He said something about cocoa and coffee, that he had been getting them, that they disagreed with him, and he had been very ill. He remarked that he thought he had been poisoned.' Mr Towers had a similar recollection of the visit:

> the conversation turned on his health. He said he had had a very violent bilious attack, or jaundice. ... He said he had had two attacks after taking coffee or cocoa, and that on one occasion he fell down in his bedroom, and was unable to go to bed; and that on another attack he was able to creep to the door and knock through to his landlady. He spoke much of this. He said he thought he had been poisoned after taking the cocoa and coffee.
>
> When we asked about Glasgow society he spoke of that; but he spoke a great deal of his own sickness. He was very fond of talking about himself. I thought him a vain person. ... I can't say he was a person who spoke much without thinking.

During these weeks Emile had established, amongst friends and colleagues, a well of suspicion, poised to overflow should any 'misfortune' appear to befall him. In effect, he had now laid the foundations for a charge of attempted murder against Madeleine and the diary, he believed, would put her guilt beyond doubt. To his flawed logic, she clearly had the motive. Their night-time appointments, perhaps witnessed by a police constable, would provide her with the opportunity and, mysteriously and at first unaccountably, Madeleine appears to have provided herself with the means. On no less than three occasions, over the next few weeks, Madeleine would be recorded as having bought arsenic, under the pretext that it was wanted to kill rats.

To understand why, we have to go back to that first diary entry on 11 February ... 'Saw Madeleine at 12 p.m. in Christina Haggart's room.' The words which passed between them that night will never be known but, if Emile's plan was to succeed, he would have to use his talent for manipulation. Madeleine's possession of arsenic was pre-requisite to the whole endeavour. It would, in the event, be a much simpler task than one might imagine. One of the most defining and enduring themes of the correspondence had been Madeleine's expected obedience to Emile's wishes and advice. On that night, in particular, she had never been more vulnerable, more willing to comply with his merest whim. While she pleaded for his forgiveness, he needed only to make an issue of her habitual disregard for his advice; he needed only to remind her of the articles in *Blackwood's* magazine which he had been good enough to point out to her, regarding the benefit of arsenic to the complexion. He was prepared to consider giving her another chance but things would have to change. The promise would be easily extracted.

All of this might rightly be dismissed as pure conjecture but for a previously unexplained anomaly in the chain of events. Emile's first 'illness' was on 19 February. He would, however, have done well to remember that Madeleine had never been handicapped by the need for absolute honesty. It is obvious that he believed that she had indeed complied with his wishes and was now in possession of the poison. On the nineteenth he wrote, 'Saw Mimi a few moments. Was very ill during the night.' It was quite true; he was very ill indeed ... but it was two days later, on the twenty-first, when Madeleine went to Murdoch's the druggist in Sauchiehall Street and made her first purchase of an ounce of arsenic 'for the garden and country house.' She signed the poisons register and had the arsenic charged to her father's account.

In other respects, Madeleine wasn't helping at all. Quite unintentionally, she was actually making Emile's task much more difficult than he might have reasonably expected. She could hardly bring herself to write to him and she was now at pains to avoid him completely. In one evasive letter, she writes:' ... I cannot see you Friday, as Mama is not away – but I think, Sunday, Papa will be away and I might see you, I think, but I shall let you know. ... My head aches so, and I am looking so bad ... but I am taking some stuff to bring back the colour.' Friday 27th:' ... I cannot see you this week, and I can fix no time to meet you.' Tuesday 3 March:' ... On Friday, we go to Stirling for a fortnight. I am so sorry, my dearest pet, I cannot see you ere we go – but I cannot. ... I hope you feel well. ... I am very well, and I think the next time we meet you will think I look better than I did the last time.' Wednesday 4 March:' ... If you would take my advice, you would go to the south of England for ten days; it would do you much good. ... I hope you wont go to Bridge of Allan, as Papa and Mama would say it was I brought you there, and it would make me feel very unhappy. ... Go to the Isle of Wight. I am exceedingly sorry, love, I cannot see you ere I go – it is impossible, but the first thing I do on my return will be to see you, sweet love.'

This was probably just a bit frustrating but, on the other hand, Emile had never lacked patience. He seems to have decided to make a virtue out of a necessity and to pass the time by doing some more work to firm up the motive. On Thursday 5 March, he wrote to Madeleine (and made a copy for himself in the office copying-press):

> My dear, sweet pet Mimi, I feel indeed very vexed that the answer I
> received yesterday to mine of Tuesday to you should prevent me from
> sending you the kind letter I had ready for you. You must not blame me,
> dear, for this but really your cold, indifferent, and reserved notes, so short,
> without a particle of love in them (especially after pledging your word
> you were to write me kindly for those letters you asked me to destroy),
> and the manner you evaded answering the questions I put to you in my
> last, with the reports I hear, fully convince me, Mimi, that there is foun-
> dation in your marriage with another; besides, the way you put off our
> union till September without a just reason is very suspicious.

I do not think, Mimi dear, that Mrs Anderson would say your mother told her things she had not, and really I could never believe Mr Houldsworth would be guilty of telling a falsehood for mere talking. No, Mimi, there is foundation for all this. You often go to Mr Minnoch's house and common sense would lead anyone to believe that if you were not on the footing reports say you are, you would avoid going near any of his friends. I know he goes with you, or at least meets you in Stirlingshire. Mimi, dear, place yourself in my position and tell me am I wrong in believing what I hear. I was happy the last time we met – yes, very happy. I was forgetting all the past, but now it is again beginning.

Mimi, I insist in having an explicit answer to the questions you evaded in my last. If you evade answering them this time, I must try some other means of coming to the truth. If not answered in a satisfactory manner, you must not expect I shall again write you personally or meet you when you return home. I do not wish you to answer this at random. I shall wait a day or so if you require it. I know you cannot write me from Stirlingshire, as the time you have to write me a letter is occupied in doing so to others. There was a time you would have found plenty of time. Answer me this, Mimi – ...Is it true that you are, directly or indirectly, engaged to Mr Minnoch or to any one else but me?

The doctor says I must go to Bridge of Allan. I cannot travel 500 miles to the Isle of Wight and 500 back. What is your object in wishing me so very much to go south? I may not go to B. of A. till Wednesday. If I can avoid going I shall do so for your sake. I shall wait to hear from you. I hope, dear, nothing will happen to check the happiness we were again enjoying. May God bless you, Pet, and with many fond and tender embraces believe me with kind love your ever affectionate husband, Emile L'Angelier.

Madeleine, at a party in January, had been wearing a necklace given to her by Billy Minnoch. When asked by another guest, Mrs Anderson, if Mr Minnoch had given her the necklace, she had replied that he hadn't; that it was a present from her father. A visitor to Mrs Anderson's, on a subsequent occasion, was a young warehouseman by the name of Mowbray (no relation to the famous arsenic victim of 1865 ... presumably). He was there when she was talking about Madeleine's denial that Billy had given her the necklace. She had also spoken of Madeleine's forthcoming marriage. Unfortunately, Mowbray worked for Huggins.

The doctor, it's worth noting, had given no advice about going anywhere, although he did remember Emile saying that he was thinking of going to the country. On Friday 6 March Madeleine, accompanied by her friend Mary Buchanan, called into Currie's pharmacy in Sauchiehall Street for another ounce of arsenic. The following day, Emile was visiting his old landlady, Mrs Clark, at the Botanic Gardens. She later remembered that he took away some gold or silver fish on that occasion.

Substantial as the case against Madeleine would be, there remained to be established one vital piece of evidence: it had to be beyond doubt, if it were to be believed that Madeleine had tried to poison him, that a meeting had actually taken place. The fact that Madeleine was doing everything she could to avoid seeing him at all certainly didn't help, but he simply had to turn up the heat to overcome that. In fact, he had already started the build-up, employing his favoured technique of veiled threat: 'If not answered in a satisfactory manner, you must not expect I shall again write you personally or meet you when you return home.' The slightest suggestion that he had changed his mind, and that her letters would have to be shown to Smith and Minnoch after all, would have Madeleine pleading for a meeting. Come the time, that is exactly what he intended to do. His problem was that he could not count on there being any witnesses to the meeting, and his solution was to stage a pantomime: he would leave Glasgow and he would make it obvious, very obvious, that his return was for no other purpose than a meeting with Madeleine.

The Smith family or, to be more precise, Mrs Smith and Madeleine, with the occasional visit from Billy and other family members coming and going, were in Bridge of Allan in Stirlingshire from 6 to 17 March. On the 18th, Madeleine was back in Currie's pharmacy buying another sixpence worth of arsenic. The following day, Thursday 19th,

Emile left for Edinburgh, en route to Bridge of Allan. His landlady Mrs Jenkins remembered that before he left he was very disappointed at not getting a letter. He told her that if it arrived she was to give it to his fellow lodger Amadee Thuau who would send it on to him. He also said that he was going on to Bridge of Allan and he would not be home until Wednesday night or Thursday morning of the following week … unless the letter arrived, in which case he may be back that night.

Madeleine meanwhile had received his note and had replied, as expected, asking for (almost certainly pleading for) a meeting. In spite of her heightened anxiety to speak with him, however, a Thursday appointment was out of the question; she and her parents had an engagement for dinner at Billy Minnoch's that Thursday night. There was no way of knowing how late that dinner party would end – 'our friends never leave till twelve o'clock' – and Billy's door is right next to Madeleine's bedroom window. The idea of her parents walking out of Billy's door to find Emile standing there left her with no option but to appoint Friday.

On Thursday afternoon Emile was in Edinburgh telling stationer Peter Pollock that he was just going to the Post Office to pick up a letter. He came back half an hour later saying that the letter hadn't arrived and he would be going on to Bridge of Allan. Later that evening, Thuau forwarded the letter. It arrived at Bridge of Allan around 9 a.m. the following morning.

That morning, Friday 20 March, Emile picked up his mail and he left his card at the Bridge of Allan Post Office. In a letter later that day to Stevenson, the warehouse manager at Huggins, he writes,

Dear William, I am happy to say I feel much better, though I fear I slept in a damp bed, for my limbs are all sore and scarcely able to bear me, but a day or two will put all to rights. What a dull place this is. I went to Stirling today but it was so cold and damp that I soon hurried home again. Are you very busy? Am I wanted? If so, I am ready to come at any time. Just drop me a line at the Post Office. You were talking of taking a few days to yourself, so I shall come up whenever you like. If any letters come, please send them to me here.

He finishes the letter with a most important line: 'I intend to be home not later than Thursday morning.' Of twofold significance, to Miss Perry, he wrote, '... I hope to be home the middle of next week. ... I should have come to see someone last night, but the letter came too late, so we are both disappointed. ... I shall be here till Wednesday.'

He has established – well and truly established – that he intends to remain in Bridge of Allan until Wednesday. Madeleine's letter will appoint a meeting and when he returns prematurely, it will be plain for all to see that this letter has brought him back. Once again, however, Madeleine was being unhelpful. She had appointed Friday night which should have suited Emile perfectly; he could easily have returned for the Friday appointment had that genuinely been his innocent intention, but something else in her letter rendered it useless. He kept only the envelope. After two years of collecting Madeleine's notes, this letter, for some uncertain reason, had to be discarded, and that presented another problem: how could he now explain his not returning on receipt of this much-spoken-of letter?

It's obvious that, since the letter was essential to establishing guilt, if something about its contents could not be seen, then the appointment had to be broken. It undermined the whole fabric of the scenario he had constructed. His solution was to pretend that Madeleine had appointed Thursday night, a device which would later be accepted, without question, by both the Crown and the defence. On Friday 20th, he wrote to Miss Perry, 'I should have come to see someone last night, but the letter came too late ...' Whatever the reason might have been for the disappearance of the letter – and there is no need to resort to conjecture since it's having existed is all that matters – the deeply significant fact remains that this letter that should have brought Emile rushing back to Glasgow was completely ignored; he remained in Bridge of Allan and waited for her next.

On Friday night, Madeleine waited, but Emile didn't show. This might not have been in the original plan but it produced the required result; she is now utterly distraught, believing that his failure to appear may mean that her worst fears have been realised; he has decided to carry out his threat. The subtext of the letter she wrote that night speaks volumes as to the height of her anxiety and apprehension:

Why my beloved did you not come to me? Oh, beloved, are you ill? Come to me sweet one. I waited and waited for you but you came not. I shall wait again tomorrow night same hour and arrangement. Do come sweet love, my own dear love of a sweetheart. Come beloved and clasp me to your heart. Come and we shall be happy. A kiss, fond love. Adieu, with tender embraces, ever believe me to be your own, ever dear fond Mimi.

The tone of this, her final letter, is in stark contrast to her preceding notes in which she has been doing everything in her power to keep him at a distance, and the dramatic irony of it could hardly be more acute. Imagining the worst, she writes in the most extravagant terms in hopes to appease and placate him. In fact, she had given Emile exactly what he wanted. She would wait in vain, for a second time, on Saturday night. The letter was posted on Saturday morning. It was addressed to Mr E. L'Angelier c/o Mrs Jenkins at Franklin Place, Glasgow, where it arrived a few hours later. When Thuau came in at 6 p.m., he immediately forwarded it to Bridge of Allan. At 10.30 on Sunday morning, the letter was delivered to the Bridge of Allan Post Office. Emile left in the early afternoon, leaving most of his belongings in his room.

He walked from Bridge of Allan to Stirling and caught the 3.30 train. He was in a good mood throughout the journey, chatting to another passenger, Thomas Ross. They both left the train at Coatbridge, the nearest point to Glasgow on that line. The guard, William Fairfoul, had also left the train. Emile asked Fairfoul where he might get something to eat, telling him that he intended to walk to Glasgow, since he didn't want to get in to the city until dark. Ross and Fairfoul accompanied him into an ale house where Emile had roast beef and porter. The waitress later remembered that he was charged one shilling and fourpence for his meal, that he complained the porter was sour, but that he wasn't given another bottle. Once on their way to Glasgow, they talked 'of scenery and localities.' Ross recalled that Emile 'walked well, and did not seem tired. … he smoked several times on the road.'

Mrs Jenkins was surprised to see Emile at her door around eight o'clock that Sunday evening. He looked well, and he said he felt a great deal better. She asked why he'd returned so early and Emile replied 'the letter you sent brought me home. When was it delivered?' She told him Saturday afternoon. He then asked her to call him early next morning because he intended to go back by the first train. About an hour later he asked Mrs Jenkins for the pass-key, saying that he was going out and might be back late.

At 9 p.m. Emile was seen on Sauchiehall Street walking in the direction of Blythswood Square. At 9.20 p.m. he visited the lodgings of an acquaintance, McAlester, who lived in Terrace Street, a short distance from the Square. The idea, presumably, was to spend some time with McAlester before telling him that he had to go off and meet Madeleine, but the man was not at home. The maid remembered that Emile hesitated for a moment, as if he might like to come in and wait. She didn't invite him to do so, which is unfortunate since his whereabouts for the next five hours are a complete mystery.

Emile's landlady, Mrs Jenkins, was awakened at 2.30 a.m. by the sound of the doorbell ringing violently. She got out of bed and called 'who's there?' Emile answered 'it is I, Mrs Jenkins. Open the door, please.' He was standing with his arms crossed on his throat as if he was in great pain. He said he was feeling very sick. Mrs Jenkins got him into his room and helped him off with his coat. He said he thought he was never going to make it home, he was so bad. She asked him if he thought he could take a cup of tea. He said he could but he asked for a glass of water first, which she got for him. He emptied the glass. She went to make him some tea and when she returned, he was half-undressed and vomiting severely. She asked if he could have eaten anything that disagreed with him and he replied that he hadn't, that he had never felt better than when he was at the coast (sic). He said he was very cold. Mrs Jenkins brought him two hot water bottles and a couple of extra blankets and he seemed to feel a bit better after that.

At around 4 o'clock, he began to feel very ill again. Mrs Jenkins asked him for his doctor's address and he told her it was Dr Thomson in Dundas Street but that it was too early in the morning and also he didn't think that she would be able to find it. About an hour later, he was suffering badly again with vomiting and diarrhoea, and Mrs Jenkins decided to go for the nearest doctor, Dr Steven. This time Emile didn't object but when she arrived at the doctor's door she found that the doctor himself was ill. He said he would call if L'Angelier didn't improve and told her to give the patient twenty-five drops of laudanum (tincture of opium), to give him hot water, and to put a mustard blister on his stomach. When she returned, Emile said that a blister wouldn't help since he was only retching. He also said that he couldn't take laudanum, that he never could take it. 'Besides', he said, 'it's not good; it has been standing without a cork.' Emile's fellow lodger Amadee Thuau would later testify that he had actually spoken to L'Angelier about his taking too much laudanum, that he had seen him take laudanum several times. Apparently, he found it helped him when he couldn't sleep but, on this morning, the last thing Emile needed to accompany a large dose of arsenic was something to promote sleep; he had to stay awake.

By seven o'clock he was looking much worse and he was dark about the eyes. Mrs Jenkins went back to Dr Steven and, this time, the doctor came immediately. He applied a mustard blister and gave him some morphia and stayed about half an hour to see its effect. Mrs Jenkins came in with some hot water, and Emile said 'oh, Mrs Jenkins, this is the worst attack I ever had.' While the doctor was sitting beside him, Emile said 'can you do anything, doctor? This is the third attack I've had. The landlady says it's bile, but I never was subject to bile.'

The one thing he couldn't even allude to was the merest suggestion of poison. The question would immediately have arisen: if you thought you were being poisoned, why did you keep going back for more? He needed someone else to point the finger, leaving him free to play the part of the unsuspecting victim. It was a just question of time. He had to wait just a bit longer before Madeleine's accuser could be brought into play. Several times he said 'oh my poor mother.' He also said how depressed he felt being so far from home and away from friends. As Mr Towers in Portobello had observed, Emile was not a person who spoke much without thinking, but how many times would he have to bemoan his isolation before Mrs Jenkins volunteered to send for a friend?

As he was leaving, Dr Steven asked Mrs Jenkins if L'Angelier was 'a person that tippled.' She said he was not. The doctor said he was like a man that tippled, and she assured him that L'Angelier was not given to drink. She said 'it is strange; this is the second time he has gone out well and returned very ill. I must speak to him and ask the cause.' The doctor said 'that will be an after-explanation', and he then told her he would return between ten and eleven. When she went back into the room, Emile asked her what the doctor had said. She said 'he thinks you will get over it.' Emile replied 'I am far worse, than the doctor thinks.' She looked in on him several times. More than once, he said 'if I could get some sleep I should be better.'

About nine o'clock, she went in to open the curtains and she finally asked Emile if there was anyone he would like to see. He said that he would like to see a Miss Perry, and gave her the address. The last time she spoke to him he said 'oh, if I could get five minutes' sleep, I think I would get better.' He would soon get his wish; the morphia was not only relieving his pain, it was probably impairing his ability to think clearly, and it was almost certainly encouraging sleep. Mrs Jenkins wrote out a message for Miss Perry and told her eleven-year-old son, Alex, to take it to 144 Renfrew Street. It was close to ten o'clock when the boy handed Miss Perry the message: 'Mr L'Angelier's compliments – he was very ill at Franklin Place, and he would be very glad if you would call.'

Dr Steven came again at 11.15 and Mrs Jenkins spoke to him in the lobby. She told him Emile had been every bit as bad as he had been earlier but that he had only recently fallen asleep and that it was a pity to waken him. The doctor said he would like to see him, and they went in. Emile was lying on his side, one arm outside the bedclothes and the other in. He seemed in a comfortable position, as if he was sleeping. Dr Steven checked for a pulse, then lifted Emile's head and let it fall. He told her L'Angelier was dead.

When the doctor left, Mrs Jenkins dispatched Alex once again, this time to her sister Mrs Kirkland and to Mr Clark, another lodger who worked at a bank nearby. Mrs Kirkland and Mr Clark came, and also Mr Chrystal, a grocer. Chrystal went in and shut L'Angelier's eyes. Clark said he would send word to Emile's employer and they also sent for an undertaker. By the time Mary Perry arrived, around noon, Emile had been laid out. Mrs Jenkins told her that he was dead and took her in to see the body. Mary Perry, in tears, overcome with shock and grief, kissed his forehead several times and said how sorry she was for his mother. She stayed for about twenty minutes. Mrs Jenkins asked her if she was Emile's fiancée and she replied 'Oh no, I am only a friend.' Mrs Jenkins then said she had heard he was going to be married, and how sorry the lady would be. Miss Perry's reply was to the effect that the less said about that the better. It was a figure of speech. As she left Franklin Place and headed for Blythswood Square she was of a mind to say everything that she believed needed to be said.

On being told of Emile's death, Kennedy and Stevenson from Huggins went firstly to the French Consul's office where they met Emile's follow-lodger Thuau. Thuau took them to Dr Thomson, Emile's doctor, and all four went on to Franklin Place, followed soon after by Dr Steven. Mrs Jenkins took them in to Emile's room. The clothes which he had taken off that night were on the sofa. Stevenson picked up Emile's jacket. He found a bit of tobacco, three finger-rings, some loose change, a bunch of keys, and a letter which he studied for a moment. It read, 'why my beloved did you not come to me? Oh, beloved, are you ill? Come to me sweet one ...' Stevenson, somewhat prematurely one might think, declared 'this explains all.' Mrs Jenkins said 'that's the letter that came on Saturday.' In Emile's desk, they also found a large number of letters in the same hand, and a memorandum book. The doctors agreed that an examination of the body was the only way in which more could be known.

Madeleine was surprised to see Miss Perry at Blythswood Square. She asked if anything was wrong. Mary Perry said, 'I have come to see your mama; I shall acquaint her with the object of my visit.' Miss Perry informed Mrs Smith that Emile L'Angelier had died that morning and that she felt Mrs Smith should know that there had been a correspondence between L'Angelier and Madeleine. Mrs Smith told her that she knew about that but that it was a long time ago, long since finished. To Mrs Smith's horror, Mary Perry replied that, on the contrary, it had continued until very recently. After Miss Perry left, Madeleine admitted to her mother that in spite of having given her word to the contrary she had carried on the correspondence and that the last letter she had written to L'Angelier had been on the Friday night.

That afternoon, the French Consul Auguste de Mean visited Mr Smith to tell him that countless letters from Madeleine had been found in L'Angelier's room, and that there was every chance that they might fall into the hands of strangers. On Smith's behalf, he went to Huggins and asked for the letters that were in L'Angelier's desk. He was informed that no-one had the authority to hand over the letters without Mr Huggins's consent. Mr Huggins, meanwhile, was visiting Dr Thomson to enquire as to the cause of his employee's sudden death. The doctor told him the symptoms were such as might have been produced by poison and that, had such a case occurred in England, a coroner's inquest would be held.

No record exists of the row that took place in the Smith household that evening. More than once Madeleine had alluded to her father's temper, and it's not impossible that when, after dinner, Mrs Smith asked Madeleine to take a walk with her, it was as much to get her out of the house for her safety as to get to the truth. Madeleine repeated to her what she had said earlier and then burst into tears, asking her mother to forgive her for breaking her word and bringing shame on the family.

Around noon, the following day, at the request of Mr Huggins, Dr Thomson and Dr Steven returned to Franklin Place to make a post-mortem examination, the result of which 'justified a suspicion of death having resulted from poison.' Later that afternoon Stevenson informed the Procurator Fiscal of the circumstances.

De Mean went again to Mr Smith's office on Wednesday. He told him about the post-mortem and then went on to explain that there was now some suspicion that Madeleine may be implicated in L'Angelier's death, that a note of hers had been found suggesting that L'Angelier's return to Glasgow had been for a meeting with Madeleine. Up until this point, James Smith had been dealing with his own fury following the scandalous revelation that Madeleine, while engaged to Billy Minnoch, had shamelessly continued in a relationship with this man L'Angelier – her behaviour disgraced the whole family. Smith was a survivor; he'd lived through crises before but now to be told that his daughter was suspected of the man's murder came as such a blow to him that it would not be an exaggeration to say that he never fully recovered for the rest of his life. As he listened to De Mean's words, his strength ebbed away from him. He became so ill that he had to go home and to his bed.

At Smith's request, De Mean came to the house and spoke to Madeleine with Mrs Smith present. He asked Madeleine if she had seen L'Angelier on the Sunday night. She replied that she had not. He pointed out that L'Angelier had come from Bridge of Allan to Glasgow at her special invitation. Madeleine said that she was not aware that L'Angelier was at Bridge of Allan before he came to Glasgow, and that she did not give him an appointment for Sunday, as she wrote to him on Friday evening, giving him the appointment for the following day, Saturday. She said that she expected L'Angelier on the Saturday, but that he did not come, and that she had not seen him on Sunday. De Mean put the question to her five or six different times, and in different ways. Her answer was always the same. He told her that he believed that she must have seen him on Sunday, that L'Angelier had come because of her letter, and it seemed unlikely that he had committed suicide without knowing why she had asked him to come to Glasgow.

He then said that the best advice that a friend could give to her, in the circumstances, was to tell the truth. The case was a very grave one; it would lead to an inquiry on the part of the authorities. If she did not speak truthfully, perhaps it would be ascertained by a servant, a policeman, or a passer-by that L'Angelier had been at the house, and that would cause a very strong suspicion as to the motive that could have led her to conceal the truth. Madeleine then got up from her chair and told De Mean, 'I swear to you, Mr DeMean, that I have not seen L'Angelier, not on that Sunday only, but not for three weeks.' He next asked her how, being engaged to be married to another man, she could have continued a clandestine correspondence with a former lover. Madeleine told him that she did it in order to try to get back her letters.

Completely unaware of what was really going on, Billy Minnoch called at the house. He, along with Madeleine, Bessie and Jack, had been invited to a dinner party with Mr Middleton, the minister who would be performing the marriage ceremony. Billy asked to speak to Mr Smith, but he was told that Mr Smith was in bed, ill. There was some discussion later, amongst the family, on account of Mr Smith's illness, as to whether or not they should go. It was decided that they should and that evening, all four dined at Middleton's. Bessie later recalled that, in spite of her father having been scolding Madeleine earlier that day, she was 'her usual cheery self' throughout the evening.

The morning of Thursday 26th, however, provides a more telling indication of her true state of mind. Janet was woken up at 5 a.m. by her sister getting out of bed and dressing. Having packed some clothes into a carpet bag, Madeleine quietly left the house. Janet was thirteen years of age, old enough to have a good idea of what was going on, but young enough to shut her eyes and go back to sleep. Just before breakfast, she told her father that Madeleine had left the house. Mr Smith went into the dining room where he found a pencil-written note from Madeleine. It was to the effect that she couldn't bear to stay at home and see her father in such distress; she had gone to the country for a couple of days 'till all would be cleared up.' Mr Smith threw the note in the fire.

Billy Minnoch turned up a while later and was told that Madeleine had gone. He could see that Mr Smith was anxious, and absorbed in thought. Smith wouldn't go into detail but told him that 'something dreadful had happened.' He said it was about 'some old love affair.' Billy urged him to do something, to make some attempt to find out where she had gone. His appraisal of the situation was that Mr Smith was, at that moment, somehow overwhelmed by the circumstances and unable to take any decisive action. Billy left to fetch Daniel Forbes, Smith's solicitor, and instructed him to advise Smith as to what should be done. He and Forbes subsequently went to the police office and informed the police captain of the circumstances.

Having suggested that Madeleine might have gone to Rowaleyn, Billy and Jack went by train to Greenock, then boarded the steamer, just about to leave for Rhu. They found her on board. Billy sent a telegram to Mr Smith, letting him know that Madeleine was safe. As they crossed the Clyde estuary, Billy questioned her as to why she would walk out of the house, leaving her family and friends so worried about her, but then he told her not to answer until later, as there were too many people present. They went on to Rowaleyn where she explained that she was distressed because her parents were so angry with her at something they believed she had done. She said they were blaming her for something very dreadful and she felt annoyed that her Papa and Mama had thought her capable of it, and yet they clearly did; they had taken it so deeply to heart. After Monday's revelations of the clandestine relationship and the correspondence, however, it's not surprising that the Smiths now felt that they didn't know their daughter at all. She asked Billy not to press her on it and said that she would tell him all by and by. They stayed there for about three-quarters of an hour while Billy and Jack persuaded Madeleine to return home. They ordered a coach and brought her back to Blythswood Square.

Madeleine was in bed throughout Friday and Saturday. Billy came in to see how she was and found her very uneasy and feverish. On the Saturday he reminded her of the promise she made to him at Rhu, that she would tell all by and by. She said that she had written to a Frenchman to get back her letters. It would be Tuesday morning before she would refer to the rumour of Emile having been poisoned and tell Billy that she had been buying arsenic for her complexion.

Emile's funeral had been held on Thursday and his body was buried in St David's (The Ramshorn) Kirk burial ground. The next morning Dr Thomson visited the Andersonian University and delivered a bottle to Dr Frederick Penny, Professor of Chemistry. It contained L'Angelier's stomach and its contents. At Dr Thomson's request, Dr Penny performed a series of tests to ascertain if there was any poison present. His experiments confirmed the presence of one-fifth of an ounce of white arsenic, and he concluded that the quantity was 'considerably more than sufficient to destroy life.'

During the previous week, the fiscal's office had been treating the investigation of L'Angelier's sudden death as a matter of routine but, following the outcome of Dr Penny's tests, on Monday 30th a warrant was requested for the exhumation of the body, on grounds of the suspicion of poisoning. Madeleine was arrested on Tuesday 31st on a charge of murder. She was interrogated at some length and her answers were recorded in the form a declaration. Under Scots Law at that time, the prisoner's declaration would be the only statement she was permitted to make in her defence. Throughout her trial, she would be bound to silence. Her infamous composure was evident as she answered all questions put to her, calmly and confidently. Her answers were given clearly and distinctly with no appearance of hesitation or reserve, but it is perhaps worth observing that this declaration was given two days after her twenty-second birthday:

My name is Madeleine Smith. I am a native of Glasgow, twenty-one years of age, and I reside with my father, James Smith, architect, at No 7 Blythswood Square, Glasgow. For about the last two years I have been acquainted with P. Emile L'Angelier, who was in the employment of W.B. Huggins & Co., in Bothwell Street, and who lodged at 11 Franklin Place. He recently paid his addresses to me, and I have met with him on a variety of occasions. I learned about his death on the afternoon of Monday, the 23rd March current, from Mama, to whom it had been mentioned by a lady named Miss Perry, a friend of Mr L'Angelier.

I had not seen Mr L'Angelier for about three weeks before his death, and the last time I saw him was on a night about half-past ten o'clock. On that occasion he tapped at my bedroom window, which is on the ground floor, and fronts Mains Street. I talked to him from the window, which is stanchioned outside, and I did not go out to him, nor did he come in to me. This occasion, which, as already said, was about three weeks before his death, was the last time I saw him. He was in the habit of writing notes to me, and I was in the habit of replying to him by notes. The last note I wrote to him was on the Friday before his death, viz., Friday, the 20th March current. I now see and identify that note, and the relative envelope, and they are each marked No. 1. In consequence of that note, I expected him to visit me on Saturday night, the 21st current, at my bedroom window, in the same way as formerly mentioned, but he did not come, and sent no notice. There was no tapping at my window on said Saturday night, or on the following night, being Sunday. I went to bed on Sunday night about eleven o'clock, and remained in bed till the usual time of getting up next morning, being eight or nine o'clock.

In the course of my meetings with L'Angelier, he and I had arranged to get married, and we had, at one time, proposed September last as the time the marriage was to take place and, subsequently, the present month of March was spoken of. It was proposed that we should reside in furnished lodgings, but we had not made any definite arrangement as to time or otherwise.

He was very unwell for some time, and had gone to Bridge of Allan for his health, and he complained of sickness, but I have no idea what was the cause of it. I remember giving him some cocoa from my window one night some time ago, but I cannot specify the time particularly. He took the cup in his hand, and barely tasted the contents, and I gave him no bread to it. I was taking some cocoa myself at the time, and had prepared it myself. It was between ten and eleven pm when I gave it to him.

I am now shown a note or letter, and envelope, which are marked respectively No 2, and I recognise them as a note and envelope which I wrote to Mr L'Angelier, and sent to the post. As I had attributed his sickness to want of food, I proposed, as stated in the note, to give him a loaf of bread, but I said that merely in a joke, and, in point of fact, I never gave him any bread.

I have bought arsenic on various occasions. The last I bought was a sixpence worth, which I bought in Currie, the apothecary's, in Sauchiehall Street and, prior to that, I bought other two quantities of arsenic, for which I paid sixpence each, one of these in Currie's, and the other in Murdoch, the apothecary's shop in Sauchiehall Street. I used it all as a cosmetic, and applied it to my face, neck, and arms, diluted with water. The arsenic I got in Currie's shop I got there on Wednesday, the 18th March, and I used it all on one occasion, having put it all in the basin where I was to wash myself.

I had been advised to the use of the arsenic in the way I have mentioned by a young lady, the daughter of an actress, and I had also seen the use of it recommended in the newspapers. The young lady's name was Guibilei, and I had met her at school at Clapton, near London. I did not wish any of my father's family to be aware that I was using the arsenic, and, therefore, never mentioned it to any of them, and I don't suppose they or any of the servants ever noticed any of it in the basin.

When I bought the arsenic in Murdoch's I am not sure whether I was asked or not what it was for, but I think I said it was for a gardener to kill rats or destroy vermin about flowers, and I only said this because I did not wish them to know that I was going to use it as a cosmetic. I don't remember whether I was asked as to the use I was going to make of the arsenic on the other two occasions, but I likely made the same statement about it as I had done in Murdoch's, and on all the three occasions, as required in the shops, I signed my name to a book in which the sales were entered. On the first occasion I was accompanied by Mary, a daughter of Dr Buchanan of Dumbarton.

For several years past, Mr Minnoch, of the firm of William Houldsworth & Co., has been coming a good deal about my father's house, and about a month ago Mr Minnoch made a proposal of marriage to me, and I gave him my hand in token of acceptance, but no time for the marriage has yet been fixed, and my object in writing the note No 1, before mentioned, was to have a meeting with Mr L'Angelier to tell him that I was engaged to Mr. Minnoch. I am now shown two notes and an envelope bearing the Glasgow postmark of 23rd January, which are respectively marked No 3, and I recognise these as in my handwriting, and they were written and sent by me to Mr L'Angelier.

On the occasion that I gave Mr L'Angelier the cocoa, as formerly mentioned, I think that I used it must have been known to the servants and members of my father's family, as the package containing the cocoa was lying on the mantelpiece in my room, but no one of the family used it except myself, as they did not seem to like it. The water which I used, I got hot from the servants. On the night of the 18th, when I used the arsenic last, I was going to a dinner party at Mr Minnoch's house.

I never administered or caused to be administered, to Mr L'Angelier arsenic or anything injurious. And this I declare to be truth.

(Signed) Madeleine Smith

Chapter Three

For the last few days the recital of an event of the most painful character has been passing from mouth to mouth, and has become the subject of almost universal excitement and inquiry. So long as the matter was confined to rumour and surmise, we did not consider that we were called upon to make any public allusion to it; but now that a young lady has been committed to prison on a most serious charge, and the names of the respective parties are in the mouths of everyone, any further delicacy in the way of withholding allusion to the case is impossible. At the same time, we fervently trust that the cloud which at present obscures a most respectable and estimable household may be speedily and most effectually removed.

It appears that on the morning of Monday the 23rd March last, a young French Protestant gentleman, named Mons. Pierre Emile L'Angelier, connected with the house of Messrs W.B. Huggins & Co died suddenly in his lodgings in Franklin Place, Great Western Road. From circumstances which came to their knowledge, the firm we have named, on their own responsibility, requested Dr Steven, who had been in attendance upon the deceased before his death, and Dr Thomson, to make a post-mortem examination. This was done, but nothing palpable was discovered. The stomach and it's contents were secured, and retained by the medical gentlemen, and their findings having been reported to the Sheriffs Fiscal who, after inquiry into the circumstances of the case, transmitted the stomach and its contents to one of our most eminent local chemists for chemical analysis. The result of the analysis was the discovery in the stomach and viscera of a considerable quantity of irritant poison. As there was not any strong presumption that Mons. L'Angelier had himself thus violently terminated his existence, an inquiry of a searching character was instituted.

It appears that the deceased had been on a short visit to the Bridge of Allan, from which he returned rather unexpectedly on the night of Sunday, 22nd ult.; and leaving his lodgings about eight o'clock, he took the check-key with him, stating he would be rather late. He did return about two o'clock on Monday morning and was then suffering great pain, in consequence of which, Dr Steven was called in, who prescribed for him without having the most distant notion that he was suffering from the effects of acrid poison. During the night, we learn that the young man was from time to time attended by his landlady, and was often convulsed with agony. He became more quiet towards the morning and was left undisturbed; but when the doctor again called on the forenoon of Monday, it was found that the patient was no more. That he was found to have died from the effects of poison we have already stated.

In the course of the investigation which followed, it came out from oral testimony, as well as from the presence of a vast number of letters, that L'Angelier was on terms of endearing intimacy with the daughter of a highly respectable architect, residing in Blythswood Square; and there is reason to believe that he left the Bridge of Allan in consequence of a letter addressed to him by the young lady, expressing a very strong desire to meet him. Whether or not the parties really did or did not meet on that Sunday night, we have no means of knowing; but in resorting to the extreme step of apprehending Miss ——, the authorities no doubt founded on the fact, which is not disputed, that on more than one occa-sion, the lady, who is only 21 years of age, procured arsenic, during the month of March, at the shops of more than one of our West End chemists.

The possession of this poison is, however, compatible with the most entire innocence; for it is known that arsenic is sometimes used by ladies, in a private way, as a cosmetic.

The thought that a highly and virtuously bred young lady could destroy her sweetheart is almost too appalling for belief; but the public voice supplies a reason in the circumstance that a gentleman in a much more prominent and promising position in life than that occupied by L'Angelier had become a suitor for the young lady's hand, and that he had been accepted by her and her parents. This we set down merely as the rumour of the day. Meanwhile we earnestly counsel the public to suspend its judgement pending the investigation now in progress. Though the young lady is in the hands of justice, there is nothing in her proceedings, so far as known to us, which is incompatible with entire innocence. And though she should be found pure and guiltless, as we trust may be the case, the family will have suffered deeply by having had one of their household even suspected of a crime so odious. We can add that Miss ——, who we understand, was judicially examined at great length before the sheriff, on Tuesday last, comported herself throughout with perfect calmness.

The idea of sub judice doesn't appear to have been of great concern to Victorian journalists. It must have been a curious feeling to be engaged as defence counsel when the whole story seemed to be in the public domain before any inquiry had begun. A more serious constraint on the defence was, it might be argued, self-imposed. Madeleine's agents had decided that she should 'run her letters' – a Scottish legal term which, analogous to a writ of *habeas corpus*, exercises the accused's right to as brief a period of imprisonment as possible before being brought to trial.

In Scots Law even today, the gathering of evidence involves two simultaneous investigations. While the prosecution are building their case, the defence are conducting their own independent investigation and it is their responsibility to ascertain the facts for themselves by interviewing potential witnesses. The precognition of witnesses, as it is called, allows the defence to hear first-hand what each witness is liable to offer in testimony. Another important feature of this Scottish system is that it affords, to the defence, the opportunity to put their own questions to the witnesses, questions that would possibly never be asked by the prosecution.

One imagines that these investigations will proceed from two entirely different standpoints, the prosecution presuming guilt and the defence innocence. In the real world, however, the defence is occasionally faced with such an array of damning evidence that there is a danger of the presumption of innocence being supplanted by a rather more pragmatic approach to the task of defending the accused. In these cases, a private tacit acknowledgement of guilt, by the defence team, is accompanied by the concession that the accused has, nevertheless, the right to a fair trial and a robust defence.

It might be argued that, when that occurs, when the presumption of innocence is tacitly abandoned by the defence, the Scottish system may tend slightly to disadvantage the accused in a very subtle way, especially where the case involves any degree of complexity. Where the defence in the English system are presented with an accumulation of information to be analysed, interpreted and disassembled, the Scottish defence team may tend to be preoccupied by the business of the collection of evidence, and the time available to focus on assimilation and critical analysis of that evidence may, possibly, be diminished. It seems possible that, especially in the early days of the investigation, the defence may have believed that they had the task of defending a guilty woman. Whether or not there is any truth in that suggestion, the complexity of the case and the time available to make sense of it all must certainly have been a factor in determining the course of the investigations on both sides.

Over the next few weeks the Crown Office undertook the immense task of building a case against Madeleine. There were to be two charges of attempted murder (19 and 22 February) and a charge of murder (22 March). In the early days it possibly seemed a particularly straightforward case. The post-mortem and chemical analysis showed that Emile had died as a result of arsenic poisoning, and the chemists had a record of each of Madeleine's purchases. No witnesses were forthcoming, however, that could place Emile at Blythswood Square on any of the nights in question; only the circumstances of his premature return on receipt of Madeleine's letter indicated the likelihood of their meeting on the 22 March.

Having found the murderer, it might be expected that as more and more facts are uncovered, things should at some point begin to fall into place, anomalies should be explained, and riddles solved. As more witnesses were interviewed, however, as more facts emerged, the case acquired an increasingly complex and contradictory nature and it was the unanswered questions that were increasing in number, the small details which didn't fit that were mounting up.

It's interesting, with the benefit of hindsight, to look at the reports of the early interviews and to see the train of thought behind the questions. Catherine MacDonald, for example, the lodging house keeper at Prospect House, Bridge of Allan, was asked if, during her stay there, Madeleine was ever in the kitchen. Did she engage in making cake or cooking in any way?

Madeleine had purchased arsenic on 6 March, the day she left for Bridge of Allan. Having made up their minds that she wasn't using it as a cosmetic, the question the Crown Office had to ask themselves was: why would she do that? A clue seemed to offer itself in her letter believed to have been written on Wednesday 25 February, just after Emile's second 'illness' when Madeleine wrote '...You did look bad Sunday night and Monday morning. I think you got sick with walking home so late, and the long want of food, so the next time we meet, I shall make you eat a loaf of bread before you go out.' Here, or so it seemed, lay the answer: she plans to put the arsenic into a cake or a loaf of bread and bring it back to Emile – a present, perhaps, from Bridge of Allan. The lodging house keeper's precognition settled the question: 'I am sure that the prisoner never was in the kitchen and that she did not engage in making cake or cooking in any way. She was too fine for anything of that sort.' They now turned

their thoughts to the notion that she bought the arsenic in prepara-
tion for the possibility that he might come to Bridge of Allan; that
she intended, should he turn up there, to murder him there, not having the wit to realise that she would be the first and indeed the only
suspect. Catherine McDonald's interview was only one of many dis-
appointments that the prosecution would have to put up with.

 That being said, they went about their business with no great
relish. James Smith was a popular figure in Glasgow society and a
personal friend of some of those who were now charged with the
task of bringing his daughter to the gallows. Messages of support
were coming in from all over the city. A subscription was raised by
Smith's employees as a mark of their esteem and of their desire to
show their support for him and for his family.

 The defence team received an early indication that things might
not be as bleak as they had first thought. The people in Dundee who
had known Emile, on reading about the case, immediately got in
touch with Mr Smith. The newspapers picked up on this new twist:

> It may be stated that evidence of great importance for the defence of Miss
> Smith, the young lady now in custody, has been obtained in Dundee, and,
> as the charge against her has attracted so much attention, and the facts
> in favour of her innocence are not generally known, it is only proper
> that we should mention that Mr L'Angelier resided in Dundee for nine
> months in 1852, and was consequently well known to many parties in
> the town with whom he was in terms of intimacy, and who heard with
> regret of his sudden and untimely end.
>
> According to the statement of those who were acquainted with him
> here, he was born and bred in Jersey, and was therefore not a Frenchman,
> as has been stated; but he was of French extraction, his father having fled
> from France at the period of the first French Revolution, and settled in
> Jersey as a nurseryman. His father dying early, the business was carried on
> for the benefit of his mother, and young L'Angelier was sent to Edinburgh
> with the view of gaining the necessary experience as a nursereyman to
> enable him to conduct the business successfully in Jersey. He obtained a

situation in the establishment of Messrs. Dixon & Co., seedsmen, which he held for upwards of six years. He then went to France where he spent about two years, and he was in Paris at the time of the revolution in 1848. He subsequently returned to Edinburgh, but was not successful at obtaining a situation on this his second visit, and indeed it is believed he did not seek very anxiously, as he was then somewhat gay in his habits, and by no means remarkable for his devotion to business. He had contracted an attachment to a young lady belonging to Fife and residing at the time in Edinburgh; but, for some cause or other – it is believed owing to the lady's want of faith in his ability to undertake the responsibilities of married life – 'the course of true love' was interrupted, and L'Angelier left Edinburgh in January 1852 for Dundee, where he obtained a situation with Mr Laird, nursereyman, Nethergate, with whom he lodged during his nine months' residence there.

Mr L'Angelier had not been long in Dundee when news arrived of the marriage of his sweetheart, which filled him with grief and for some time he was uncommonly melancholy, declaring that he was miserable and retched on account of his blighted hopes. Indeed, so much did he feel the disappointment, that he at one time threatened in the hearing of more than one person, to commit suicide – even threatening to stab himself with a knife, a fact which is considered of great importance in connection with the present case, as it shows that it was by no means an incredible thing that a young man of such excitable temperament might, while smarting under a love disappointment, actually commit the rash act which, under similar circumstances in Dundee, he had threatened to do. It is also reported – although we have not been able to verify the statement, that, in another instance, when not so successful in a love affair as he desired, he threatened to drown himself. Indeed he is represented by all who knew him as being of a romantic, excitable, thoroughly Gallican temperament; either greatly elevated or dejected, exceedingly happy or exceedingly miserable; lively, frolicsome, and ambitious to make conquests among the ladies in a station far above his own.

He was very proud of his family descent, and fond of talking of the counts, marquises and dukes of the old French nobility to whom he was related, but when in Dundee was so poor that those to whom he spoke of his high connections used to joke with him, and say it was a pity his aristocratic friends did not remember him. He was not in a position to move in society when here; but as a smart, pleasant young fellow, had numerous acquaintances, with whom, however, he did not, after leaving the town, keep up any correspondence; and many of them heard of him for the first time since his departure when they read the account of his unfortunate end in the public prints.

From this statement, it will be seen that there is ample reason for the public suspending their judgement until the case comes to trial. The parties here most intimately acquainted with the youth at once wrote to the young lady's father on learning from the papers the nature of the charge against her, and a legal gentleman from Glasgow has already visited Dundee, and collected such evidence as is considered material for the defence.

Madeleine had been in prison for three months. To all appearances, she had remained in good spirits and confident, throughout, of the outcome. At eight o'clock on the morning of Tuesday 30 June, crowds besieging the High Court of Justiciary in Edinburgh flooded in as the doors were opened. The areas of the courtroom reserved for the general public were instantly filled. While no journalist was so bold as to allude to the tricoteurs, it was noted that about a dozen women were in court, 'and some of them evinced such a determination to sit out the proceedings that they brought their work with them and commenced stitching as soon as they sat down.' About 10.20 a.m., the three presiding judges – the Lord Justice-Clerk, and the Lords Ivory and Handyside – took their seats and shortly after, with all eyes upon her, accompanied by a female warder, Madeleine ascended the trap stair 'with a firm step and composed air', to take her place at the bar.

Reporters described her as 'a very pretty girl' and

more than ordinarily prepossessing … her eyes are large and dark and full of sensibility … she looks younger than her reputed age of 21 … she was elegantly but simply attired in a white straw bonnet, trimmed with white ribbon and mounted with a figured veil which, however, she did not make much use of to conceal her face … her gown was of brown silk … she held in her gloved hands a cambric handkerchief and a silver mounted smelling-bottle … she took her seat with perfect composure and maintained the same demeanour throughout the day; at the same time, she evidently gave the keenest attention to all the proceedings and examined the Court with all the curiosity of a mere spectator.

The proceedings were held up for almost two hours by one of the main prosecution witnesses failing to appear on time. On his arrival, the court resumed with the Lord Justice-Clerk calling Dr Penny into court and telling him that 'the court have been kept waiting two hours during the time you were absent. You were cited for 10 o'clock?' Penny answered 'I was.' 'Then why', he was asked, 'did you not attend?' Penny's reply was a foretaste of what was to come: 'I was not aware that I would be required so soon.' He was informed that:

the object of the citation is to compel witnesses to attend, and it is a great contempt of Court to imagine that you are to judge of the time. In this case, you have kept the jury and court waiting for more than two hours. We cannot suppose for a moment that this was anything but a singular disregard of the order and forms of citation, and I trust that this exposure will prevent a like occurrence in future.

One of the first witnesses to testify was Emile's landlady Mrs Jenkins. The Lord Advocate James Moncrieff, leading for the Crown, asked her about Emile's first illness. On that first night Emile had asked for the pass-key, saying he might be back late. At eight in the morning Mrs Jenkins had knocked on his door and he said 'come in, if you please.' When she went into his room, he said 'I have been very unwell. Look what I have vomited.' Mrs Jenkins asked him why he hadn't called upon her, and he said 'I was not able to ring the bell. On the road home, I was seized with a violent pain in my bowels and stomach, and when I was taking off my clothes, I lay down on the carpet and thought I should have died, and no-one would have seen me.' He also complained of being very thirsty and asked her to make him some tea. That afternoon he visited the doctor and he was prescribed some medicine. When he returned, he said he felt very cold and he lay down on the sofa. Mrs Jenkins put a railway rug on him.

The Lord Advocate asked if the illness had made a change to his appearance. 'A great change', Mrs Jenkins replied. 'He looked yellow, and not like what he used to be. His skin became dark under the eyes, and the red on his cheeks became more broken.' Asked how quickly he had recovered, Mrs Jenkins said 'well, he never was the same afterwards. He got a little better but, when I asked how he was, he said he never felt well.'

Mrs Jenkins described Emile's second illness in similar terms. She told how, during the night, she had covered him with blankets, placed hot water bottles at his feet and stomach, made him tea and brought him a great number of drinks such as lemon and water, and toast and water. She had looked in on him again, about six in the morning, and he seemed a little better. The doctor later visited Emile and prescribed for him. Emile was off work for a week. He told Mrs Jenkins that the powders that the doctor had prescribed were not 'doing him the good he expected', and he said 'the doctor always says I'm a little better but I do not feel I am getting well.'

After identifying a number of letters and a photograph of Madeleine that Emile had kept in his room, Mrs Jenkins, referring to the photograph, said she had once asked Emile 'is that your intended, Sir?' He had replied 'perhaps, someday.' She also recalled Emile, toward the end of September, having asked her if she would provide a dining room and bedroom. He had told her that he was going to be married about the end of March and he would like it if she would take them in.

Mrs Jenkins then testified as to the period preceding his final illness: Emile's anxiety to receive a letter, his disappointment at its not arriving before his excursion to Bridge of Allan, and her surprise at his subsequent unexpected return on receipt of the letter. He had told her that he would not be back before Wednesday or Thursday. After identifying the letter, Mrs Jenkins recounted the ordeal of Emile's final hours, Miss Perry's arrival and someone's (Stevenson) finding of the letter in Emile's waistcoat pocket. 'Some person – I don't remember who it was – said, "this explains all."' 'Did you see that letter?', the Lord Advocate asked. She replied 'I said "that's the letter that came on Saturday".'

In the cross-examination, John Inglis (Dean of the Faculty of Advocates) who was conducting the defence, seems to the have had an unnerving effect on poor Mrs Jenkins who in her capacity as Emile's landlady had surely suffered enough. 'You have told us of an illness on the 22nd of February, and there was an illness before that of which you say you cannot tell the exact date?' 'Yes.' 'How long might it be before the second illness?' 'It might be eight or ten days, but I cannot speak as to that. I have no remembrance of the proper time.' 'When did he first begin to complain of his health at all?' 'In January, he complained of a sore thumb, then there was a little boil broke out on his neck, and shortly after that, another, but I don't recollect the proper dates. I think it would be about the end of the month.'

On that first day, testimony was also heard from Peter Pollock, the Edinburgh stationer to whom Emile had explained that he had hoped for a letter but that it hadn't arrived; Mrs Jayne Bayne, the Bridge of Allan lodging house keeper who remembered that Emile had intended to stay longer; Charles Rutherford, the Bridge of Allan Postmaster with whom Emile had left his card prior to collecting the letter he was expecting; William Fairfoul, the guard on the mail train who recalled that Emile did not wish to get into Glasgow before dark; and Thomas Ross, the Glasgow auctioneer who had accompanied Emile on his trek from Coatbridge to Glasgow.

Last to take the stand was William Stevenson from Huggins. He read out Emile's letter – the one sent from Bridge of Allan in which he had said that he would be home no later than Thursday. He then read out the letter that he found in Emile's waistcoat pocket – 'Why my beloved did you not come to me? Oh, beloved, are you ill? …'

He had remarked that it explained why Emile was in Glasgow so soon. Stevenson then identified Emile's memorandum book. He had found it in the lodgings but he already knew of its existence; he had seen it before, at the office. Emile had complained to him that the lock on his desk was in a frail state and when he went to look and opened the drawer, the memorandum book had been there.

On the second day, Stevenson continued his testimony. Having taken charge on the morning of Emile's death, he was subject to some fairly intense and prolonged questioning as to his involvement in the gathering and labelling of the numerous letters that were found in Emile's lodgings. Before the court had resumed that morning, he had told the Fiscal's clerks, effectively, that he had had more than enough questioning about the letters and wanted no more to do with it. The volume of testimony required of him, together with the relentless probing of the Dean of Faculty in his determined search for the slightest break in the chain of proof had, seemingly, left Stevenson feeling 'exceedingly uncomfortable and very unwell.' Perhaps he had hoped that they could have found a way to bring the girl to the gallows without putting him through the ordeal of such a protracted and involved investigation.

Dr Thomson, who had attended Emile after his first two illnesses, described the symptoms that he had observed and which led him to prescribe for a 'bilious fever'. The Lord Advocate asked 'were the symptoms such as you would have expected to follow, if you had known that he had taken an irritant poison?' Dr Thomson answered 'Yes, they were.' The court then heard him read the reports of the preliminary and post-exhumation post-mortems.

Edward Maitland, the Solicitor-General, questioned Dr Steven, as to Emile's last hours and the Lord Justice-Clerk then assisted in establishing that the bottle containing the stomach and its contents had been thoroughly clean and fit for use. The Solicitor-General had asked if it was a pickle bottle that was used. Dr Steven replied 'Yes.' 'Was it washed out?' Dr Steven said he saw it repeatedly washed out and had then washed it out himself. The Lord Justice-Clerk, possibly with the benefit of his own experience of the difficulty of completely removing this particular contaminant, said 'I daresay you tasted the stuff, the last time, to see if it was free from the taste of pickles.' 'No my Lord, but it was repeatedly washed out in my presence and I washed it myself afterwards.' The examination then continued with the Solicitor-General asking Dr Steven, 'on the occasion of the second post-mortem, did anything strike you about the preservation of the body?' He replied that it was remarkably well-preserved; all of which juxtaposing must have been somewhat confusing for the jury.

Dr Penny, Professor of Chemistry, was called to testify, firstly as to the presence of arsenic in the stomach. His report was concise and conclusive:

> The stomach and a reddish-coloured fluid were carefully analysed and chemically examined with a view of ascertaining whether they contained any poisonous substances. The liquid contents of the stomach measured eight and a half ounces which, on being allowed to repose, deposited a white powder, which was found on examination to possess the external characteristics and all the chemical properties peculiar to arsenious acid – the common white arsenic of the shops.

The various tests used in examination of the powder were then outlined. As to the quantity, the stomach and its contents had contained nearly eighty-three grains of arsenic, nearly one-fifth of an ounce. The report concluded by stating that,

> these results show unequivocally that the said white powder was arsenious acid; that is, the preparation of arsenic which is usually sold in commerce, and administered or taken as a poison under the name of arsenic or oxide of arsenic. Having carefully considered the results of this investigation, I am clearly of opinion that they are conclusive in showing: firstly, that the matters subjected to examination and analysis contained arsenic; and, secondly, that the quantity, of arsenic found was considerably more than sufficient to destroy life.

When asked how much would be sufficient to destroy life, Dr Penny said, 'it is not easy to give a precise answer ... from four to six grains is generally regarded as likely to destroy life.'

The Lord Advocate moved to the second post-mortem. Again, the presence of arsenic was confirmed. Dr Penny then testified as to tests he had made on the arsenic sold by the chemists Murdoch and Currie. Murdoch's arsenic, as required by law, contained a small proportion of soot, and Currie's, likewise, was coloured by a small amount of indigo. When asked, 'could that colouring matter be removed by washing?' he answered, 'the greater part of it might, by peculiar and dextrous manipulation, be removed, and the arsenic would afterwards appear white to the unassisted eye.' This was an important question since Dr Penny's report specifically refers to his having observed a white powder. Given that the Procurators Fiscal were fully aware that Madeleine had purchased stained arsenic, it is hard to understand from a distance of 150 years why a more thorough examination was not undertaken to establish, unequivocally, the presence or absence of any colouring matter. The Lord Advocate continued: 'if a sufficient portion of that arsenic was administered, so as to cause death, and, prior to death, vomiting to a great and violent extent had taken place, would you have expected to have found, on analysis, any part of the colouring matter?' Dr Penny replied, 'not of the indigo.'

It has to be noted that Dr Penny's 'expectations' in this respect, should not be taken necessarily to qualify as expert testimony; he was being asked to express an opinion which may have called for some practical experience. In point of fact, he was later recalled, having performed an experiment involving two unfortunate dogs – one destroyed by arsenic stained with soot and the other by indigo-stained arsenic. He testified that he had found no difficulty in detecting the colouring matter in post-mortem examination of both dogs.

In cross-examination, the Dean of Faculty sought from Dr Penny an estimate of total amount of arsenic that L'Angelier had ingested, and an opinion as to the difficulty of administering a large dose.

Dr Penny confirmed that it would be 'very difficult to give a large dose in a liquid', and that such cases as he had read of, in which a similar amount was involved, had been cases of suicide. In re-examination however, the Lord Advocate asked, 'would you tell us whether substances such as cocoa or chocolate might be used to administer a considerable amount of arsenic without detection?' Dr Penny answered:

> It might. Allow me to explain. There are great differences between giving rise to suspicion and actual detection. I have found, on experiment, that when 30 or 40 grains of arsenic are put into a warm cup of chocolate, a large portion of the arsenic settles down in the bottom of the cup, and I think that a person drinking that poisonous chocolate would suspect something when the gritty particles came into his mouth and teeth. But if that same quantity or even a larger quantity were boiled up in the chocolate, instead of merely being mixed or stirred, then none of it settles down, and it might be gulped over.

For such an important case, the scientific contribution seems to have been particularly loose. The Lord Advocate's inference that the viscosity of the medium would be an important factor in determining the proportion of arsenic that might be held in suspension was absolutely valid but, if that was to be offered as an explanation for the mystery of the immense quantity swallowed, it surely could have been supported by some analysis of the actual stomach contents. Since almost eighty-eight grains of arsenic had remained in the stomach, some remnants of a thick chocolate drink that had held it in suspension might also have been evident, but no attempt at all seems to have been made to determine the nature of the whole contents of the stomach.

Although the Dean of Faculty would later deal with the implications of the quantity of arsenic, in his address to the jury he seems, at this moment, to have been caught slightly off-guard by Dr Penny's statement. He asked, 'in the case where the chocolate is boiled with the arsenic, what is the reason why the arsenic does not subside?'

Dr Penny answered, 'because a large proportion dissolves with the boiling fluid.' The Dean continued, 'then the arsenic, in the case you have been supposing, would be, you think, held in solution by the chocolate?' 'I am not supposing,' Dr Penny replied, 'it is by actual experiment, and that is what I found to be the case.'

It had all the appearance of a good point having been made for the Crown. It is, of course, facile for someone who has a scientific aptitude and the benefit of hindsight to criticise this testimony, but the fact remains that sometimes it is essential to talk in figures. Woolly experiments are worse than useless and, in a case such as this, they are irresponsible. What temperature, we should have been told, is the highest that can be considered drinkable? What then, was the quantity of arsenic that precipitated out of solution at that temperature? It might also have been asked what the results of that same experiment might have been had it been conducted out of doors, on a cold March night, when the temperature difference between the first and second gulps would have been that much greater. How much of the forty grains would remain either in solution or in suspension by the second gulp?

Without the answers to such questions, the experiment was next to worthless but, there was an even more fundamental error that rendered this testimony not merely inadequate but thoroughly misleading. Dr Penny seems to have forgotten entirely the reason for his appearance in the High Court. Including 5.2 grains of arsenic that was first found to have precipitated to the bottom of the jar, a total of 87.9 grains of arsenic had been held in the stomach alone. This, in addition to the arsenic found in the intestines and other organs, was still only that which remained after an entire night of vomiting and purging. The actual amount of arsenic that L'Angelier had ingested may have been anything between 160 to 240 grains. Dr Penny's experiment, persuasive as it was, was based on only a fraction of the quantity L'Angelier had actually swallowed. With an appropriate quantity of arsenic in the cup, he might have found that the solution was saturated well above drinking temperature with more than half of the arsenic refusing to dissolve at all.

Dr Penny left the witness box after a somewhat disturbing compliment from the Lord Justice-Clerk who said he had 'never heard more clear, distinct or satisfactory evidence.'

Dr Robert Christison, something of an expert in arsenic poisoning, confirmed Dr Penny's conclusions as to the presence of arsenic and spoke to the symptoms, as might be expected. He then spoke about the colouring matter in Murdoch's and Currie's arsenic. He stated that, judging from the depth of colour, he could infer that Murdoch's contained the due proportion of soot, and that Currie's, however, contained something less than the quality and proportions of indigo required by the Act. He pointed out that there was only one-36th part when there should have been one-32nd part.

Right after his very particular assessment of the quality and proportions of the colouring matter sold by Murdoch and Currie, he was asked by the Dean of Faculty if he had seen any colouring matter in the organs he had examined. 'I did not detect colouring matter in the dead body,' Christison replied. 'My attention was not directed to it. I got only one article in which it might have been found, if my attention had been directed to it, viz., the small intestine; the others had been subjected to previous analysis. I was not asked to attend to colouring matter. I did not see it, and I did not search for it.'

If the fact that the proportion of Curries colouring matter was a 36th part, when it should have been a 32nd part, seemed to Christison to be relevant to the case — and it cannot be disputed that it had some relevance — then the presence or absence of colouring matter in the organs was significantly more relevant. If it can be believed that this man would not have noticed the fact that the arsenic that he had found was stained, and that a specific request to distinguish white from non-white would be necessary before he could either see or report the difference he was, at the very least, singularly lacking in initiative and common sense.

A few minutes later, still under cross-examination, he said, 'I was informed by Dr Penny of the quantity he found in the stomach — more than eighty grains. There was also a white powder found, in addition.' Christison was quite aware that the 'white powder' had been tested by Dr Penny. It weighed 5.2 grains and it was found to be pure white arsenic.

The day closed after testimony from Amadee Thuau, Emile's fellow lodger and Auguste De Mean, the French Consul. Thuau joined the ever-growing list of people who had not expected Emile to return so soon from Bridge of Allan, whereas De Mean – recalling in cross-examination L'Angelier's digestive problems, his always-ready bottle of laudanum, and his half-hour discussion about how much arsenic a person could consume without injury – seemed to do more work for the Defence than the Crown.

The trial resumed the following morning at 10 a.m. As before, every available seat had been occupied from 8 a.m. It was noted that 'the prisoner, on taking her seat at the bar, appeared as composed and apparently free from nervousness as on the two former days. On entering the bar she smiled and shook hands with her agent, and spoke for a few moments with every appearance of confidence and cheerfulness with the Dean of Faculty.'

Testimony was heard from: Madeleine's best friend Mary Buchanan, who had accompanied Madeleine into the chemist's; Augusta Guibilei Walcot, a pupil teacher at Miss Gorton's School for young ladies, who denied that she had ever advised the use of arsenic as a cosmetic; the Smiths' houseboy William Murray, whom Madeleine had sent for the Prussic Acid; the chemists and their assistants who had been involved in the sale of arsenic to her; William Campsie, the Smiths' gardener at Rowaleyn, who told the Court that he had never received any arsenic from Miss Smith for the purpose of killing rats; Billy Minnoch whose matter-of-fact testimony, it should be observed, was later to lead armchair students of the case to portray him as boring and sombre which, in fact, could not have been further from the truth of the man.

Thomas Kennedy, Emile's friend and the cashier at Huggins, spoke of Emile as being a well-behaved, well-principled, religious young man, whom he held in some regard. He testified as to Emile's absence from work, his illnesses, identified a number of letters, and spoke of the morning that Emile had come into his office crying, having received Madeleine's letter wishing an end to the relationship. Mrs Clark, L'Angelier's landlady when he had lodged at the curator's house in the Botanic Gardens, spoke highly as to his character. She remembered him taking away some gold or silver fish on the occasion of his visit around 6 March. In cross-examination, Mrs Clark was not asked if arsenic was kept at the Botanic Gardens and where it was kept; she was not asked whether it was kept under lock and key, and she was not asked whether Emile could have had access to it without her knowledge. Mr Clark was not called.

An objection from the Dean of Faculty interrupted John Murray, a Glasgow sheriff officer, who was testifying that his investigations indicated that no person of the name L'Angelier had purchased arsenic between the months of December and March. The Lord Justice-Clerk said that what was brought forward was simply to prove that L'Angelier had not bought arsenic under his own name, not that he might not have bought it under another name. He, therefore, thought it a proper question. Murray resumed his testimony: 'I examined all the chemist's shops in Glasgow, and extended my inquiries to Coatbridge, Bridge of Allan, and the road to Stirling, and found no such entry regarding a person named L'Angelier.' The third day came to a close with an important discussion on the procedure for collection of evidence, with the Dean of Faculty complaining that the Defence had been put at a disadvantage. Once again, Madeleine had remained at the bar from start to finish, refusing any refreshment.

Friday's business began at the usual time with the Dean of Faculty calling the attention of the Court to a circular that had been printed, announcing that the *Scotch Thistle* of Saturday would contain a report of the trial, and of all the letters between the prisoner and L'Angelier. He said that 'the letters in print – upwards of 100 – were being set up in this newspaper office, with the view of being published to-morrow.' The circular was signed, 'James Cunningham.' In these circumstances it appeared to him that the proposed publication was a gross breach of public decorum. 'I am,' he said, 'much disposed to leave this matter in the hands of the Court, but I must take the liberty of urging that some proceedings should be taken for preventing the proposed publication.' The Lord Advocate added that if the circular to which the Dean referred had fallen into his hands he would have taken the decisive course his learned friend had taken, and he agreed with his learned friend in the extreme and gross impropriety of this publication, and he was perfectly ready to co-operate in any proceedings that might be necessary. The Lord Justice-Clerk ordered the immediate attendance of James Cunningham.

Several witnesses then spoke of the clandestine nature of the correspondence itself. They spoke of letters being sent to Christina Haggart and addressed by L'Angelier's colleagues at Huggins to conceal from Mrs Smith the fact that the correspondence was continuing. There were also letters addressed to a fictitious Miss Bruce, Rhu Post Office, to be called for.

Christina herself gave a seemingly charming and convincing monosyllabic performance, and gave away no more than was absolutely necessary. She told of her own complicity in conveying L'Angelier's letters to Madeleine when the family lived at India Street. Around that time she had also opened the back gate on more than one occasion to let him in.

'Did you ever see him come into the house in India Street?' – 'Yes.'

'Come into it?' – 'Yes.'

'Who admitted him?' – 'I was asked to open the gate.'

'By whom?' – 'By Miss Smith.'

'Which gate do you mean?' – 'The back gate.'

'The back gate in India Street?' – 'Yes.'

'When was this?' – 'During the day.'

'Were the family at home?' – 'I think they were all in church, except the younger sister.'

'That would be a Sunday?' – 'Yes.'

'Into what apartment did he go?' – 'The laundry.'

'Who took him in there?' – 'Miss Smith.'

'And she went in with him?' – 'Yes.'

'Was the door shut when they went in?' – 'Yes.'

'How long did he remain there?' – 'I do not remember exactly.'

'Some minutes or a considerable time?' – 'About half an hour.'

'Did he come back to India Street on other occasions?' – 'At night.'

'How often?' – 'I do not remember.'

'Was it once or oftener?' – 'Oftener.'

'Five or six times?' – 'I don't think more than three or four times.'

'You say "at night." What hour?' – 'About ten o'clock.'

'After the family had retired for bed?' – 'No.'

'Before they retired to their rooms?' – 'Yes.'

'Did he always go to the laundry?' – 'No.'

'Where did he go?' – 'He stood at the back gate.'

'Did he not come into the house at all?' – 'Not to my knowledge.'

'Did you open the back gate to him?' – 'Yes.'

'By Miss Smith's directions?' – 'Yes.'

'Did you set it open when there was no-one there, or open it when he was there?' – 'I opened it when he was there, and I opened it when he was not there.'

'On some occasions, when you went to open the gate, you found him standing there and, at other times, you did not?' – 'Yes.'

'Did Miss Smith, on those occasions, go out to him?' – 'I did not see her.'

'Did you leave the back doors which led to the gate open?' – 'Yes.'

'Was there anyone in the laundry at that time?' – 'No.'

'Might Miss Smith and this gentleman have gone into the laundry, without you seeing them?' – 'Yes.'

The Court heard that Christina had also played a part in L'Angelier's more recent visit to Blythswood Square. At Madeleine's request, she had opened the back door into the lane, returned to the house and gone into the kitchen, where she remained for some time. She was asked if she had remained rather longer than usual in the kitchen. She replied that she had, that Miss Smith had asked her to do so in order that she might see her friend, but she had not said where she would be seeing him. 'Did you think she was in your bedroom?' – 'I had no doubt but I did not know of my own knowledge.' As to 22 March, Christina remembered that she hadn't been well that day and had stayed in bed until 5 or 6 p.m. Her fiancé, Duncan MacKenzie, had visited her that evening and he had waited downstairs while she attended family worship at 9 p.m. She had last seen Miss Smith in the dining room before going back downstairs to her boyfriend. She saw MacKenzie out by the back gate shortly after 10 p.m.

Duncan MacKenzie then spoke of having met L'Angelier when the family lived in India Street. L'Angelier had asked him if he was going into the house, if he knew Christina, and if he would ask her to come out. He was present when they met but did not hear what they said. 'I was not jealous of them talking,' he said, 'although Christina thought I was.' He later received a letter from Madeleine saying it was her friend he had seen and that she hoped nothing would arise between Christina and him.

Following some testimony as to L'Angelier's proximity to Blythswood Square on the evening of the 22nd, Mrs and then Mr Towers entered the witness box to recount the tale of L'Angelier's visit to their home in Portobello, his lengthy conversation on the subject of his own health, his illnesses and his story of the poisoned coffee and chocolate.

Miss Perry was next to come into the Court. An audible intake of breath accompanied her entrance as the public got their first sight of the woman whom they believed to have been L'Angelier's girlfriend prior to Madeleine. Rumour had it that L'Angelier had first settled upon Mary Perry and would, in all likelihood, have settled for her had not Madeleine come into view. They expected 'a dashing young creature – a second string to L'Angelier's bow.' Instead, they beheld, 'a little old maid, in quiet black bonnet and brown dress, with an intellectual cast of countenance, and a pair of spectacles imparting a quaintness to her face.'

Her evidence was particularly interesting, not so much in its content, but in her use of untenable forced construction. Emile, having said, 'if she were to poison me, I would forgive her,' her own words to him had been, 'you ought not to allow such thoughts to pass through your mind. What motive could she have for giving you anything to hurt you?' He had replied, 'I don't know that; perhaps she might not be sorry to be rid of me.' Patently conscious of one of the Crown's several impending predicaments – the difficulty of explaining why a man who believed he was being poisoned would go back for more – and their consequent need to downplay Emile's suspicions, she then testified that, 'all this was said in earnest, but I interpreted the expression "to be rid of me" to mean rid of her engagement.' An even more remarkable recourse to blatant dissembling came in cross-examination when the Dean of Faculty asked her about L'Angelier's threat to show the letters to Mr Smith:

> … he offered to give the letters to her father. I did not understand the meaning to be that he threatened to show the letters to her father. I understood that to be a consent, by him, to give up the engagement, and he so represented it. Miss Smith would not accede to that proposal and the engagement remained unbroken at Miss Smith's desire.

L'Angelier and Miss Perry seem to have been well-suited.

Finally that day, Mr Cunningham of the *Scotch Thistle* came before the bench and disappointed everyone in the public gallery by denying that he had any letters at all and assuring the Court that he intended to print only those letters that were read in Court.

Saturday 4 July, the fifth day of the trial, brought the evidence that Mr Cunningham knew would sell more copies of the *Scotch Thistle* than ever before: the letters. The day began with some more 'expert' testimony from Dr Christison but once that was out of the way the public gallery was treated to the strange incongruity of Madeleine's love letters being read in the flat, matter-of-fact tones of the Clerk of Court. The whole course of the affair was traced out in these notes. The trivial and the mundane, together with her private thoughts and the expression of her most secret feelings, intended to be read only by her lover, or rather the man this young girl believed she was in love with; all were read aloud to the Court. By Monday, they would be printed in almost every newspaper in the country. The *Glasgow Herald* trumpeted its high regard for public decorum: 'We have found it necessary to omit from the letters, as read, various passages as unfit for publication on the ground of great indelicacy …'

After the last letter was read, the Lord Advocate proposed to tender the entries in L'Angelier's memorandum book. Following an objection by Mr Young, and argument on both sides, the Court postponed its decision.

The *Herald* reported that:

> there was a marked change in the appearance and demeanour of the unfortunate prisoner today. On coming up to the dock, she had a more saddened and less elastic gait than formerly and, during the day, her colour went and came – sometimes her cheeks were flushed and, at others, they were pale, while there was a frequent compression and quivering of the lip. Altogether, she seemed to be at times much distressed.

The Court opened on Monday with the decision of the judges on the admissibility of L'Angelier's memorandum book, the Lord Justice-Clerk and Lord Handyside being against, and Lord Ivory in favour of its admission.

Mrs Janet Anderson was the last witness for the Crown. Her name had appeared in L'Angelier's copy-press letter: 'I do not think, Mimi dear, that Mrs Anderson would say your mother told her things she had not.' She testified that she had met Madeleine at a party and asked about her necklace. 'I asked if she had got it from Mr Minnoch, and she denied that.' The Lord Advocate asked Mrs Anderson if she had spoken of this to anyone. She replied that she didn't recollect speaking to anybody and then she said, 'I may have mentioned that I thought she got it from Mr Minnoch.' This testimony closed the case for the Crown.

In opening the case for the Defence, the Dean of Faculty announced that, in the course of the examination of some of the first witnesses, reference will be made to affairs of some little delicacy in which L'Angelier had been engaged in some previous part of his life, but I am extremely reluctant to drag names before the public in this examination, and I hope my learned friend, the Lord Advocate, will assist me in this.

So, neither the name nor the person of the Lady in Fife was to be brought into the trial. It might seem that, with a girl on trial for her life, the good name of another should not have been given such generous consideration but it was apparent to the Defence that her testimony could not have any substantial bearing on the case. That being said, she was actually in a very unique position. She had not only been a victim of L'Angelier's ambitions but, unlike Madeleine, she was free to speak. She could have told the court, first-hand, what kind of man L'Angelier really was in his relationship with her. It might also have been valuable to know how her parents had dealt with him. That testimony, however, would only have had some significance in context of the Defence intending, from the first, to present an entirely different case, portraying Madeleine as the victim and the object of L'Angelier's revenge. While his death remained a mystery, her testimony could not have advanced Madeleine's defence to any degree, and would have achieved only the ruin of another reputation.

We have already essentially heard in the earlier part of our story, the various recollections provided by the witnesses for the Defence. Such testimony as has been omitted has generally either been effectively duplicated by other witnesses or is merely corroborative of other testimony. Charles Baird, for example, spoke of finding him very unwell in his lodgings at Franklin Place:

I think it was either in the last fortnight of September or the first fortnight of October last. When I went up in the evening he said he had returned straight from the office. He ordered some tea. He took very ill suddenly, and put his hand on his stomach, and, as it were, doubled himself up. He lay down on the sofa, screaming with pain. This continued for about fifteen minutes. I advised him to send for a medical man, and left him, and I believe he did so. He was going to bed when I left. It was about ten o'clock when I went, and about eleven when I left. I saw him the following morning between nine and ten. I asked him how he was, and he said he had a very bad night of it, that he had sent for a medical man – I believe a Dr. Steven, Great Western Road, who had been employed by him before. He said he had vomited a great deal during the night.

Of extracts from the correspondence put in evidence by the Dean of Faculty, the first, in September 1855, began,

Beloved Emile, I have just received your note. I shall meet you. I do not care though I bring disgrace upon myself. To see you, I would do anything. Emile, you shall yet be happy; you deserve it. You are young; you, who ought to desire life, wishing to end it! Oh, for the sake of your once-loved Mimi, desire to live and succeed in this life. Everyone must meet with disappointment. I have suffered from disappointment. I long to see you and speak to you.

In another, written in October 1855, Madeleine had written,

Beloved Emile, your kind letter I received this morning. Emile, you are wrong in thinking I love you for your appearance. I did and do admire you, but it was for yourself alone that I loved you. I can give you no other reason, for I have got no other. If you had been a young man of some Glasgow family, I have no doubt there would have been no objection to you. But because you are unknown, he has rejected you. Dear Emile, explain this sentence in your note: 'Before long, I shall rid you and all the world of my presence.' God forbid that you ever do. My last letter was not filled with rash promises. No, these promises written in my last letter shall be kept – must be kept. Not a moment passes but I think of you.

Such rare glimpses of L'Angelier's personality, in his own hand – infantile and self-obsessed as in this melodramatic attempt to invoke guilt and sympathy – are, of course, invaluable in this case where we have such a wealth of opportunity to criticise and pass judgement upon the volumes of text written by Madeleine, set against a handful of lines written by L'Angelier, and each one of these, presumably, being lines that he somehow believed would reflect well upon him.

Janet, Madeleine's thirteen-year-old sister, appeared for the defence and told the Court about both Madeleine and herself going to bed after 10.30 on the night of 22 March. Some testimony was led regarding the ease with which white arsenic could be obtained, mainly from printers and dyers and their suppliers. Doctors were brought in to speak of cases of suicide by arsenic – none had confessed before death to having taken the poison – and to recount their experiments proving the relative safety of washing with arsenic. Various druggists spoke of a man fitting L'Angelier's description having visited their shops on 22 March, although this evidence was now contradicted by the more solid and persuasive testimony of the railway guard Fairfoul and of Ross, the auctioneer who had walked with L'Angelier from Coatbridge.

With the conclusion of the case for the Defence, it was reported in the *Glasgow Herald* that,

> the prisoner had been very unwell and suffered much from exhaustion on Sunday. But today she was well, quite composed, and evidently in good spirits. When any jocular remark was made, she laughed quietly. She was quite unmoved when her sister appeared in the box, and when Janet, before leaving, stood for a moment under the bench to look at the prisoner, the latter gave her a pleasant smile of recognition.

The *Glasgow Courier* went into more detail although, reading between the lines, they seem to have reached a verdict already:

> The personal appearance of Miss Smith, the central figure in this remarkable case, is the point on which most attraction seems to be fixed in the court by the spectators with which it is thronged, and which is most

talked of amongst the less privileged outside world. Eager crowds gather in the early morning at the Jail and in Parliament Square to catch a glimpse of the prisoner as she is taken to the Court. In the evenings, thousands gather in the streets to see the cab in which she is borne back from the Court-room to the prison. Every day sees hundreds at the door of the court who would willingly expend guineas in obtaining a look at the young lady. Hundreds are daily passed in for a few minutes by official friends to get a glimpse of the prisoner, and may be seen departing with the air of satisfied curiosity upon their anxious countenances. Others who are privileged to sit in the court through the whole day may be seen surveying the slight figure in the dock, with eyes that never weary of gazing upon it, from the opening of the diet until its close.

In the midst of all this excitement – passing through the eager crowd, from and to prison – seated at the bar with hundreds of eyes steadily upon her – Madeleine Smith is the only unmoved, cool, serene personage to be seen. From the first moment to the last, she has preserved that undaunted, defiant attitude of perfect repose which has struck every spectator with astonishment. She passes from the cab to the courtroom – or rather to the cell beneath the dock – with an air of a belle entering a ball-room. She ascends the narrow staircase leading into the dock with a cool, jaunty air, an unveiled countenance, the same perpetual smile – or smirk, rather, for it lacks all the elements of a genuine smile – the same healthy glow of colour, and the same confident ease. The female turnkey at her side looks more of the prisoner, for while she is still and scarcely ever lifts her eyes, Miss Smith never ceases surveying all that goes on around her – watching every word of every witness, returning every stare with compound interest, glancing every second minute at the down-turned eyes in the side galleries, and even turning right round upon the reporters immediately behind her, to see how they get along with that note-taking which is carrying her name and deeds into every British home.

When judges and jurymen retire for lunch, she refuses even so much as a small packet of sandwiches. Others may be thirsty amid the hot excitement but, when the female attendant offers her a glass of water, she will not have it. Others may be under the necessity of retiring for a few minutes;

she knows no such necessity. There she sits, refusing meat and drink or a moment's retirement in her cell, with a smelling-bottle in her dainty little hand, which she never uses – a splendid specimen of physical power, and of such endurance as only a will of terrible strength could attain. When she is called upon to plead, she says, in a clear, sweet treble – no trace of huskiness or emotion perceptible in the voice, no trembling on her tongue – 'Not guilty!'

The Dean of Faculty, her leading counsel, bids her good morning or says a word to her when the proceedings close for the day, and she smiles so cheerily that you listen to hear her laugh. Whoever speaks, counsel or witness, must be sensible of the fixed, penetrating glance of her large dark eyes. Her head is perpetually turning from the gentlemen of the long robe to the responsive witness-box, as the questions are put and answered.

Dr Penny describes his analytical investigations of the portions of her old sweetheart's body, and the ribbons of her bonnet are so still that you clearly perceive there is not even a hidden shudder passing through her frame. Dr Steven narrates how L'Angelier's body was exhumed, and she only leans forward on the railing before the dock to study the doctor's face, and hear the words the more easily. The poor Frenchman's land-lady relates, with pathetic simplicity, how L'Angelier died, and Madeleine meets the eye of the honest matron without blanching for a moment. She sees her old school-companion and friend, Mary Buchanan, in tears; but the smirk does not desert her, and she cannot shed a responsive tear to those of the girl who was to have been her bridesmaid. The wife of the curator of the Botanic Gardens turns her honest, large grey eyes upon the woman who deserted her old lodger, of whom she thought so highly, and whom she now laments so sincerely; but Madeleine is too much for the matron, and the witness is the first to lift away her gaze. Even Mr Minnoch in the witness-box – placed in that position so peculiar and trying, solely by her influence – fails to steal from her a single particle of equanimity, and she looks steadily at that deeply injured merchant, who has too keen a sense of his own humiliation to direct even a solitary glance in the direction of the dock! It requires the vividly pictorial and earnest story of Mons. de Mean to bring a crimson blush to her cheek, or to make a momentary shadow of concern darken her brow.

The scene in the courtroom is such as the High Court of Justiciary has never before presented in the present century. The whole of the Faculty of Advocates would seem to be there, filling more than their own gallery; a goodly array of writers to the signet appear in their gowns; upwards of a score of reporters to the press ply their busy pencils; the western side of the gallery abounds in the moustachioed scions of the aristocracy; ministers of the gospel are there gathering materials for discourse; and civic dignitaries are in abundance. A few women who may expect to be called ladies are mingling in the throng. Among the clergy we notice Principle Lee, William Pulsford; the celebrated Independent preacher, Dr Andrew Thomson, professor Harper, and Mr Hibbs, an Episcopalian priest, who 'goes fu' for preaching about Palmer and Dove, and will, no doubt, have a morning sermon on one of these Sabbaths devoted to Madeleine Smith. Lords Cowan and Ardmillan, after they are relived from their judicial duties elsewhere, come and sit on the bench; so does the venerable Lord Murray and Lords Wood, Deas and others.

The fee given to the Dean of Faculty, the senior counsel for the defence, is said to be a hundred guineas, but this retainer will be supplemented likely by a daily 'refresher' during the trial. It is believed that he feels peculiarly interested in the case, and has so mastered it that he will leave no stone unturned to secure the deliverance of his unfortunate client.

Chapter Four

THE LORD ADVOCATE'S ADDRESS

For six days the jury had listened and observed as successive witnesses appeared before them, some of them very young, some old and wise and learned. Some had told a simple story, honest, convincing and unequivocal; others had, with erudition and scientific clarity, muddied the waters, good and proper. And now, out of the chaos of this aggregate, the advocates must try to bring order, structure and light. It was the task, firstly of James Moncrieff, the Lord Advocate, and then John Inglis, the Dean of Faculty, to make sense of the bewildering array of complex and often conflicting evidence. Shortly after 10 a.m. on Tuesday 7 July, the Lord Advocate rose to his feet to address the fifteen men who would decide the truth of it.

Gentlemen of the jury, after an investigation which for its length has proved unexampled, I believe, in the criminal annals of this country, I have now to discharge perhaps the most painful public duty that ever fell to my lot. I am quite sure, gentlemen, that I shall meet with that attention which the deep importance of this case requires, and which you have paid to its details from the commencement.

It is now my duty, as clearly and as fully as I can, to draw these details together, and to present to you, if I can, in a connected shape, the links of that chain of evidence which we have been engaged for the last week in constructing. Gentlemen, I could have rejoiced if the result of this inquiry would have justified us in withdrawing our charge against the prisoner. I grieve to say that so far is that from being the result to which we come that, if you give me your attention, you will arrive at the conclusion that every link is so firmly fastened, every loophole is so completely stopped, that there does not remain the possibility of escape for the unhappy prisoner from the net that she has woven for herself.

Gentlemen, the indictment charges three separate crimes: two separate acts of administering poison with intent to kill; and the third charge is the successful administering of poison with intent to kill, viz., murder.

In stating to you the evidence on which we think that these charges must be found proved, I shall avoid, as far as possible, travelling into a region which this case affords too great materials for. I mean the almost incredible evidence which it has afforded of disgrace, and sin, and degradation, the fearful domestic results which must inevitably follow, those feelings of commiseration and horror which the age, the sex, and the condition of the prisoner must produce in every mind. All these are things into which I shall not travel. They might unnerve me for the discharge of my painful public duty. Besides, no language of mine, no language of my eloquent and learned friend, can convey to the mind one-tenth of the impression which the bare recital of the details of this case has already created throughout the whole of this country. The only other remark of that kind which I shall make is this, that while a prisoner in the position of this unfortunate lady is entitled, justly entitled, to say that such a crime shall not be lightly presumed or proved against her; yet, gentlemen, if the charges in the indictment be true, if the tale which I have to tell be a true one, you are trying a case of as cool, premeditated, deliberate homicide as ever justly brought its perpetrator within the compass and penalty of the law.

Gentlemen, the first fact on which I found is one into which it will not be necessary for me to go in any great detail. It is a very important fact in the inquiry, but it is one on which you can have no doubt whatever: this unfortunate man, Emile L'Angelier, died of arsenic. There can be no doubt about that. The symptoms which he exhibited on the night of the 22nd and morning of the 23rd March were in all respects the symptoms of poisoning by arsenic. His body was opened, and the stomach was analysed by Dr Penny, who found an immense quantity of arsenic in it; the other parts of the body which were taken out at the exhumation were analysed by Dr Christison, and he found traces of arsenic in every one of them; and therefore, gentlemen, I think you will come to the conclusion – and it is not a conclusion on which it is necessary for me to dwell – that the inquiry starts with this ascertained and certain fact, that L'Angelier died on the morning of the 23rd March in consequence of the administration of arsenic, whether given him by another, or taken by himself, in whatever way he swallowed it. The cause of his death was unquestionably arsenic.

The next question which arises is, by whom was that poison administered? That truly constitutes the inquiry which you have now to answer. What is the evidence that connects the prisoner at the bar with the death of L'Angelier? My story is short. This young lady returned from a London boarding school in the year 1853. She met L'Angelier somewhere, I believe, about the end of 1854. L'Angelier's history has not been very clearly brought out. It is plain, unquestionably, that in 1851 he was in very poor and destitute circumstances. Of his character I say nothing at present but this: that it is quite clear that, by energy and attention, he had worked his way up to a position that was at least respectable, a position in which those who came in contact with him plainly had for him a very considerable regard. It is no part of my case to maintain the character of the unhappy deceased. The facts in this case make it impossible to speak of him in any terms but those of very strong condemnation. Nor am I at all inclined to say that from first to last his conduct was that of a man of honour. But still it is plain that, when Miss Smith became first acquainted with L'Angelier, he was a man moving in a respectable position, bearing a respectable character, liked by all those who came in contact with him, spoken of by the three landladies with whom he lodged, in the highest possible terms, a man of whom the chancellor of the French Consulate spoke as respectable and steady, a man spoken of by his employers and by his fellow-clerks in Huggins's warehouse also in the highest terms. I do not say anything of that at present, but such is the fact.

These two persons met; they were introduced, I assume, clandestinely. After a time, it seems, an attachment commenced, which was forbidden by her parents. It is only right to say that the earlier letters of the prisoner at that time show good feeling, proper affection, and a proper sense of duty. Time went on; the intercourse was again renewed, and in the course of 1856, as you must have found, it assumed a criminal aspect. From that time down to the end of the year, not once or twice, but, I have evidence to show, repeatedly, acts of improper connection took place. It will be necessary for you to take into your consideration that she had so completely committed herself by the end of 1856, that she was, I will not say in L'Angelier's power – he was in her power – but she belonged to him, and could with honour belong to no one else. But her affection began to cool; another suitor appeared; she endeavoured to break off her connection with L'Angelier by coldness, and asked him to return her letters. He refused, and threatened to put them into the hands of her father; and it seemed to be said that this was a kind of dishonourable threat. There is much that is dishonourable in this case, but not in that. It would not have been honourable to allow the prisoner at the bar to become the wife of any other man.

It was then she saw the position she was in. She knew what letters she had written to L'Angelier; she knew what he could reveal; she knew that, if those letters were sent to her father, not only would her marriage with Mr Minnoch be broken off, but that she could not hold up her head again. She writes in despair to him to give her back her letters; he refuses. There is one interview; she attempts to buy prussic acid. There is another interview; she has bought arsenic. There is a third interview; she has bought arsenic again. Her letters, instead of being cold, instead of demands for the recovery of her letters being contained in them, again assume all the warmth of affection they had the year before. On the 12th of March she has been with Mr Minnoch making arrangements for her marriage in June; on the 2st she invites L'Angelier, with all the ardour of passion, to come to see her. She buys arsenic on the 18th, and L'Angelier dies of poison on the morning of the 23rd.

Chapter Four

The story is strange, in its horrors almost incredible, and no one can wonder that such a story should carry a thrill of horror into every family in the land. Well may my learned friend require me to bring strong proof of it, for certainly, without clear proof, no one would believe it. The prisoner is well-entitled to every presumption of innocence which law and reason can give her, but if, as I am certainly bound to do, I bring before you such proof as to carry conviction to your minds that no reasonable man can doubt then, incredible as the story is, and fearful as the result of your verdict must be, we have no alternative, in the discharge of our public duty, but myself to ask, and you to give, that verdict which the facts of the case, if proved, demand.

But what that proof is to be, you must consider very seriously. In cases of this kind – in occult crimes especially – the ends of justice would be perpetually defeated if you were to say you shall not convict a man unless you find some person who saw the crime committed. But in the case of administration of poison, that remark applies with peculiar force. In truth, the fact of administering poison before witnesses is so far from affording, in the first instance, a presumption of guilt, that it sometimes is the strongest proof of innocence. I remember a case which attracted as much attention in a sister country as this has done in ours. The culprit there sat by the bedside of his victim, surrounded by medical attendants, gave him the poison in their presence – sat and witnessed its effects – saw his dying agonies with a coolness that could hardly be believed. There could hardly be a stronger presumption of his innocence than that; and the result was that he very nearly had entirely escaped suspicion from the fact that the thing was done openly. And, therefore, in the case of the administration of poison, the fact of there being no eye-witness to the administration is not an element of much weight in the inquiry. You may assume that if it was done with a guilty intention it was done secretly. The question is, whether we have evidence to trace the crime from the course of the circumstances.

Now, having thus given you an outline of the nature of the evidence, I go on to consider that evidence in detail. The first letter which it is necessary for me to refer to is the letter dated 29th April '56. In that letter she says, 'Dearest, I must see you; it is fearful never to see you; but I am sure I don't know when I shall see you. P. has not been a night in town for some time, but the first night he is off I shall see you. We shall spend an hour of bliss. There shall be no risk; only C.H. shall know' – this C.H. being Christina Haggart, who was made the confidant of this amour since its commencement, and the vehicle through whom the letters were transmitted.

On Friday, May 3rd, '56, the prisoner says, 'P. has been in bed two days. If he should not feel well and come down on Tuesday, it shall make no difference. Just you come; only darling, I think if he is in the boat, you should get out at Helensburgh. Well, beloved, you shall come to the gate – you know it – and wait till I come. And then, oh happiness, won't I kiss you, my love, my own beloved Emile, my husband dear? I don't think there is any risk. Well, Tuesday, 6th May – the gate – half-past ten; you understand, darling.'

The next is dated Wednesday morning, five o'clock, you have these words 'My own, my beloved husband – I trust to God you got home safe, and were not much the worse of out. Thank you, my love, for coming so far to see your Mimi. It is truly a pleasure to see my Emile. Beloved, if we did wrong last night, it was in the excitement of our love. Yes, beloved, I did truly love you with my soul.' Then she says further down, 'Am I not your wife? Yes, I am. And you may rest assured, after what has passed, that I cannot be the wife of any other but dear, dear Emile.' Then after referring to a journey to Lima, which L'Angelier had proposed making, she goes on to say, 'I shall write dear Mary soon. What would she say if she knew we were so intimate? She would lose all her good opinion of us both – would she not?' That letter speaks language not to be mistaken.

From that period dates the commencement of the criminal intimacy between the parties. The letters between that date of 7th May and the end of the year are written in a strain that really I do not think I should comment upon. I can say this, that the expressions in these letters – the language in which they are couched – the matters to which they refer, show so entire an overthrow of the moral sense – the sense of moral delicacy and decency as to create a picture which I do not know ever had its parallel in an inquiry of this sort. That is the character of these letters from May, 1856, down to the end. Where the prisoner had learned this depraved moral state of thought and feeling it is not for me to say. If my learned friend means to say that L'Angelier had his own share in corrupting her moral sense, I shall not much dispute it. It does not matter to this inquiry whether that was so or not. There is scarcely one of these letters down to the end of December, 1856, or beyond that period, that does not allude in direct terms to such things as are alluded to in the letters already quoted from.

I next refer to a letter of Friday, 27th May, from which I take the following as a specimen of the letters which passed at this time. In that letter she says 'I think I would be wishing you to love me, if I were with you, but I don't suppose you would refuse me, for I know you will like to love your Mimi' – three scores being made under 'love.' In a letter, which has no date, she swears she will never marry any one else, and in another letter, enclosed in the same envelope, she says 'Our intimacy has not been criminal, as I am your wife before God.' Then she says 'I promise to you, you shall have it (my likeness) some day, so that promise won't be broken. If I did not sign my name, it was for no reason. Unless it is to a stranger, I never do put Smith, only Madeleine.' The conclusion of that letter is in the same strain as the rest.

The correspondence proceeds, and we have a letter dated Saturday night, and bearing the Helensburgh post-mark, July, '56. In that letter she says, 'I shall not see you till the nights are a little darker. I can trust C.H. She will never tell about our meeting. She intends to be married in November; but she may change her mind.' In point of fact, C.H., or Christina Haggart, was married in May last.

The next I refer to is one dated on Thursday evening, in which the prisoner says, 'I cannot see you ere you go, for which I am sorry. You forget that my little sister is in my bedroom, and I could not go out by the window, or leave the house, and she there. It is only when P. is away I can see you, for then Janet sleeps with M.' She then refers to his visit to Badgemore. My learned friend requested that the last passage in that letter should be read, for the purpose of showing that she had read an article in *Blackwood's Magazine* about arsenic. That shows plainly, at any rate, that it was written in the month of September. At the bottom of the page is this passage, 'I did tell you at one time that I did not like [William is first written, but scored out] Minnoch, but he was so pleasant that he quite raised himself in my estimation.' That must have been in September, 1856, and you will see that in the correspondence to the end of the year there are constant allusions to Minnoch, by way of preparing L'Angelier for something in connection with that man. And it turns out, in point of fact, that L'Angelier did become extremely jealous of his attentions.

The next letter has the post-mark, Helensburgh, 29th September. She begins by saying, 'I did not write you on Saturday, as C.H. was not at home, so I could not get it posted. I don't think I can see you this week. But I think next Monday I shall, as P. and M. are to be in Edinburgh. But my only thought is Janet; what am I to do with her? I shall have to wait till she is asleep, which may be near eleven o'clock. But you may be sure I shall do it as soon as I can.' Further on she goes on to say, 'Mr Minnoch has been here since Friday. He is most agreeable. I think we shall see him very often this winter. He says we shall, and P. being so fond of him, I am sure he will ask him in often.'

You will recollect that Mr Minnoch's house is next to Mr Smith's in Blythswood Square. The last letter is clearly written just before the family left Helensburgh to go, for the first time, to the Blythswood Square house. In the next, writing from Helensburgh on Tuesday she says, 'I forgot to tell you last night that I shall not be able, of an evening, to let you in. My room is next to B., and on the same floor as the front door. (This refers to the Blythswood Square house, which he had never yet seen). I shall never be able to spend the happy hours we did last winter.' You will find by and by that she got over that difficulty.

On Sunday 19th October, she says, 'Papa is very busy with some election matters … Janet is not well; she has a bad cold. Do you know I have taken a great dislike to C.H. I shall try and do without her aid in the winter. She has been with us four years, and I am tired of her, but I won't show it to her.'

In the next, on Friday 17th November, she says, 'Sweet love, you should get those brown envelopes; they would not be so much seen as white ones put down into my window. You should just stoop down to tie your shoe, and then slip it in. The back door is closed. M. keeps the key, for fear our servant boy would go out of an evening. We have got blinds for our windows.' She had so arranged that, instead of having her room on the same floor with the front door, she should have it on the same floor as the low front door, so that the window of her room, being on a level with the pavement, might be a depository for their correspondence. This is the first letter, then, in which instructions are given as to how the correspondence is to take place at the Blythswood Square house.

And now you will see the course that the correspondence taken. In one letter she says, 'I don't think I can take you in as I did in India Street,' plainly showing that she had taken him in there. Then she says, in the next letter bearing the post-mark of Friday, November 21, 'Now, about writing, I wish you to write me and give me the note on Tuesday evening next. You will, about eight o'clock, come and put the letter down into the window – (just drop it in – I won't be there at the time) – the window next to Minnoch's close door. There are two windows together with white blinds. Don't be seen near the house on Sunday, as M. won't be at church, and she will watch. In your letter, dear love, tell me what night of the week will be best for you to leave the letter for me. If M. and P. were from home I would take you in very well at the front door, just the same way as I did in India Street, and I won't let a chance pass, I won't, sweet pet of my soul, my only best-loved darling.'

She could perfectly well take him in at the front door. She could leave her own room, go upstairs, and she had only to open the hall door sufficiently to enable L'Angelier to get into the drawing-room, so as to prevent the possibility of being heard from any of the back rooms of the house. And this letter proves that that is not a mere theory, but what she proposed to do.

Gentlemen, it seems plain that there was, at this time, a serious intention on the part of these persons to make an elopement. You had it proved by many witnesses. You had it proved by the landlady, Mrs Clark, as to the intention to have the banns proclaimed on Sunday, and the marriage to take place on Monday.

In her next letter, she says she was going with Mr Minnoch to a concert, and she says, 'You say you heard I took M. to the concert against his inclination, and forced him to go. I told you the right way when I wrote. But from your statement in your letter of tonight you did not believe my word. Emile, I would not have done this to you. Even now I would write and tell you. I would not believe every idle report. No, I would not. I would, my beloved Emile, believe my husband's word before any other, but you always listen to reports about me if they are bad. You know I could not sit a whole evening without talking, but I have not flirted.'

Gentlemen, there is evidence here, which you have under the hand of the prisoner further on, that after the first paroxysms had subsided, her affection towards L'Angelier had cooled. The reason of that it is not necessary that we should discern. He seems to have been rather exacting; but whatever the reason might be, it is quite plain that a change came over her affection about this time. I have now brought them down to the 18th December, 1856, and she says herself in a subsequent letter that her coolness began in November, when they came to Glasgow. Not only so, but she begins to do what L'Angelier called flirting with Mr Minnoch. Mr Minnoch has told you that at this time and during the whole of this winter there was a tacit understanding between them that they were lovers. She alludes to this in her letter when she refers to the reports about her, and denies that there is any truth in them. On the next day she says, 'For your sake I shall be very cold to everybody. I am rather more fond of C.H. She is very civil. I will trust her.' Gentlemen, there is in the rest of this letter what I will not read, but there is a plain and obvious reference to the possibility of her becoming a mother, which, under the circumstances, it is impossible not to see the force of.

The next letter was written before Christmas, 1856. She says, 'Beloved Emile, we must meet. If you love me you will come to me when P. and M. go to Edinburgh, which will be the 7th or 10th January ... Will you give me a letter on Friday at six o'clock, as I have promised to go with Jack to the pantomime ... If P. and M. go, will you not, sweet love, come to your Mimi? Do you think I would ask you if I saw danger in the house? No, love, I would not. I shall let you in; no one shall see you.

We can make it late – twelve, if you please. You have no long walk. No, my own beloved. My sweet, dear Emile. Emile, I see your sweet smile. I hear you say you will come and see your Mimi, clasp her to your bosom, and kiss her, call her your own pet, your wife. Emile will not refuse me. I need not wish you a merry Christmas, but I shall wish that we may spend the next together and that we shall then be happy.'

This means that he shall come into the house as he had done before, and it speaks of his clasping her to his heart. In the next letter she says 'Now, I must tell you something you may hear. I was at the theatre and people, my love, may tell you that M. was there too. Well, M. was there, but he did not know of my going. He was in the Club Box, and I did not even bow to him. To-day, when B., Mamma, and I were walking, M. joined us, took a walk with us, and came home. He was most civil and kind. He sent Janet such a lovely flower to-night, to wear on Monday evening. Now, I have told you this, sweet pet, I know you will be angry; but I would rather bear your anger than that you should perhaps blame me for not telling you, and someone will be sure to inform you of me.'

And now, gentlemen, having traced the correspondence down to this date proving the greatest intimacy between the parties, proving the correspondence to be of such a character that no eye could see it without her character being utterly blasted – proving also vows, over and over repeated, that, after her intimacy with him, she could be his wife and that of no other, as to be so would be a sin, having intimated in as strong language as she could, that for Mr Minnoch she had no affection whatever, that she had at no time whatever flirted with him or any one else, being his wife – having proved all this down to the end of 1856, we now come to the crisis, and I must ask you to keep the dates in mind from this time forward.

The next act in this tragedy begins, you will see, on the 9th January, 1857. In this letter she says, 'It is past eleven o'clock, and no letter from you, my own, ever dear, beloved husband. Why this, sweet one? I think I heard your stick this evening. Pray, do not make any sounds whatever at my window. If it were possible, sweet one, would you not leave my notes at six as at ten o'clock? The moon is up, and it is light. I hope, my own, ever dear, beloved one, you feel better and that you are in better spirits. Sweet, dear Emile, I do truly and, fondly love you with my heart and soul. But you, I know, think me cool and indifferent.' And then she goes on to say 'How do you keep yourself warm in bed? I have Janet beside me; but I often wish you were with me. Would you not put your arms round your Mimi, and fondly embrace her and keep her warm? Ah, yes, I know you would.' Then she wonders if the time would ever come, and then, on the next page, she says, 'I wish I could see you; but I must not even look out of the window, so just leave your note and go away.' This was a general intimation, as much as to say, 'If you come to my window, and I don't look out, you must assume there is some reason why I pretend not to see you, so just leave my note and go away.'

The next, Saturday 10th of January, says, 'My own dear, beloved Emile, I cannot tell you how sorry I was last night at not hearing from you … If you would risk it, my sweet, beloved pet, we would have time to kiss each other and a dear fond embrace; and though, sweet love, it is only for a minute, do you not think it is better than not meeting at all?' Observe that the preceding day was January the 9th. In the next letter there is nothing material. She tells him that her father wished they had a larger place than Rhu, and that they would not likely go back there again. Now, at this very time Mr Minnoch has told you that a few days afterwards he asked the prisoner to be his wife, and yet she writes to L'Angelier on Monday night, 'Sweet love, come if you can.'

Gentlemen, let me make this remark, that though the expressions from this time forward are much the same in effect, there is a manifest chill in them – the letters are shorter and curter and colder than before. 'My sweet Emile, I hope you are well. I did not sleep all night thinking of my pet. I went to Govan with M., and when I got home I was looking so ill M. made me go and take a walk to get some colour, so B. Pattison and I took a long walk on the Dumbarton Road. When I told you, love, to write me for to-night I forgot I am to be out.' This is on Monday, 19th January, and she writes further, 'As we go at nine o'clock your letter will not be here, but I shall tell C.H. to take it in. Dearest Emile, all this day I have wished for you one moment to kiss you; to lay my head on your breast; would make me happy. I think I shall see you Thursday night. I think P. is not at home. But, you shall hear. Adieu, my loved one. My husband. My own little pet. Adieu. God bless you. I am your wife. Your own Mimi L'Angelier. P.S. – I don't think I should send you this scroll but I could not help …' She goes on to say in it, 'I am your wife; I did love you so much when you were at the window last night.' And so, he was at the window on Sunday the 18th January.

Now, gentlemen, go back to the letter of the 9th January; you will see that it contains this passage, 'When we shall meet again I cannot tell.' In the letter of the 10th January she says, 'My sweet, dear pet, I should so like to spend three or four hours with you just to talk over some things; but I don't know when we can meet, not for ten days. I might say Monday, same as last.' This proves that they had met. 'If you would risk it, my sweet, beloved pet, we would have time to kiss each other, and a dear, fond embrace; and though, sweet love, it is only for a minute, do you not think it is better than not meeting at all?' In the course of ten days they were to meet; they had met before, but their meeting was postponed for the present.

On Sunday 18th she writes, 'Emile, my own beloved, you have just left me. Oh, sweet darling, at this moment my heart and soul burns with love for thee, my husband, my sweet one. Emile, what would I not give at this moment to be your fond wife. My night-dress was on when you saw me; would to God you had been in the same attire.'

On Monday the 19th says, 'I did love you so much last night when you were at the window.' The next date is Wednesday 21st January. This is a very short letter. It says 'I have just five minutes to spare. Why no letter, pet? On Monday night it was such a disappointment to your Mimi. I cannot see you on Thursday as I hoped.'

The next letter is dated Thursday, 22nd January. She had said in the former letter, 'I cannot see you on Thursday as I hoped.' Then she writes in this letter, 'I was so very sorry that I could not see you tonight. I had expected an hour's chat with you; but we must just hope for better the next time … M. is not well enough to go from home; and my dear, sweet, little pet, I don't see we could manage in Edinburgh, because I could not leave a friends house without their knowing it. So, sweet pet, it must at present be put off till a better time. I see no chance before March, but rest assured, my dear love, Emile, if I see any chance I shall let you know of it.'

Now, gentlemen, mark this. On the 28th of the month of January the prisoner accepts Minnoch. On the 2nd February, she writes, 'I felt truly astonished to have my last letter returned to me, but it will be the last you shall have an opportunity of returning. When you are not pleased with the letters I send you, then our correspondence shall be at an end; and as there is a coolness on both sides, our engagement had better be broken.'

Now, these are the very words that Kennedy told you L'Angelier repeated to him on the morning when he entered the counting-house so much distressed. She says, 'You have more than once returned me my letters, and my mind was made up that I should not stand the same thing again. And you also annoyed me much on Saturday by your conduct in coming so near me; altogether, I think, owing to coolness and indifference (nothing else) that we had better for the future consider ourselves strangers. I trust to your honour as a gentleman that you will not reveal anything that may have passed between us. I shall feel obliged by your bringing me my letters and likeness on Thursday evening at seven. Be at the area gate, and C.H. (Christina Haggart) will take the parcel from you. On Friday night I shall send you all your letters, likeness, &c. I trust that you may yet be happy, and get one more worthy of you than I. – On Thursday at seven o'clock.'

She says that she had found coolness and indifference on both sides, and for that reason, and as she affirms for nothing else, the engagement had better be broken off. But remember, gentlemen, four days before that letter was written she had been engaged to Mr Minnoch. She was to return L'Angelier's letters to him; therefore she had them. On the 2nd of February, 1857, she had his letters; she was to return them on the Friday; and she was also to return L'Angelier's likeness. It was found in her chamber. What became of these letters we have no explanation of whatever.

There is a postscript to this important letter. She says, 'You may be astonished at this sudden change, but for some time back you must have noticed a coolness in my notes. My love for you has ceased, and that is why I was cool. I did love you truly and fondly, but for some time back I have lost much of that love. There is no other reason for my conduct, and I think it but fair to let you know this. I might have gone on and become your wife, but I could not have loved you as I ought. (She was engaged at this time to another man.) My conduct you will condemn, but I did at one time love you with my heart and soul. It has cost me much to tell you – sleepless nights – but it was necessary that you should know. If you remain in Glasgow or go away, I hope you may succeed in all your endeavours. I know you will never injure the character of one you so fondly loved. No, Emile, I know you have honour, and are a gentleman. What has passed you will not mention. I know when I ask you that you will comply. Adieu.'

Gentlemen, what a labyrinth of bewilderment this unhappy girl, first by her lapse of virtue, and then by her want of truth, was driving herself into! She tries to break off this engagement because she says there was coolness on both sides, which I daresay on her part was not affected. She says she has no other reason for her conduct but that she has lost her love for L'Angelier – she says this when she knows that the actual reason is that she has pledged her word to another. She tells L'Angelier that her affection was withdrawn, in the hope that his indignant spirit would induce him to turn her off, when she would be free to form another engagement. But, gentlemen, she had the dreadful recollection of the existence of the correspondence. She probably did not know how much L'Angelier had preserved of it, but she knew that she was completely in his power.

Gentlemen, she did not hear from L'Angelier for more than a week. She, accordingly wrote this second letter, which bears the post-mark of the 9th February: 'I attribute to your having a cold that I had no answer to my last note. On Thursday evening you were, I suppose, afraid of the night air. I fear your cold is not better. I again appoint Thursday night first – same place – street gate – seven o'clock. – M.'

Now, gentlemen, this letter was written after the 5th February, and some days before the 12th. She adds in the same letter, 'If you bring me the parcel on Thursday, please write a note saying when you shall bring it, and address it to C.H. Send it by post.' She had heard nothing, got no answer to the demand for her letters, and she writes this cold letter in the tone of the former, saying everything is broken off, and making a second appointment for the delivery of her letters. Gentlemen, L'Angelier refused to give up the letters. He refused to give them up to her. He told Miss Perry, and he told Mr Kennedy, and I think he told others, that he would not give up the letters, but that, on the contrary, he would show them to her father.

Now, gentlemen, in other circumstances, and had matters not gone so far between these unfortunate persons, it might have been considered a dishonourable and ungenerous thing in a man in L'Angelier's position to take that line of conduct. But whether it was or no is not material to the matter in hand. I must say, however, that in the position in which the prisoner and L'Angelier stood, I do not see how he, as a man of honour, could allow this marriage with Mr Minnoch to take place and remain silent. It may be doubted whether they were not man and wife by the law of the land. It is needless to discuss this question. There certainly were materials in that correspondence to show that this view might be maintained by L'Angelier had he chosen to do it, and that he considered the prisoner his wife though they had not been married in a regular and respectable manner. He considered her his wife, and so thinking, he had a right not to give up the letters. I do not think, therefore, that much can be said about L'Angelier not giving up these letters. It matters not. The fact is he refused, and the fact is you will find he made the threat to herself, as he said to Kennedy he would do, as well as to Miss Perry and others.

Gentlemen, just listen to this. It is a letter dated Monday 9th February; it is posted in Glasgow on the 10th; the appointment is made for the 13th, and recollecting the strain of the letters that went before, listen to this, 'Monday night. – Emile, I have just had your note. Emile, for the love you once had for me do nothing till, I see you …' [The Lord Advocate read the entire letter.]

Now, gentlemen, we have traced the matter up to this point. She is so committed that she cannot extricate herself, and yet, if not extricated, her character, her fame, her reputation, her position, are forfeited for ever. But she does receive a letter from L'Angelier which we don't possess; and on the Tuesday evening she again writes to him. This is one of the letters found in his desk. It was not posted at all. It was delivered, and was found in an envelope; but it refers plainly to the letter that went before, and to the assignation that was made. I shall read every word of that letter, long as it is, for it is perhaps the point on which this case turns, 'Emile, I have this night received your note. Oh, it is kind of you to write to me. Emile, no one can know the intense agony of mind I have suffered last night and today. Emile, my father's wrath would kill me; you little know his temper. Emile, for the love you once had for me do not denounce me to my Papa … [The Lord Advocate read the entire letter.] … I will take you within the door. The area gate will be open. I shall see you from my window, 12 o'c. I will wait till 1 o'c.'

Doubtless, poor creature, she had done that, and throughout this unhappy history of the gradual progress of an ill-regulated mind, one cannot see all this without, what I am sure I feel from the bottom of my heart, the deepest commiseration. Doubtless L'Angelier had abused his opportunities in a way that no man of honour ought to have done, and had stolen into that family and destroyed their peace for over. She had no doubt put on paper what she should not. Gentlemen, I never in my life had so harrowing a task as raking up and bringing before such a tribunal and audience as this, the outpourings of such a despairing spirit, in such a position as this miserable girl was. Such words as these paraded in public under any circumstances would be intolerable agony, but the circumstances of this case throw all these considerations utterly into the shade, and if for a moment they do obtrude themselves upon us they must be repelled, for our duty is a stern one, and cannot yield to such considerations.

And, gentlemen, pausing here for a moment, let me take in some of the surrounding circumstances and see what they are. L'Angelier, whatever were his faults, was certainly true to her. He spoke to Kennedy about her. He said his love for her was infatuation, and that it would be the death of him. It was not revenge that he wanted; he wanted his wife. That is quite clear; and he plainly has told her that he would not permit his engagement to be broken, and that he would put these letters into her father's hands. As I have already said, I do not know that in the circumstances he was altogether wrong in so doing but, gentlemen, at this time a very remarkable incident takes place. On the second week in February, the prisoner asked the boy, the page who served in the family, to go to a druggist's with a line for a bottle of prussic acid. You have seen the state of mind she was in. Some extrication or other was inevitable if she hoped to save her character, and with a strength of will, which I think you will see she exhibited more than once in this case, she resolved she would not go back to L'Angelier; she had accepted the love of another, and had determined to marry that other. And throughout all this, while she is in utter despair, and tries to move him by her protestations, there is not the slightest indication of any intention to go back to him, to love him and be his wife. Quite the contrary; but on that day, at the door of her own bedroom, she gives Murray a line for prussic acid. For what purpose? For what purpose or earth could she want it? And for what purpose did she say she wanted it? For her hands.

This is the first indication we have that her mind is running in that way. This is the first suggestion we have of the means she proposes for her extrication from this labyrinth of difficulty. And why did she want prussic acid? For her hands as a cosmetic. Did you ever hear, gentlemen, of prussic acid being used as a cosmetic for the hands? There has been, among a great deal of curious medical evidence which we have had in this case, no suggestion that prussic acid was ever used for the hands. But it will not have escaped your notice, that not only is her mind now beginning to run upon poison, but that it is also beginning to run on the excuse for wanting it. She did not get the prussic acid; but it is perfectly clear that the time when she wanted it was the date of this despairing letter, and immediately before the meeting she had appointed for Wednesday the 11th, and regarding which she says, 'If I cannot get you in at the back door I will take you in at the front door.'

Another incident happened at this time. An interview took place between the prisoner and L'Angelier in the house in Blythswood Square.

Chapter Four

Christina Haggart did not see L'Angelier, but she told you plainly she
knew it was he, and that he and the prisoner remained alone for nearly
an hour in her room, and that she (Christina Haggart) remained in the
kitchen while L'Angelier and the prisoner were together. There can be
no doubt about the date, though my learned friend tried to throw some
obscurity over it. A meeting was fixed for Wednesday the 11th February.

But, gentlemen, when M. De Mean asked the prisoner how she and
L'Angelier met, she denied he had ever been in the house at all, plainly
and positively. I have shown to you from her letters he had been more
than once in that house before, but probably not in the course of 1857.
But she positively, denied he ever had been there at all. You will find
allusions; throughout the letters to embraces, kisses, and interviews, and
things that could only have taken place had he been in the house, and
she says distinctly that he might come without fear, for no one would
see him, and that they might have an interview. That one interview took
place we have the direct testimony of one witness.

What took place at that interview we cannot tell; but we find this,
that in one way or another this feud had been made up, that the whole
thing had been arranged; and how arranged? Not certainly, gentlemen,
on the footing of giving up the letters! – not certainly on the footing of
the prisoner not continuing her engagement with L'Angelier; but, on the
opposite footing, upon the footing of the engagement continuing. How
was that to extricate the prisoner? What did she propose to herself to do?
She had found that L'Angelier would not give up the letters. She did not
persevere in her endeavour to induce him to do so by despairing protes-
tation. She took another line, and that line was by pretending – because
it could not be real – pretending to adopt the old tone of love and affection; all this time keeping up the engagement with Minnoch, receiving
the congratulations of his friends, receiving presents from him, and being
engaged in fixing the time of their union.

But they met that day; and in the next letter on Saturday, 14th, she says:
'My dear Emile, I have got my finger cut and can't write; so, dear, I wish
you would excuse me. I was glad to see you looking so well yesterday.'
I don't think that that refers to this interview; she was in the habit of

passing his window and looking up to it; and the probability is that this refers to come glimpse she had got of him in that way, or she might have met him on the street. The interview took place, as I have shown, on Wednesday night. She goes on: 'I hope to see you very soon. Write me for Thursday, and then I shall tell you when I can see you. I want the first time we meet that you will bring me all my cool letters back – the last four I have written – and I will give you others in their place.' These are the only letters she asks for now – the cool letters; she asks for those letters that she had written in her cool moments, to convince L'Angelier that she is as true to him as ever; but remark she makes an appointment for Thursday. Plainly the quarrel has been made up. The day was Thursday, 19th February. Be kind enough to bear that in mind.

He saw Madeleine next on the 19th, and in the middle of the night he was seized with a sudden illness. You heard it described by his landlady, Mrs Jenkins. It was vomiting, purging, vomiting of a green stuff, and excessive pain. He lay on the floor all night; he was so ill that he could not call for assistance for some time; and his landlady found him in the morning. At last he was relieved, but only after a great deal of suffering. These symptoms were the symptoms of arsenic. He recovered; and he went out on the day after, on the 20th. On the 21st, the prisoner purchased arsenic at the shop of Mr Murdoch – a very singular purchase, gentlemen, for a person in her position to make. But it was not the first time in the history of this case that she had tried to buy poison. She had tried to buy poison before that meeting of Wednesday 11th.

I shall not stop just now to discuss the question of the reason which she gave for it, because my object at present is simply to give you the facts historically, although if you should find that the excuse she gave for the buying of the poison was a false one, it is evident how strong and inevitable the conclusion is which you must necessarily draw from that single fact. She went to Murdoch's shop; she asked for the arsenic openly, but the story she told in regard to its use was, upon her own confession, an absolute falsehood; she said she wanted it to poison the rats at Rhu. A different excuse is afterwards given for the purchase of it, but you have this singular and startling fact, that on the 21st she goes into Mr Murdoch's shop alone; she asks for arsenic; says that the gardener at Rhu wants it to poison rats; she says he has tried phosphorus paste, but that that will not do, and that he wants to try arsenic. Gentlemen, that was an utter falsehood, an admitted falsehood. We shall see immediately what she says the real reason was, and whether it was more correct than the one she gave in the shop.

Having purchased that arsenic on the 21st, according to my statement, L'Angelier saw her on the 22nd, which was a Sunday, and on the night of the 22nd and the morning of the 23rd he was again seized with the very symptoms that he had had before, everything, in short, which you would expect in a case of arsenical poisoning.

Now, gentlemen, it is most material to give me your attention at this particular part of the case. L'Angelier saw the prisoner on the 19th, and had been ill immediately after; he was ill after the 22nd, and he told Miss Perry that these two illnesses had followed after receiving coffee one time and chocolate another time from the hands of the prisoner. In corroboration of that, will you listen to this letter? I think you will consider this of the deepest importance. Its date was Wednesday, 25th February: 'Dearest, Sweet Emile, – I am sorry to hear you are ill. I hope to God you will soon be better; take care of yourself; do not go to the office this week, just stay at home till Monday. Sweet love, it will please me to hear you are well. I have not felt very well these two last days – sick and headache. Everyone is complaining; it must be something in the air. I can see you Friday, if M. is not away, but I think Sunday P. will be away, and I might see you, I think, but I shall let you know. I shall not be at home on Saturday, but I shall try, sweet love, and give you even if it should be a word. I cannot pass your windows or I would, as you ask me to do it; do not come and walk about, and become ill again. You did look bad Sunday night and Monday morning.'

'I think you got sick with walking home so late and the long want of food, so the next time we meet I shall make you eat a loaf of bread before you go out. I am longing to meet you again, sweet love. My head aches so, and I am looking so bad that I cannot sit up as I used to do; but I am taking some stuff to bring back the colour. I shall see you soon again. Put up with short notes for a little time.'

Now, gentlemen, that was written on the 25th. It proves that he saw her on Sunday the 22nd. It proves that he was sick at that time, and was looking very bad. According to my statement, he was ill on the 19th. It proves that she was thinking about giving him food; that she was laying a foundation for seeing him, that she was taking stuff to bring back her colour. It proves that she was holding out a kind of explanation of the symptoms which he had, because she says she is ill herself; and it proves that all this took place the day after she had bought the arsenic at Murdoch's. L'Angelier had said that his illness had taken place after receiving a cup of coffee from herself; and she says in her own declaration that upon one occasion she did give him a cup of cocoa.

No doubt the illness of the 19th takes place when I cannot prove the prisoner had any arsenic in her possession – that is perfectly true. The prisoner's counsel took some pains to prove that arsenic might be had without being purchased in a druggist's shop, but you will look at the surrounding circumstances in the case, at the fact that L'Angelier said his two first illnesses had arisen immediately after receiving a cup of coffee one time and a cup of cocoa or chocolate the other; that she admits she did give him a cup of cocoa; that she had the means of making it in the house; that the illness the second time was the same as the first time; and that upon both occasions these illnesses were symptomatic of arsenic. You will also consider, what weighs on my mind, what was the nature of the arrangement between L'Angelier and Miss Smith. How did she propose to extricate herself from the difficulties in which she found herself placed? She had everything at stake: character, fame, fortune, and everything else. She knew she could not get back her letters by entreaties, and she did not endeavour to get them by that means any longer, but professed to adhere to their engagement. What did she contemplate at that moment? For the first time she begins to purchase, or endeavour to purchase, prussic acid.

And now, gentlemen, for the arsenic. What reason does she give for the purchase of arsenic? She says she had been told when at school in England, by a Miss Guibilei, that arsenic is good for the complexion. She came from school in 1853, and, singular enough, it is not till that week of February prior to the 22nd that she ever thinks of arsenic for that purpose. Why, gentlemen, should that be? At that moment I have shown you she was frightened at the danger she was in, in the highest degree, and is it likely that at that time she was looking for a new cosmetic? But what is the truth as to what she had heard, or very likely read? What is the use of the arsenic, and what does she say? She says that she poured it all into a basin and washed her face with it. Gentlemen, do you believe that? If she was following out what she found in the magazines, that was not what she found there, for they say that the way to use arsenic is internally. Therefore, do you believe that she got the arsenic for the purpose she says?

A very respectable gentleman came into the box yesterday to swear that arsenic might be safely used in that way, and he actually had the courage to try the experiment on Saturday. I should not like to say anything to shake the nerves of that gentleman, but the experiment cannot be said to be yet completed. With all deference to Drs Maclagan and Lawrie, we have heard from the two first authorities in Europe that such practices may be attended with danger. Before you can take such a preposterous story, she must show that in some reasonable and rational manner she was led to believe that this cosmetic might he usefully and safely used. But all that has been referred to is the swallowing of arsenic. She says she used the whole quantity each time in a basin of water. I fear, gentlemen, there is but one conclusion, and that is, that there is not a word of truth in the excuse; and if, therefore, you think there are two falsehoods here about the poisoning – the first told in the druggist's shop, and the second made in her declaration – I fear the conclusion is inevitable that the purpose for which she had purchased it was a criminal one, and that, taking all the circumstances together, you cannot possibly doubt that the object was to use it for the purpose of poisoning L'Angelier.

But this time it failed; he is excessively ill, but recovers. How she got the poison on the 19th, I say at once I am unable to account for, and the prisoner is entitled to any benefit that may give her. But you will recollect what the symptoms were. You will also recollect the letter, and that this letter proves the conclusiveness of what has been said before, that

L'Angelier was sick at the time of their meeting. And that reminds me of what I had forgotten. The witness Thuau, you will remember (his fellow-lodger), asked L'Angelier if he had seen Miss Smith on the occasion of his first illness, and he said he had. If that took place on the 19th – and I think I have proved it – then you have additional evidence that the 19th was the day.

He gets better, and on the 27th of February a letter is sent from the prisoner in these terms: 'My dear, sweet Emile, I cannot see you this week, and I can fix no time to meet with you. I do hope you are better; keep well, and take care of yourself. I saw you at your window. I am better, but have got a bad cold. I shall write you, sweet one, in the beginning of the week. I hope we may meet soon. We go, I think, to Stirling about the 10th of March for a fortnight.'

Now, what was L'Angelier about all this time? We have very clear evidence of that from Kennedy, Miss Perry, and Dr Thomson. The man was entirely changed; he never recovered his looks; he never recovered his health; he appeared in the office, as Miller told you, with his complexion gone, and a deep hectic spot on either cheek. He appeared in Miss Perry's on the 2nd March a frail and tottering man, entirely altered from what he used to be. He was advised to go away from his office; he followed the advice given him, and did not return till next week; and it is proved by Mrs Jenkins, Dr Thomson, and Kennedy that this was the only occasion on which he was detained by illness from the office. He was recommended to leave town for the good of his health, and he got leave of absence from the office.

While I am here, let me just allude in a single sentence to the conversation that took place between Miss Perry and L'Angelier. Gentlemen, you could not fail to be struck with it. He said his love for Miss Smith was a fascination, and he used the remarkable expression, 'If she were to poison me I would forgive her.' He had said before, in a looser way, to Kennedy that he was perfectly infatuated about her, and that she would be the death of him; but this time he uses these remarkable words. He used the expression, 'If she were to poison me I would forgive her,' in connection with the statement that his illness had immediately followed his taking a cup of coffee or cocoa from her. Unless it were true that he had felt ill with a cup of coffee on one occasion and a cup of cocoa on the other, what could have put it into his head to say, 'If she was to poison me I would forgive her'? If you believe Miss Perry's story, that he got a cup of coffee the first time and a cup of cocoa the second and take into account the effects that followed, would you think it strange that he should say, 'If she was to poison me I would forgive her'?

With the other evidence I have brought to bear upon this critical period – from 19th to 27th February, I leave you to judge whether, at all events, it is not certain, first, that they met on these two occasions; second, that he got something from her on both occasions; and, third, that his illness succeeded immediately after having got a cup of coffee in the first place, and a cup of cocoa in the second; and that, in the last place, these illnesses took place under circumstances which led him to say, half in joke, half in earnest, 'If she were to poison me I would forgive her.' Miss Perry does not say this was a serious belief. It would appear to have been a floating notion which coursed through his brain, and I suppose he drove it away. We shall see what happened to drive it away; we shall see protestations of renewed love, which probably made him believe that that phantom, suddenly conjured up, was, after all, a mere delusion of his brain.

While L'Angelier was recovering, the prisoner writes a letter dated Tuesday, the 3rd of March. It appears that L'Angelier had proposed to go to the Bridge of Allan, and on Tuesday, the 3rd of March, the prisoner writes this letter to say that they intend to go to Stirling for a fortnight, and to go on Friday, the 6th. But it seems that L'Angelier had some thoughts of going to the Bridge of Allan: 'My dearest Emile, I hope by this time you are quite well, and able to be out. I saw you at your window, but I could not tell how you looked – well, I hope. I am very well. I was in Edinburgh on Saturday, to be at a luncheon-party at the Castle. It was a most charming day, and we enjoyed our, trip very much. On Friday we go to Stirling for a fortnight. I am so sorry, my dearest pet, I cannot see you ere we go – but I cannot. Will you, sweet one, write me for Thursday, eight o'clock, and I shall get it before ten o'clock, which will be a comfort to me, as I shall not hear from you till I come home again? I am very well, and I think the next time we meet, you will think I look better than I did the last time. You won't have a letter from me this Saturday, as I shall be off, but I shall write the beginning of the week. Write me for Thursday, sweet love; and with kind love, ever believe me to be yours, with love and affection, Mimi.'

She writes the next day a letter posted on the 4th March: 'Dearest Emile, I have just time to write you a line. I could not come to the window, as B. and M. were there, but I saw you. If you would take my advice you would go to the South of England for ten days; it would do you much good. In fact, sweet pet, it would make you feel quite well. Do try and do this. You will please me by getting strong and well again. I hope you won't go to B. of Allan, as P. and M. would say it was I brought you there, and it would make me to feel very unhappy. Stirling you need not go to, as it is a nasty, dirty little town. Go to the Isle of Wight. I am exceedingly sorry, love, that I cannot see you ere I go. It is impossible, but the first thing I do on my return will be to see you, sweet love. I must stop, as it is post time. So adieu, with love and kisses, and much love. I am, with love and affection, ever yours, Mimi.' She had made the attempt at poison on two occasions, and had failed. Apparently her heart was somewhat touched, and probably she thought that if she could get him out of the way she might have her marriage with Mr Minnoch over without his knowledge, after which it would be easy to get her letters, as there would be no motive for keeping them.

You will see what L'Angelier says to this proposition to go to the Isle of Wight. It cannot but have struck you that these last letters, though written in the words, are not written in the old spirit of the letters between these persons. And as it must have struck you so it struck L'Angelier himself. And I am now to read to you what, I regret to say, is the only scrap of evidence under the hand of this young man that I am able to lay before you. But that letter is of some consequence. It shows the tone of his mind, and his position altogether, after what had taken place between them since the reconciliation, and indicates very plainly what, at that time, his suspicions were.

[The Lord Advocate read, entire, L'Angelier's press copy of his letter]: 'My dear, sweet pet Mimi, I feel indeed very vexed that the answer I received yesterday to mine of Tuesday to you should prevent me from sending you the kind letter I had ready for you. You must not blame me, dear, for this but really your cold, indifferent, and reserved notes, so short, without a particle of love in them (especially after pledging your word you were to write me kindly for those letters you asked me to destroy), and the manner you evaded answering the questions I put to you in my last, with the reports I hear, fully convince me, Mimi, that there is foundation in your marriage with another; besides, the way you put off our union till September without a just reason is very suspicious …'

Observe, gentlemen, that in that letter he says very plainly that, after the meeting of the 22nd, he was 'forgetting all the past.' Whatever had floated through his mind on the subject of the strange coincidence of his illnesses on the one hand, and his visits to the prisoner on the other, all that he put away. 'But now,' he says, 'it is again beginning. Mimi, I insist on having an explicit answer to the questions you evaded in my last. If you evade answering this time, I must try some other means of coming to the truth.'

This was written on the 5th March. He says he won't go to the Isle of Wight, and that the doctor tells him he must go to the Bridge of Allan. The prisoner buys her second ounce of arsenic next day. But before she does it, she writes this letter on the 5th: 'My dear, sweet pet, I am sorry you should be so vexed; believe nothing, sweet one, till I tell you myself. It is a report I am sorry about, but it has been six months spoken about … We shall speak of our union when we meet.' Keeping it up you see, gentlemen, till the last; for when she was at the Bridge of Allan she made all her arrangements for her marriage with Mr Minnoch in June. 'I wish, love, you could manage to remain in town till we come home, as I know it will be a grand row with me if you are seen there … Neither M. nor his sisters go with us.' No, but she knew that they were going there at the same time. 'If you do not go to Bridge of Allan till we come home, come up Mains Street tomorrow, and if you go, come your own way.' As I told you, next morning she went into Currie's shop with Miss Buchanan to purchase arsenic for the alleged purpose of killing rats in the Blythswood Square house. She asked for sixpence worth, having bought the very same quantity on the 21st February. After she gets a letter from L'Angelier, saying, 'If you won't answer my questions, I will not any longer put them to you, but will find another way of satisfying myself,' she writes him 'Do not come to Bridge of Allan, but go to the Isle of Wight. If you come to Bridge of Allan, come your own way.' And on 6th March, in the expectation that he might come to Bridge of Allan, she buys arsenic again.

The prisoner purchased that arsenic unquestionably upon a false moment. The statement was that it was rats that were to be poisoned, and that there would be no danger, as the house was to be shut up, and all the servants were to be away. Well, all that story was absolute falsehood; the servants were not leaving the Blythswood Square house, and there were no rats there to kill. Again, it was said to be for her complexion. Do you really think that it did her so much good the time before that she came back for more of it?

But when the prisoner found the toils coming closer around her – L'Angelier determined not to be put off and she herself pledged to an absolute falsehood, viz., that the report of her marriage is not true – she purchases another dose of arsenic. Draw your own conclusions, gentlemen; I fear you will find but one at which it is possible for you to arrive. It is said, what did she do, with all this arsenic she could not use the half, the tenth, the twentieth part on the former occasions. It is not difficult to account for that; whenever she used so much as she required, the rest was thrown into the fire. He did not go to the Bridge of Allan, and she had therefore no occasion to use it there; and when she found she had no use for it, she disposed of what she had bought.

The two last letters she wrote were from the Bridge of Allan. They are cold letters enough. The first of them bears the postmark Bridge of Allan, 10th March, and she says, among other things in it, that she shall be home on Monday or Tuesday, and will write him when they shall have an interview. Observe that it is an interview she speaks of, and you will immediately see with what feverish impatience L'Angelier waited for receipt of that letter appointing the interview. The last letter from her at the Bridge of Allan has the postmark 13th March, and in it she said 'I think we shall be home on Tuesday, so I shall let you know, my own beloved sweet pet, when we shall have a dear, sweet interview, when I may be pressed to your heart, and kissed by you, my own sweet love.' Then she says, 'I hope you will enjoy your visit here.' By that time it had been arranged that L'Angelier should postpone his visit till the Smiths came back.

The marriage with Minnoch at this time was all settled – the day was fixed – the prisoner was committed beyond all hope of recovery, and had but one way out. But leaving her there for the present, let us follow the fortunes of L'Angelier for the next most critical ten days of his life. He gets leave of absence on the 6th, goes to Edinburgh for a week, sees a variety of persons, and gets much better. Several witnesses have told you how he ate, how he talked about his illness, and you have heard how he repeated in the house of Mr Towers the singular statement he had before made to Miss Perry, that he had got coffee and cocoa from somebody, and that illness immediately succeeded on taking these two substances. He says 'I do not wonder so much that I should be ill after cocoa, for I am not accustomed to that, but that I should be ill after coffee, which I take regularly, I cannot account for.' And they were so much struck with the remark, that they said to him, 'Has any one any motive in poisoning you?' To that he made no answer; but you will not omit to see the corroboration that gives to the story of Miss Perry, and to the real circumstances, as I have explained them to you.

The week after, he was to have a letter appointing an interview. He had not had one since the 22nd, and he was longing for it with impatience. He came back to Glasgow on Tuesday 17th and said, 'Is there no letter waiting for me?' For they were to be home on the 17th, and she was to write and say when the interview was to be. He stayed at home all Wednesday, better in health, but low in spirits, expecting a letter. He went to Bridge of Allan on Thursday, the 19th, and after he had gone, a letter came. He did not get that letter at his lodgings, but he had left his address with M. Thuau, with instructions to forward any letter which came; and the envelope is found addressed to his lodgings, and posted on Thursday. That letter has never been found. We do not know what became of it, but this is certain, that the envelope without the letter was found in his bag. I regret the absence of that letter as much as my learned friend can, though I think there is exceptional evidence of what that letter set forth. It arrived, however, on the 19th March, Thursday, and Thuau on the same day addressed it to the Post Office at Stirling; and that was posted at Franklin Place on the night of the 19th March, and reached Stirling about nine o'clock on the 20th. On the 20th L'Angelier writes to Miss Perry, and says, 'I should have come to see some one last night, but the letter came too late, so we are both disappointed.' After a letter or two, which are not material now for me to read – though they were material as identifying the course L'Angelier took, as proved otherwise – after a letter or two from Mr Stevenson and others, we come to the last of the series, with postmark 'Glasgow, March 21': 'Why, my beloved, did you not come to me. Oh, beloved, are you ill? Come to me, sweet one. I waited and waited for you, but you came not. I shall wait again to-morrow night, same hour and arrangement. Do come, sweet love, my own dear love of a sweetheart. Come, beloved, and clasp me to your heart. Come and we shall be happy. A kiss, fond love. Adieu, with tender embraces. Ever believe me to be your own ever dear, fond Mimi.'

That letter was posted in Glasgow, if at a box, between 9 a.m. and 12.30 p.m., and if at the General Post Office, between 11.45 a.m. and 1 p.m. That letter was found in the pocket of the coat. About that letter and envelope there is no dispute nor question whatsoever. There was an appointment for Thursday, the 19th. On Wednesday, the 18th, she bought her third packet of arsenic. She went back to Currie's shop on the 18th, told him that the first rats had been killed that they had found a great many large ones lying in the house; and, as she had got arsenic before, appeared to be a respectable person, and told her story without hesitation, on the 18th March, she got her third packet of arsenic.

That letter was enclosed by Thuau to L'Angelier on the same day with the rest. He enclosed it in a letter of his own, in which he says that the letter came at half-past twelve, and that he hastened to put it into the post, if there is time. L'Angelier got that letter after nine o'clock at Stirling on

Sunday morning. He left shortly after the afternoon service had begun. It is proved by his landlady that he left at that time – it is proved by the postmaster that he got a letter – it is proved that he was in his usual health. He walked to Stirling, started instantly, taking the letter as an appointment for Sunday night. The question whether it was so or not is immaterial. The guard recognised him as a gentleman who travelled from Stirling to Coatbridge, handed him over to Ross, the auctioneer, and he swears these two were the only passengers in that train who stopped at Coatbridge. They had food together in the inn; the guard, Fairfoul, saw him start with Ross in perfect health at Coatbridge to walk to Glasgow. Ross swears that he walked with him to Glasgow, that he was quite well, walked briskly, did not tire, stopped at no place on the road, and arrived in his lodgings a little after eight, and, Mrs Jenkins says, looking infinitely improved since he left her on the 19th. He came home in the greatest spirits, and told them that the letter had brought him home. They knew, and he made no secret of, why he had come home. The landlady knew so well that when he went out at night he was going to see his sweetheart, that she never asked him any questions on these occasions. He stayed in the house, took some tea, and left the house in his usual health a little after or before nine o'clock.

He is seen sauntering along in the direction of Blythswood Square about twenty minutes past nine. It is too early. He knows the ways of the house, and knows that they have prayers on Sunday night. He must beguile the time a little, and so he goes past Blythswood Square, down to the other side, and makes a call on his acquaintance McAlester, in Terrace Street, but does not find him at home. The maid-servant recognised him, and says he was there about half-past nine. Here my clue fails me. We lose sight of him for the period of two or three hours, and my learned friends on the other side are equally unsuccessful in their endeavours to trace him; but there is no attempt to show that any mortal man saw him anywhere else than the only place he was going to.

He went out with the determination of seeing her; and believing that he had an appointment at that place, you cannot doubt that, after coming from the Bridge of Allan, post haste, to see her, walking first from Bridge of Allan to Stirling, then travelling from Stirling to Coatbridge, walking from Coatbridge to Glasgow, and then walking from his lodgings in the direction of Blythswood Square – you cannot believe that he would give up his purpose within a hundred yards of the house. The thing is incredible, impossible.

Well, gentlemen, as I said, he knew the ways of the house; he know when it was the habit of the family to retire to rest, and that he would have to wait till Janet was asleep. Can you believe – is it reasonable to believe – that after all these preparations, L'Angelier should have returned without going to the house? The thing is impossible. But if he did go to the house, what do you suppose he did? He went of course to the window and made his presence known. He could do it with certainty. The prisoner denies she heard anything that night. Is that within the region of possibility? She writes him a letter to come to her. I know she says the appointment was for Saturday. But do you suppose that in the course of that correspondence, even if that were true, she would not have waited for him next night on the chance of his being out of town?

The interview was long delayed, anxiously looked for – the interview at which everything was to be explained, in an explanation which she knew he was waiting for. Is it possible that she went to sleep that night, and never woke till the morning? Gentlemen, whatever else you may think, I think you will come to this inevitable conclusion, that L'Angelier did go to the house, did make his presence known; and if he did that, what means the denial, in the prisoner's declaration, that L'Angelier was there that night at all? It is utterly inconceivable and impossible. You have no other trace of him. The policeman, it is true, did not see him, but neither did he see him in many a midnight walk, for you know what a policeman's beat is, and how easy it would be to avoid him. But that he was there is certain.

This was the critical night, when the question was to be decided of her fame and reputation for ever. When and how do we see him next? He is found at his own door, without strength to open the latch, at two o'clock in the morning, doubled up with agony, speechless with exhaustion and pain, parched with thirst, and burning with fever; vomiting commences instantly, and the former symptoms, with great aggravations, go on from two till about eleven o'clock, when the man dies of arsenic. So ends this unhappy tale that I have taken so long to tell you. His last words are few. No one asks him where he has been. They know where he has been, and that is why they do not ask; so says his landlady. She knows where he has been, but asks no questions; but she was a kindly, attentive woman, and she does say to the doctor, 'What can be the meaning of this, that while he has gone out in good health twice, he has come back ill? We must have this inquired into, for I cannot comprehend it.' The unfortunate victim himself is unwilling plainly to admit to himself what doubtless he suspected. He says, 'I never had bile before; I do not know what it is; I never felt this way before; I am very cold; cover me up.'

On the first proposal to send for the doctor, he says – for he certainly does seem to have been a kind-hearted creature – he says to his landlady, 'it is too far for you to go.' After a while, as he is worse, the landlady again proposes to go for a doctor, one who is near at hand, and he says, 'If he is a good doctor, bring him.' She goes, and comes back with a prescription. He makes some difficulty about taking the laudanum; for though it appears from Thuau that he did occasionally take it, he had an aversion to all drugs, thinking that as he had got round before without laudanum, he would get round again. But the symptoms get worse, and he tells Mrs Jenkins to go again for Dr Steven, who comes.

Now, gentlemen, I shall have to speak of the allegation of suicide immediately. But was it not remarkable that not a single question was asked of the doctor by my learned friends as to whether L'Angelier seemed to wish to get better or not? The evidence of Mrs Jenkins, from first to last, shows that L'Angelier was most anxious to recover. And among the very last things he said was, 'Oh, if I could only get a little sleep, I think I should recover.' At last, Mrs Jenkins, taking alarm, says, 'is there any one you would like to see?' He replies, 'I should like to see Miss Perry.' He does not say, 'I should like to see Miss Smith.' If he thought that his life was really in danger, surely the natural feeling is, that he should wish to see her whom of all the world he was most devotedly attached to. But he expresses a wish only to see Miss Perry; and, doubtless, if he had seen

Miss Perry, we should have known more about this case than we do now. But before Miss Perry saw him, death had sealed his mouth; it had caught him more quickly than the doctor or his landlady expected, and more quickly than he had any idea of himself. And so, when the doctor raised his head from the pillow, it fell back; the man was dead; and the mystery of that night remains sealed, so far as the tongue of the unhappy victim is concerned.

Now, gentlemen, I have told you this long and sad tale, and I am very much mistaken indeed if it does not produce an effect on your mind leading to one inevitable result. I don't wish to strain any one point against the unhappy prisoner at the bar. The case is one of such magnitude, the amount of evidence so intricate, and depending as it does upon minute circumstances, the more so from the position in which I am now obliged to present the case – I have found it necessary to select all the little facts and put them all together, in order to construct, as I say, a chain of evidence that appears to me completely irrefutable. But, notwithstanding that, I have no desire whatever to press you beyond the legitimate consequences of the facts which I have now established and I shall therefore go on to consider, with all the candour that I can, the defence that has been set up.

Just let me, before I do so, recapitulate that which we have proved. We have brought these unhappy persons down to the end of December, bound to each other in a way which truly was indissoluble, because the prisoner was so committed in her letters that, except with L'Angelier's consent, she never could have got quit of him. You find her engaging herself to another, and trying to break off from L'Angelier by mere coldness, and not succeeding; you find the threats of L'Angelier; you find her despairing letters; you then find a meeting fixed, and the first indications of poison being given; the meeting takes place, a reconciliation is effected, but the engagement with Mr Minnoch goes on. In about a fortnight or ten days he is taken ill after the purchase of arsenic on one occasion – I have not been able to prove the purchase on the other occasion – but it is proved by her own statement that he was taken ill after getting something from her; he proposes to go to the Bridge of Allan; she entreats him not to go, because Mr Minnoch is there; and by-the-by I forgot to read, although I will not now stop to read, the letter which on the 16th March – the very time she appointed for the last meeting with L'Angelier – she wrote to Mr Minnoch, her intended husband; he takes ill, talks of going to Bridge of Allan; she tries to dissuade him from going, but he goes; she buys arsenic on the 18th; she writes to make an appointment for the 19th, and she buys arsenic the same day; he does not keep his appointment for the 19th, but he does so on Sunday in answer to a second invitation from her, which is found in his pocket; he goes back to Glasgow for the express purpose of keeping the appointment; he goes out that night to keep the appointment; and he comes home and dies of arsenic within twelve or fifteen hours.

Gentlemen, I have concluded that part which I considered necessary relative to the case of the prosecution. But it is right that I should now read the letter which the prisoner addressed to Mr Minnoch. It is dated the 16th of March, the day before the family returned from the Bridge of Allan. I read it to show you the inextricable difficulty in which the unhappy prisoner had placed herself. 'My dearest William, it is but fair, after your kindness to me, that I should write you a note. The day I part from friends I always feel sad. But to part from one I love, as I do you, makes me feel truly sad and dull. My only consolation is that we meet soon. Tomorrow we shall be home. I do so wish you were here today. We might take a long walk. Our walk to Dunblane I shall ever remember with pleasure. That walk fixed a day on which we are to begin a new life, a life which I hope may be of happiness and long duration to both of us. My aim through life shall be to please and study, you. Dear William, I must conclude as Mama is ready to go to Stirling. I do not go with the same pleasure as I did the last time. I hope you got to town safe, and found your sisters well. Accept my warmest, kindest love, and ever believe me to be yours with affection, Madeleine.'

This letter was written two days before she wrote making the assignation with L'Angelier only a very few days before his death. There is one other incident to which I must call your attention, and it is this: apparently the prisoner had shown no particular agitation at the news of

L'Angelier's death. Gentlemen, if she is capable of committing the crime charged, you will not wonder at her self-possession; but news came on the Thursday; something on that day reached her ears. What it was we do not know. One morning she was missed from her father's house. Whether she had been in bed or not is not certain. Janet, her sister, says she was not in bed when she awoke in the morning. She was not seen in the morning by any of the servants. She was found by Mr Minnoch at half-past three o'clock in the Helensburgh steamer at Greenock. Where she was that evening we cannot discover. But it has been shown that she was absent from half-past seven o'clock in the morning, when she was missed, till half-past three, when she was found by Mr Minnoch. So much is certain. I do not press this incident for more than it is worth, for the mere discovery of the letters was enough to induce her to fly from her father's house. But still the fact remains that these letters were discovered, and that the prisoner flies. She is brought back by Mr Minnoch. From a very gentlemanly feeling he asks no questions, and she never explains, and never has explained, what she did on that occasion. This incident bears, therefore, on the case for the prosecution.

As I said before, I have nothing but a public duty to perform. I have no desire to plead this cause as an advocate. My duty is to bring the case before you, as the ends of truth and justice require. But I would be wanting in my duty if I had not brought out these elements, and culled these details, to show you how they bear upon the accusation in the indictment.

I now go to the defence which, as I gather, will probably be set up. As I said before, I will go into it, in the spirit of candour, as well as justice. Now, the first thing may be taken from the declaration of the panel herself. Let us see what it says. Although the declaration of a prisoner is never evidence in his or her favour, yet, in this case, if it be truth, I have no desire to prevent it from having its legitimate effect upon your minds. If she can tell a consistent story – a story consistent with the evidence – there is no desire to deprive her of the benefit of it. [The Lord Advocate read the Prisoner's Declaration.]

Gentlemen, in regard to the last letter, you will see that the prisoner does not tell that the letter referred to was written on any previous occasion.

She says he had been unwell, and had gone to the Bridge of Allan, and she is shown a letter, and I can only refer the writing of it to the sickness before his death. In reference to the use of the arsenic, I do not, of course, know what my learned friend is going to say, but I have not been able to find, either in the publications of the Messrs. Blackwood or the Messrs. Chambers, the shadow of a statement to the effect that arsenic, diluted in water, is ever used in the manner spoken of by the prisoner, and you have the evidence of the lady (Madame Guibilei), who told you that in the story read in the school at Clapton, it was said that arsenic was used internally by the Styrian peasants for the purpose of making their wind stronger, and also for improving the appearance of their complexion. Now, gentlemen, that is her account of what took place.

She denies entirely that she saw L'Angelier on the night before his death; she denies that she heard him at the window the night before his death. You will consider, gentlemen, if that is consistent with any reasonable probability. No doubt the girl Janet slept with her. She said she found her there when she awoke in the morning, and that she went to bed with her at the same time that night, my learned friend did not ask her, and perhaps properly, whether she had heard any noise during the night, and the prisoner is quite entitled to the benefit of the supposition that her sister did not hear any noise during the night. Again, the footboy, who slept in the front of the house, declares he heard nothing, and the two maids, who slept in the room behind, swear they heard nothing. But, gentlemen, so far as regards Janet, you have it positively proved that L'Angelier was in the habit of coming night after night to the window. You have it proved that on many occasions he did come to the house, and you certainly have it proved that on some occasions he was in the house with the prisoner. It does not appear that Janet knew anything about these meetings; and you have her referred to sometimes in the letters, in which she says she could not get Janet asleep last night, as an excuse for not having been at the window to receive him.

In regard to the servants, you will recollect how the house stands by the plan; and that nothing could be easier than for the prisoner, if she had a mind, to go upstairs and open the front door to receive him into the drawing-room; or, if the area gate were left open, she could, with great ease (for the boy slept soundly, and footboys are rather apt to sleep soundly), open the area door, and let him in that way. Whether she could let him in by the back door, without the connivance of Christina Haggert, is another question. Christina Haggert swears that she did not connive at it on that occasion; and it may be doubtful, therefore, whether that mode of access was open to her; and, therefore, while there is nothing in what these witnesses say to imply that they did meet that night there is certainly nothing to exclude the possibility of it.

As to the prisoners account of the use for which she bought the arsenic, as I said before, you must he satisfied that it is a reasonable and credible account before you make up your mind on this case; because, unless it can be presented to you in some intelligible way that this arsenic was bought and used for this purpose, I am afraid the prisoner stands in the position of having in her possession the very poison by which her lover died without being able to account satisfactorily for the possession of it. I do not mean now to go back on the observations I have already made, but you will consider whether – the poison having only been purchased on these three occasions, and never before – that is a true statement which she makes with regard to the use of it. You have to consider whether there is the slightest probability – a probability which any reasonable man can entertain – that she made these three solitary purchases on these three days, and that she used the whole arsenic for that purpose, and that the coincidences of her meeting with L'Angelier on these particular occasions, and immediately after these purchases, is a mere coincidence. If you come to that conclusion, gentlemen, no doubt it will go very far indeed to maintain the defence, but if you cannot, then I am very much afraid the opposite result follows inevitably.

But then it is said, and said with some plausibility, that the meeting which was intended to take place was a meeting trysted for the Saturday, and not for the Sunday. Now, gentlemen, the way I put it to you is this, that either of these two suppositions is quite possible. The letter may have been posted after eleven o'clock, in that case there can be no doubt that the tryst or meeting was for the Sunday; it may have been posted at nine o'clock, in which case probably it would have been the night before, and though it bears no date, it may possibly have meant that the tryst was to be held on Saturday. But I may make this remark, that while throughout this correspondence the Thursdays and Fridays and Sundays are the nights generally appointed for the meetings, I have found no instance – perhaps my learned friend may find one – of meetings appointed for the Saturday. But still, gentlemen, that is within the bounds of probability, and it will be for you to consider, even supposing she expected L'Angelier on the Saturday, whether, knowing he was at Bridge of Allan, which, in her declaration, she says she knew, it is at all likely she should not have waited on the Sunday also, in the case of his not having returned to town on the Saturday – that even if it had been the Saturday evening, the question is, is it within the bounds of probability in this case that he did not go to the window that night, and make himself heard in the usual way?

But, Gentlemen, it is one of the main theories on which the defence is founded, that L'Angelier may have committed suicide. Of course, that is a matter with which I am bound to deal, and can deal only with the anxiety to discover truth. Why, if we had found in this case anything indicating, with reasonable certainty, a case of suicide, we might have disregarded all these facts on which this prosecution is founded. I own, gentlemen, however, and I say it with regret, that I have been unable to see, from first to last, in the evidence for the prosecution or the defence, anything that warrants me in believing that this could possibly be a case of suicide. You must deal with that, gentlemen, you must consider the question as between murder and suicide; and, of course, if you are not satisfied that it was a case of murder, you must give the prisoner the benefit of any doubt you may entertain on the subject. But, gentlemen, we have also to consider, is there any other conceivable cause for what has taken place? Therefore, before I deal with the question of suicide, let us see whether other contingencies are altogether excluded. It seems to have been said that L'Angelier was an eater of arsenic, and that he may have poisoned himself by an overdose. Gentlemen, I think that rests on evidence so little entitled to credit that I need not deal with it; and if my learned friend takes that defence, I am quite content to leave it in the hands of the Court, to direct you as they may think fit.

The only evidence of L'Angelier ever having spoken of arsenic is the evidence of two parties who know him in Dundee in the year 1852. On one occasion he is said to have given it to horses; but the evidence on that point is entirely uncorroborated. And as to the other case – the lad who found a parcel of arsenic, but who never recollected the conversation with L'Angelier until a very few days before this trial, I must throw his evidence out of view altogether. There is not, from the time he came to Glasgow, the smallest suspicion that he was in the habit of taking arsenic; he is not proved to have bought it on any single occasion; and it is not proved that he had it in the house at any time. The supposition, therefore, that he was in the habit of taking it we must altogether reject; neither is the slightest evidence that it would he possible, even by the practice of eating arsenic, regarding which I am very incredulous, to have arranged the matter that the amount of 106 grains should have been found in the stomach of the man. It is so completely out of the bounds of reason that I dismiss the hypothesis as beyond the range of possibility.

It seems, however, to be said, that perhaps at the Bridge of Allan he had accidentally got arsenic. But, gentlemen, that won't do; that is impossible. The cases in which arsenic shows itself only after five hours are very rare indeed. Dr Christison told you that active exercise would accelerate the action of the poison, and that from half an hour to two hours is the ordinary time that it takes to operate. But L'Angelier left the Bridge of Allan at three o'clock. He walked to Stirling and was found at Coatbridge quite well, and he walked to Glasgow quite well, looking better than he had done for three weeks. He left his own house looking quite well, at nine o'clock, and he is seen at Mrs Parr's at half-past nine in perfect health. You thus have him traced for upwards of six hours from leaving Bridge of Allan, and he is quite well, and you have no indication that at Bridge of Allan, Coatbridge, or anywhere else, he had arsenic, or could have had it. Therefore, gentlemen, it seems to me that accidental administration is out of the question, or the administration by any one else. It is not suggested that he saw anybody that night except the prisoner, and you are therefore left to no conjecture, unless it be either a case of suicide or a case of murder.

Now this, as I said before, is a most important matter for you to consider, and you are bound to consider it most deliberately. If the case be suicide, within the limits of the evidence, of course you will say so; but it is my duty to put these facts in the light in which they ought to stand; and I say that I do not think the facts admit the possibility of this being, within any reasonable compass or probability, a case of suicide. Under any circumstances we should have to consider and place in the balance the probabilities of the case, because, although a great deal of evidence has been led as to L'Angelier's temperament, I don't think much importance is to be attached to this matter. You do not discern from a man's temperament whether he is likely to commit suicide or not, and I don't think we can learn from the statistics of suicide that the men whose temperament would be supposed as likely to lead them to commit suicide are those who do so.

In regard to L'Angelier's history, we have had a great deal of evidence, but it did not affect my mind in the slightest degree. There was evidence from one or two men who knew L'Angelier at a time when he was of a poorer class in life, and they told about his having wished to put himself out of the world. Well, but listen, even these witnesses proved to you that at that very time L'Angelier was a kind of gasconading, boasting man, such as a Jersey man might be; that he was in the habit of boasting of his acquaintance with high families, of saying what he knew not to be true. I do not know that they proved all he said not to be true, because that gentleman from Dublin, who seemed to think he was a vain, lying fellow – and you will set his evidence against that of the persons from Glasgow who knew the deceased – admitted that his story about the Fife lady was true, and it turned out that L'Angelier had a somewhat, winning way among ladies.

But it is said that he talked about committing suicide. He did so, but he did not do it. He said at one time that if any lady jilted him he would put a knife in his breast; but he was jilted, and he did not do it. The man that is going to commit suicide does not go to the window when his companion is in bed, and wait till he gets out of it. The man desiring to commit suicide does not go down with a companion to Leith Pier and say that he is going to drown himself. The man that commits suicide does not take a knife in his hand and say to his companions that he is going to plunge it into his breast. I think this temperament is much the reverse of the suicidal. It is more the characteristic of our neighbours on the other side of the Channel, but it does not to my mind load in the slightest degree to a conclusion one way or other in regard to L'Angelier having committed suicide. I think you must deal with this matter altogether independently of these considerations. No doubt a variable temperament is a matter of some consequence. Rapid transition from extreme elevation to extreme depression is a matter to be considered in such a case as this. But I think his conversation with Mr Miller in regard to the abstract question of suicide is perhaps the only thing that is proved on the other side that can bear on this part of the case.

But then, gentlemen, you will have to consider the circumstances under which this supposed suicide was committed. L'Angelier had taken up his position. He had a strong suspicion that there was something in the rumours about Mr Minnoch. He did not mean to kill himself if they were true, but he said, 'I will show these letters to her father.' That is what he meant to do. Well, he came from the Bridge of Allan for the purpose of seeing Miss Smith, the prisoner – very happy, in good spirits, cheerful – he had a kind note from her in his pocket. He went out at night, to go to Blythswood Square. He certainly had no thoughts of suicide. Well, now, is it conceivable that, without having gone near the house, he committed suicide? Is it within the bounds of evidence or probability? Where did he get the arsenic to buy that night? Not surely at Todd & Higginbotham's store, not in any of the chemical works, certainly not in any of the druggists' shops. That is not conceivable. Is it in the least likely that a man in his position would go out to Blythswood Square and swallow dry arsenic there, and then totter home, and die? Gentlemen, that is a supposition that is entirely inconceivable.

There is the possibility, no doubt, that he went to see Miss Smith, and that she told him she was going to give him up, and that this had a great impression on his mind; but if she saw him, what comes of the declaration that she has made that she did not see him that night? And if she did see him that night, is there any link awanting in the chain of evidence that I have laid before you? I can conceive of no possibility of it being a case of suicide that does not imply that they met, and if they met, then the evidence of her guilt is overwhelming. The only chance of escape for the prisoner is to maintain the truth of her declaration that they did not meet that night; and, if they did not meet, I cannot see how the case can be considered as one of suicide.

You may, no doubt, consider whether the truth is that he went to the house, and finding he was not admitted, and that Miss Smith did not hear him, went away in disgust. This is an observation that may be made; but you will consider, in the first place, whether it is possible that, having fixed a meeting the night before, L'Angelier, if he went to the window, would have desisted till he had attracted Miss Smith's attention. And, if he attracted her attention, then they met that night. Therefore, gentlemen, it must be maintained by the prisoner that he did not go to the window, or make a noise there, for she says in her declaration that she never heard him. And, if that be so, I say again I do not see how this can be treated as a case of suicide.

But then it is said that the quantity of arsenic found in the stomach clearly denoted a case of suicide, because so much could not have been given and successfully administered. Gentlemen, I don't think this is made out, but quite the reverse, because if the poison were given in cocoa, as it probably was, it has been proved by Dr Penny that a very large quantity can be held in suspension in it, and Dr Maclagan proved the same thing, though my learned friend the Dean of Faculty did not ask him what amount might or might not be held in suspension in cocoa. No doubt it would require to be boiled in it. But, gentlemen, if the defence that is to be set up is that the prisoner saw certain things in *Blackwood's Magazine*, then she was not without some knowledge of the properties of arsenic. She had access to the kitchen, the fire of which was close to her bedroom. She had a fire in her bedroom, and she might have boiled it without the least danger. This, therefore, presented no difficulty. There is no proof that she did so but, on the other hand, there is no proof on the other side in the slightest degree to exclude the probability of it. And that there should be a large dose is quite consistent with reason and the facts of this case.

If we are right in saying that there were two former cases of administration which were unsuccessful, – and it is proved that a slight dose might be given in coffee – is it not plain, if the thing were to be done that night, that it should have been done with certainty? And consequently there is nothing surprising in the fact that the third dose was a very large quantity.

It is said, gentlemen, and probably will be maintained, that this arsenic was also mixed, that traces of it must have been found in the stomach, and that therefore the arsenic must have been got by L'Angelier and administered by himself. But as to that taken by L'Angelier a month before, no traces of carbonaceous matter could by any possibility have been expected. If Currie's arsenic had been coloured with indigo, probably the colouring matter would have been detected in the stomach. But it was not coloured with indigo; it was coloured with waste indigo; and by experiment, as well as by theory, this was found to leave no trace. There were, no doubt, experiments made by Dr Penny, in which very minute particles of carbonaceous matter were found in the stomach mixed with the arsenic. But, gentlemen, when Dr Penny, in the first place, examined the stomach his attention was not directed to this subject at all, and it was his subsequent experiments that were directed to this matter. Dr Christison also told you that, unless in one part, he could not have expected to find traces of the colouring matter indigo; and it is quite easy to conceive, independently of the fact that the analysts were not looking for it, that a large quantity of the carbonaceous matter, which is lighter than arsenic, might have been thrown off the stomach in the violent vomiting. And, therefore, gentlemen, I must own that this suspicion of suicide does not appear to me to have any probability.

The only thing peculiar about his demeanour was this: he did not say where he had got it; the landlady did not ask him, because she thought she knew; she had no doubt he had been visiting Miss Smith. If he had not gone there, I think you would have expected him to say so. But while that is quite true, you can very easily see, especially in a man with the temperament which he is described by the witnesses to have had, that if he had got anything which disagreed with him there, he would rather die than disclose it. You can easily understand that. Whether, when he sent for Miss Perry, he intended to disclose it is a different question. But during the whole of the illness there seems not to have been the slightest desire for death or the slightest aversion, to life, but, on the contrary, the last thing that he said was, 'If I could only get a little sleep I think I should be well.' The sleep he got was the sleep of death.

Now, gentlemen, I have gone through all this case; there has been a great deal of medical evidence led, but I think I have touched upon all the important portions of it. Evidence was led as to the character of L'Angelier. It is not for me to refer further to that. I think you will understand perfectly well what sort of a man he was. That he was in very low circumstances in 1851, and in a position in which he might well have been weary of life, is perfectly certain. That he had good friends in different parts of the country has at all events not been disproved, and that he himself may have been well connected, as many French refugees are, though in a low position in point of fortune, is at least possible, though there is no proof of it.

And now, gentlemen, having detained you so long, having gone over this case with an amount of trouble and anxiety which I would fain have spared, I leave it entirely in your hands. I am quite sure that the verdict which you give will be a verdict constant with your oath, and with your opinion of the case. I have nothing but a public duty to discharge. I have endeavoured in my argument in this case throughout to show you, as powerfully as I could, how the circumstances which have been proved in evidence bear upon the prisoner. Nor should I have done so if a solemn sense of duty, and my own belief in the justice of the case had not led me to do so. If I had thought that there were any elements of doubt or of disproof in the case that would have justified me in retiring from the painful task which I have now to discharge, believe me, gentlemen, there is not a man in this Court who would have rejoiced more at that result than myself for, of all the persons engaged in this trial, apart from the unfortunate object of it, I believe the task laid upon me is at once the most difficult and the most painful.

I have now discharged my duty. I am quite certain that in the case which I have submitted to you I have not overstrained the evidence.

I do not believe that in any instance I have strained the facts beyond what they would naturally bear. If I have, you yourselves, my learned friend on the other side, and the Court, will correct me. And now, gentlemen, as I have said, I leave the case in your hands. I see no outlet, for this unhappy prisoner, and if you come to the same result as I have done, there is but one course open to you, and that is to return a verdict of guilty of this charge.

On the suggestion of the Lord Justice-Clerk, the Dean of Faculty delayed his address till the next day, and the Court adjourned at 3.30 p.m. One of the reporters asked Madeleine what she had thought of the Lord Advocate's address. She replied, 'When I hear the Dean of Faculty, I will tell you. I never like to give an opinion till I have heard both sides.'

The *Glasgow Herald* commented that:

the unfortunate prisoner had today a very pale, careworn and anxious look. She held down her head for a considerable part of the day and, for the first time, assumed the aspect of someone who feels ashamed. She brightened up on one occasion. A very fine sketch of the bench, bar, jury, and prisoner was taken by a gentleman from the *Illustrated London News*. During the brief interval which took place, this sketch was being examined by the gentlemen in the Glasgow reporters' seat, which is at the right side of the panel's dock. Miss Smith evidently knew what it was at once, and exhibited considerable interest, but, in all likelihood, the feeling was mixed with pain.

1 David Hamilton, architect

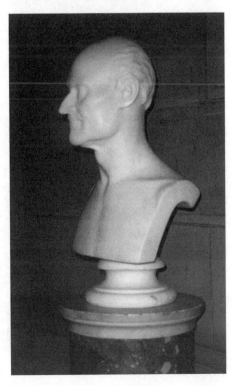

2 Bust of David Hamilton, architect

3 The rear wall of the McLellan Galleries, directly opposite 144 Renfrew Street

4 Miss Perry's house at 144 Renfrew Street

5 Rowaleyn

6 No. 7 Blythswood Square

Above: 7 The Smith family. The three youngest are believed to be Madeleine's cousins, members of the Ogilvy family

Left: 8 Emile L'Angelier

9 Catherine McDonald's boarding house, Bridge of Allan

10 The High Court of Justiciary, Parliament Square, Edinburgh

11 The curator's house at the Botanic Gardens where L'Angelier lodged

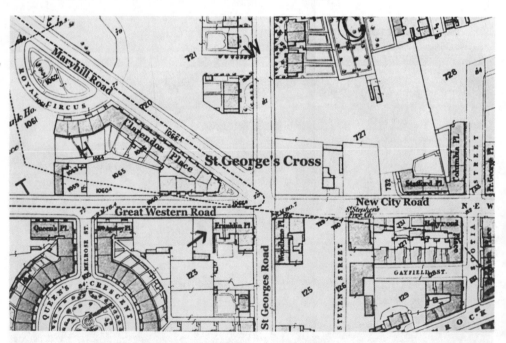

12 Nineteenth-century map showing Franklin Place (now demolished)

13, 14, 15 The scene in Court as captured by the artist for *London Illustrated*

Above: 16 The front area at
Blythswood Square

Left: 17 Bust of Madeleine which
stood for many years in Rowaleyn

18, 19 George Wardle's drawings in the V&A. Madeleine and George were married in 1861

20 Copy of a section of Lady Wardle's Bayeux Tapestry replica. Madeleine was one of those whose stitching contributed to this project of her sister-in-law's Leek Embroidery Society

21 The Wardle Family house in Leek

22 Madeleine's son Tom, his wife Anitta and their children

23 Madeleine at around eighty-nine years old. Her great-granddaughter is on the right of the picture (the other children are no relation)

24 Madeleine's grave at Mount Hope Cemetery

Chapter Five

THE DEAN OF FACULTY'S ADDRESS

The press had now devoted a full week to the case. On 3 July, *The Scotsman* had reported that its previous day's impressions were several thousand above the record-breaking sales of the edition that had covered the fall of Sebastopol. Stories that would normally have filled the front pages had been pushed aside. Fearful accounts of mutiny and massacre had been received from India; another railway catastrophe had struck in England; an animated debate on the ballot was heating up in Parliament; Queen Victoria's visit to Manchester enjoyed a brief passing mention; but it was the trial of Madeleine Smith that captured the imagination throughout the country. And on Wednesday, 8 July, the eighth day of the trial, came yet another historic moment when forty-six-year-old John Inglis, the Dean of the Faculty, would deliver an address to the jury that is remembered to this day as a benchmark for excellence:

> Gentlemen of the jury, the charge against the prisoner is murder, and the
> punishment of murder is death; and that simple statement is sufficient
> to suggest to us the awful solemnity of the occasion which brings you
> and me face to face. But, gentlemen, there are peculiarities in the present
> case of so singular a kind – there is such an air of romance and mystery

investing it from beginning to end – there is something so touching and exciting in the age, and the sex, and the social position of the accused aye, and I must add, the public attention is so directed to the trial, that they watch our proceedings and hang on our very accents with such an anxiety and eagerness of expectation, that I feel almost bowed down and overwhelmed by the magnitude of the task that is imposed on me. You are invited and encouraged by the prosecutor to snap the thread of that young life, and to consign to an ignominious death on the scaffold one who, within a few short months, was known only as a gentle and confiding and affectionate girl, the ornament and pride of her happy home.

Gentlemen, the tone in which my learned friend, the Lord Advocate, addressed you yesterday could not fail to strike you as most remarkable. It was characterised by great moderation, by such moderation as I think must have convinced you that he could hardly expect a verdict at your hands and, in the course of that address, for which I give him the highest credit, he could not resist the expression of his own deep feeling of commiseration for the position in which the prisoner is placed, which was but an involuntary homage paid by the official prosecutor to the kind and generous nature of the man. But, gentlemen, I am going to ask you for something very different from commiseration; I am going to ask you for that which I will not condescend to beg, but which I will loudly and importunately demand: that to which every prisoner is entitled, whether she be the lowest and vilest of her sex or the maiden whose purity is as the unsunned snow. I ask you for justice; and if you will kindly lend me your attention for the requisite period, and if heaven grant me patience and strength for the task, I shall tear to tatters that web of sophistry in which the prosecutor has striven to involve this poor girl and her sad, strange story.

Somewhat less than two years ago, accident brought her acquainted with the deceased L'Angelier; and yet I can hardly call it accident, for it was due unfortunately in a great measure to the indiscretion of a young man whom you saw before you the day before yesterday. He introduced her to L'Angelier on the open street, in circumstances which plainly show that he could not procure an introduction otherwise or elsewhere.

And what was he who thus intruded himself upon the society of this young lady, and then clandestinely introduced himself into her father's house? He was an unknown adventurer; utterly unknown at that time, so far as we can see. For how he procured his introduction into the employment of Huggins & Co. does not appear; and even the persons who knew him there, know nothing of his history or antecedents.

We have been enabled in some degree to throw light upon his origin and his history. We find that he is a native of Jersey; and we have discovered that at a very early period of his life, in the year 1843, he was in Scotland; he was known for three years at that time to one of the witnesses as being in Edinburgh, and the impression which he made as a very young man, which he then was, was certainly, to say the least of it, not of a very favourable kind. He goes to the Continent; he is there during the French Revolution, and he returns to this country, and is found in Edinburgh again in the year 1851. And in what condition is he then? In great poverty, in deep dejection, living upon the bounty of a tavern-keeper, associating and sleeping in the same bed with the waiter of that establishment. He goes from Edinburgh to Dundee, and we trace his history there. At length we find him in Glasgow in 1853. And in 1855, as I said before, his acquaintance with the prisoner commenced.

In considering the character and conduct of the individual, whose history it is impossible to dissociate from this inquiry, we are bound to form as just an estimate as we can of what his qualities were, of what his character was, of what were the principles and motives that were likely to influence his conduct. We find him, according to the confession of all those who observed him then most narrowly, vain, conceited, pretentious, with a great opinion of his own personal attractions, and a very silly expectation of admiration from the other sex. That he was to a certain extent successful in attracting such admiration may be the fact, but, at all events, his own prevailing idea seems to have been that he was calculated to be very successful in paying attentions to ladies, and that he was looking to push his fortune by that means. And, accordingly, once and again, we find him engaged in attempts to get married to women of some station at least in society. We have heard of one disappointment which he met with in England, and another we heard a great deal of connected with a lady in the county of Fife. And the manner in which he bore his disappointment on those two occasions is perhaps the best indication and light we have as to the true character of the man. He was depressed and melancholy beyond description; he threatened – whether he intended or not – to commit suicide in consequence of his disappointment. He was not a person of strong health, and it is extremely probable that this, among other things, had a very important effect in depressing his spirits, rendering him changeable and uncertain, now uplifted, as one of the witnesses said, and now most deeply depressed, of a mercurial temperament, as another described it, very variable, never to be depended on.

Such was the individual with whom the prisoner unfortunately became acquainted in the manner that I have stated. The progress of their acquaintance is soon told. My learned friend the Lord Advocate said to you that, although the correspondence must have been from the outset an improper correspondence, because it was clandestine, yet the letters of the young lady at that first period of their connection breathed nothing but gentleness and propriety. I thank my learned friend for the admission; but even with that admission, I must ask you to bear with me while I call your attention for a few moments to one or two incidents in the course of that early period of their history which I think are very important for your guidance in judging of the conduct of the prisoner.

The correspondence in its commencement shows that if L'Angelier had it in his mind originally to corrupt and seduce this poor girl, he entered upon the attempt with considerable ingenuity and skill; for the very first letter of the series which we have contains a passage in which she says 'I am to break myself off all my very bad habits. It is you I have to thank for this, which I do sincerely from my heart.' He had been noticing, therefore, her faults, whatever they were. He had been suggesting to her improvement in her conduct or in something else. He had thus been insinuating himself into her confidence. And she no doubt yielded a great deal too easily to the pleasures of this new acquaintance, but pleasures comparatively of a most innocent kind at the time to which I am now referring. And yet it seems to have occurred to her own mind at a very early period that it was impossible to maintain this correspondence consistently with propriety or with due regard to her own welfare. For so early as the month of April, 1855 – indeed in the very month in which apparently the acquaintance began – she writes to him in these terms: 'I now perform the promise I made in parting to write to you. We are to be in Glasgow tomorrow (Thursday), but as my time shall not be at my own disposal I cannot fix any time to see you. Chance may throw you in my way. I think you will agree with me in what I intend proposing, viz., that for the present the correspondence had better stop. I know your good feeling will not take this unkind; it is meant quite the reverse. By continuing to correspond harm may arise; in discontinuing it nothing can be said.'

Accordingly, for a time, so far as appears, the correspondence did cease. Again, gentlemen, I beg to call your attention to the fact that in the end of this same year the connection was broken off altogether. That appears from the letter which the prisoner wrote to Miss Perry in the end of September: 'Dearest Miss Perry, many many, kind thanks for all your kindness to me. Emile will tell you I have bid him adieu. My papa would not give his consent, so I am in duty bound to obey him. Comfort dear Emile. I had hoped some day to have been happy with him but, alas, it was not intended. We were doomed to be disappointed. You have been a kind friend to him. Oh, continue so. I hope and trust he may prosper in the step he is about to take. I am glad now he is leaving this country, for it would have caused me great pain to have met him. Think my conduct not unkind. I have a father to please, and a kind father, too. Farewell, dear Miss Perry, and, with much love, believe me yours most sincerely, – Mimi.'

Once more, in the spring of 1856, it would appear – the correspondence having in the interval been renewed, how, we do not know, but is it not unfair to suppose, rather on the importunate entreaty of the gentleman than on the suggestion of the lady who wrote such a letter as I have just read? – the correspondence was discovered by the family of Miss Smith. On that occasion she wrote thus to her confidante, Miss Perry: 'Dearest Mary, M. has discovered the correspondence. I am truly glad that it is known; but, strange to say, a fortnight has passed and not a word has been said. I cannot understand it. Now that it is known, I do not mean to give way. I intend to state in plain terms that I intend to be dear Emile's wife. Nothing shall deter me. I shall be of age soon, and then I have a right to decide for myself. Can you blame me for not giving in to my parents in a matter of so serious importance as the choice of a husband? I had been intended to marry a man of money, but is not affection before all things, and in marrying Emile I will take the man whom I love. I know my friends will forsake me, but for that I do not care so long as I possess the affection of Emile and, to possess and retain his affection, I shall try to please him in all things, by acting according to his directions, and he shall cure me of my faults ... I am sorry not to be able to see you, as we are going to Edinburgh in a week or ten days.' Now, what follows from this you have heard from some of the witnesses. The correspondence was put an end to by the interference of Mr Smith, and for a time that interference had effect.

But, alas, the next scene is the most painful of all. This which we have been speaking of is in the end of 1855. In the spring of 1856 the corrupting influence of the seducer was successful, and his victim fell. It is recorded in a letter bearing the post-mark of the 7th May, which you have heard read. And how corrupting that influence must have been how vile the arts to which he resorted for accomplishing his nefarious purpose, can never be proved so well as by the altered tone and language of the unhappy prisoner's letters. She had lost not her virtue merely, but, as the Lord Advocate said, her sense of decency. Gentlemen, whose fault was that; whose doing was that? Think you that, without temptation, without evil teaching, a poor girl falls into such depths of degradation? No, influence from without, most corrupting influence, can alone account for such a fall. And yet, through the midst of this frightful correspondence – and I wish to God that it could have been concealed from you, gentlemen, and from the world, and I am sure the Lord Advocate would have spared us, if he had not felt it necessary for the ends of justice – I say that even through the midst of this frightful correspondence there breathes a spirit of devoted affection towards the man who had destroyed her that strikes me as most touching.

The history of the affair is soon told. I do not think it necessary to carry you through all the details of their intercourse from the spring of 1856 down to the end of that year. It is in the neighbourhood of Helensburgh, almost entirely, that that correspondence took place. In November the family of the Smiths came back to Glasgow. And that becomes a very important era in the history of the case, for that was the first time at which they came to live in the house in Blythswood Square, which you have heard so much about. There were many meetings between them in the other house in India Street in 1855. They met still more frequently at Rhu, but what we are chiefly concerned with is to know what meetings took place between them in that last winter in the house in Blythswood Square, how these took place, and what it was necessary for them to do in order to come together, for these things have a most important bearing on the question which you are here to try.

In a letter which bears postmark '17th December,' she says, 'I would give anything to have an hour's chat with you. Beloved Emile, I don't see how we can. M. is not going from home, and when P. is away Janet does not sleep with M. She won't leave me, as I have a fire on in my room and M. has none. Do you think, beloved, you could not see me some night for a few moments at the door under the front door? But perhaps it would not be safe. Someone might pass as you were coming in. We had better not.' Now you will recollect that Christina Haggart told us that upon one occasion, and one only, there was a meeting in that place, arranged in the way spoken of in this letter. A meeting, that is to say, at the door, under the front door, to which, of course, he required to be admitted through the area gate; and that was accomplished through the assistance of Christina Haggart.

Then, again, there is reference in the next letter, which bears the postmark of the 19th, to a desire for a meeting: 'My beloved, my darling, do you for a second think I could feel happy this evening, knowing you were in low spirits, and that I am the cause? … Oh, would to God we could meet. I would not mind for M. If P. and M. are from home, the first time they are, you shall be here. Yes, my love, I must see you, I must be pressed to your heart. … Oh yes, my beloved, we must make a bold effort.' Here again is the same condition, and the impossibility of carrying the meeting through unless in absence of the parents; but the first opportunity which occurs she will certainly avail herself of.

Then in another letter, dated 29th, she writes, 'If you love me you will come to me when P. and M. are away in Edinburgh, which I think will be about the 7th or 10th of January.' In the same letter also, she says, 'If P. and M. go, will you not, sweet love, come to your own Mimi? Do you think I would ask you if I saw danger in the house?' On the 9th of January she writes again a letter, in which you will find a repetition of the same warning how to conduct himself at the window: 'It is just eleven o'clock, and no letter from you, my own over dear beloved husband. Why this, my sweet one? I think I heard your stick this evening (pray do not make any sounds whatever at my window).' Further, she says in the same letter, 'I think you are again at my window, but I shall not go down stairs, as P. would wonder why, and only he and I are up waiting for Jack. I wish to see you; but no, you must not look up to the window in case any one should see me. So, beloved, think it not unkind if I never by any chance look at you. Just leave my note and go away.' In the next letter, dated the 11th, she says, 'I would so like to spend three or four hours with you, just to talk over some things, but I don't know when we can; perhaps in the course of ten days. ... If you would risk it, my sweet beloved pet, we would have time to kiss each other and a dear, fond embrace and though, sweet love, it is only for a minute, do you not think it is better than not meeting at all? ... Same as last.' Plainly that was the short meeting which Christina Haggart told us of as occurring in the area under the front door, and, so far as I can see, there is not a vestige or tittle of written evidence of any meeting whatever, except that short meeting in the area, down to the time of which I am now speaking, that is to say, from the 18th of November till the date of this letter, which is the 11th January.

Then, on the 13th January, she writes a letter, which is also very important with reference to the events at this period, because at that time he had been very unwell. The 13th of January is the date of the letter: 'Monday night.' – it is posted on the 14th, but as she almost always wrote her letters at night, you will easily understand that it was written on the night of the 13th – 'I am glad you are sound. That is a great matter, I had a fear you were not, and I feared that you would die; but now I am easy on that point. I am very well.' In the same letter she says, 'I don't hear of M. or P. going from home, so, my dear pet, I see no chance for us. I fear we shall have to wait a bit.' That may have reference either to the possibility of their meeting, or to the possibility of their carrying out their design of an elopement. It matters not very much.

Then on the 18th January we have this: 'I did love you so much last night when you were at the window.' Now, whether that last phrase indicates that there was a conversation at that meeting or not does not very clearly appear; but, at all events, it can have been nothing more than a meeting at the window. She says, 'I think I shall see you Thursday night.' I suppose the same kind of meeting that she refers to immediately after. Whether that meeting on Thursday night ever took place or not does not appear; but it is not very important, because, pray observe, gentlemen, that that Thursday night is a night of January; this being written on Monday, the 19th, Thursday would have been the 22nd.

In the next letter, bearing the post-mark 21st January, she says, 'I have not got home till after two o'clock for the last two nights. If you can I shall look for a note on Friday, eight or ten, not six.' In the next, dated 22nd January, she says, 'I was so sorry that I could not see you to-night; I had expected an hour's chat with you; we must just hope for better the next time. ... I don't see the least chance for us, my dear love. M. is not well enough to go from home, and, my dear little sweet pet, I don't see we could manage in Edinburgh, because I could not leave a friend's house without their knowing of it; so, sweet pet, it must at present be put off till a better time. I see no chance before March.' In the same cover there is another letter, dated Sunday night, where there is reference to a meeting, but my learned friend the Lord Advocate very properly admitted that that was a meeting at the window, nothing more, and therefore I need say no more of it. He was convinced of that by referring back to letter No. 93, and comparing them together. He admitted the meeting there was merely at the window.

Now, gentlemen, that concludes the month of January. There are no more letters of that month. There is not another, so far as I can see, referring to any meeting whatever in that house. Christina Haggart told you, when she was examined, that in the course that winter, and when the family were living in Blythswood Square, they met but twice; and it is clear that they could not meet without the intervention of Christina Haggart. I don't mean that it was physically impossible, but when the young lady saw so much danger, so much obstruction in the way of her accomplishing her object, unless she could secure the aid of Christina Haggart, there is not the slightest tittle of evidence that without that assistance she ever made the attempt. I mean, of course, you must understand, meetings within the house. I don't dispute the existence of the correspondence which was carried on at the window, and I don't doubt that even on occasions they may have exchanged words at the window, and had short conversations there. But I am speaking of meetings within the house. The only evidence at all as to meetings within the house is confined to the meeting in the area under the front door, and the other meeting that took place on the occasion when Christina Haggart introduced L'Angelier at the back door.

Now, I am sure you will agree with me that this is a most important part of the case; and I bring you down thus to the commencement of the month of February with this, I think, distinctly proved or at least I am entitled to say, without a shadow of evidence to the contrary that they were not in the habit of coming into personal contact. On the contrary, they had only met in this way on two occasions in the course of the winter. But now we have come to a very important stage of the case. On the 28th of January Mr Minnoch proposes, and, if I understand the theory of my learned friend's case aright, from that day the whole character of this girl's mind and feelings was changed, and she set herself to prepare for the perpetration of what my learned friend has called one of the most foul, cool, deliberate murders that ever was committed.

Gentlemen, I will not say that such a thing is absolutely impossible; but I shall venture to say it is well-nigh incredible. He will be a bold man who will seek to set limits to the depths of human depravity; but this at least all past experience teaches us, that perfection, even in depravity, is not rapidly attained, and that it is not by such short and easy stages as the prosecutor has been able to trace in the career of Madeleine Smith, that a gentle, loving girl passes at once into the savage grandeur of a Medea, or the appalling wickedness of a Borgia. No, gentlemen, such a thing is not possible. There is and must be a certain progress in guilt, and it is quite out of all human experience, judging from the tone of the letters which I have last read to you, that there should be such a sudden transition from affection to the savage desire of removing by any means the obstruction to her wishes and purposes, that the prosecutor imputes to the prisoner.

Think, Gentlemen, how foul and unnatural a murder it is, the murder of one who, within a very short space, was the object of her love – an unworthy object, an unholy love – but yet while it lasted – and its endurance was not very brief – it was a deep, absorbing, unselfish, devoted passion. And the object of that passion she now conceives the purpose of murdering. Such is the theory that you are desired to believe. Before you will believe it, will you not ask for demonstration? Will you be content with conjecture; will you be content with suspicion, however pregnant, or will you be so unreasonable as to put it to me in this form: that the man having died of poison, the theory of the prosecutor is the most probable that it offered? Oh, gentlemen, is that the manner in which a jury should treat such a case? Is that the kind of proof on which you could convict of a capital offence?

On the 19th of February, on the 22nd of February, and on the 22nd of March – for the prosecutor has now absolutely fixed on these dates – he charges the prisoner with administering poison. I observe, he does not ask you to suppose merely that by some means or other the prisoner conveyed poison to L'Angelier, but he asks you to affirm on your oaths the fact that, on those three occasions, she, with her own hands, administered the poison. Look at the indictment and see if I have not correctly represented to you what the prosecutor demands at your hands. He says in the first charge that she 'wickedly and feloniously administered to Emile L'Angelier, now deceased.' Again, in the second charge, he alleges that she did 'wickedly and feloniously administer to him a quantity or quantities of arsenic' and, in the third charge, that she did 'wickedly and feloniously administer to, or cause to be taken by, the said deceased Emile L'Angelier, a quantity of arsenic, of which he died and was thus murdered' by her.

There are three separate acts of administration, not I pray you to observe, general psychological facts, which you may deduce from a great variety of moral considerations, but plain physical facts – facts which, if anybody had seen, would have been proved to demonstration, but which, in the absence of eyewitnesses, I do not dispute may be proved by circumstantial evidence. But then you must always bear in mind that the circumstantial evidence must come up to this – that it must convince you of the perpetration of these acts.

Now, then, in dealing with such circumstantial proof of such facts as I have been speaking of, what should you expect to find? Of course, the means must be in the prisoner's hands of committing the crime. The possession of poison will be the first thing that is absolutely necessary and, on the other hand, the fact that the deceased was, on the first occasion, ill from the consequences of poison, on the second occasion was ill in the same manner from the consequences of poison, and, on the third occasion, died from the same cause. But it would be the most defective of all proofs of poisoning to stop at such facts as these, for one person may be in the possession of poison, and another person die from the effects of poison, and yet that proves nothing. You must have a third element. You must not merely have a motive – and I shall speak of motive by and by. You must not merely have a motive, but opportunity – the most important of all elements. You must have the opportunity of the parties coming into personal contact, or of the poison being conveyed to the murdered person through the medium of another. Now, you shall see how far there is the slightest room for such a suspicion here.

As regards the first charge, it is alleged to have taken place on the evening of the 19th February, and the illness, on the same theory, followed either in the course of that night, or rather the next morning. Now, in the first place, as to date, is it by any means clear? Mrs Jenkins – than whom I never saw a more accurate or more trustworthy witness – Mrs Jenkins swears that, to the best of her recollection and belief, the first illness preceded the second by eight or ten days. Eight or ten days from the 22nd, which was the date of the second illness, will bring us back to the 13th February, and he was very ill about the 13th February, as was proved by the letter I read to you, and proved also by the testimony of Mr Miller. Now, if the first illness was on the 13th February, do you think that another illness could have intervened between that and the 22nd without Mrs Jenkins being aware of it? Certainly that won't do. Therefore, if Mrs Jenkins is correct, that the first illness was eight or ten days before, that is one and a most important blow against the prosecutor's case on this first charge.

Let us look now, if you please, at what is said on the other side as to the date. It is said by Miss Perry that not only was that the date of his illness, but that he had a meeting with the prisoner on the 19th. Miss Perry's evidence upon that point, I take leave to say, is not much worth. She had no recollection of that day when she was examined first by the Procurator Fiscal; no, nor the second time, nor the third time; and it was only when, by a most improper interference on the part of one of the clerks of the Fiscal, a statement was read to her out of a book which has been rejected as worthless in fixing dates, that she then for the first time took up the notion that it was the 19th which L'Angelier had referred to in the conversations which he had with her. And, after all, what do these conversations amount to? To this, that on the 17th, when he dined with her, he said he expected to meet the prisoner on the 19th. But did he say afterwards that he had met her on the 19th? The Lord Advocate supposed that he had, but he was mistaken. Miss Perry said nothing of the sort. She said that when she saw him again on the 2nd March, he did not tell her of any meeting on the 19th.

Well, gentlemen, let us look now, in that state of the evidence, as to the probabilities of the case. This first illness, you will keep in view, whenever it took place, was a very serious one – a very serious one indeed. Mrs Jenkins was very much alarmed by it, and the deceased himself suffered intensely. There can be no doubt about that. Now, if the theory of the prosecutor be right, it was on the morning of the 20th that he was in this state of intense suffering, and upon the 21st, the next day, he bought the largest piece of beef that is to be found in his pass-book from his butcher; and he had fresh herrings for dinner in such a quantity as to alarm his landlady, and a still more alarming quantity and variety of vegetables.

Here is a dinner for a sick person! All that took place upon the 21st, and yet the man was near death's door on the morning of the 20th, by that irritation of stomach, no matter how produced, which necessarily leaves behind it the most debilitating and sickening effects. I say, gentlemen, there is real evidence that the date is not the date which the prosecutor says it is.

But, gentlemen, supposing that the date were otherwise, was the illness caused by arsenic? Such I understand to be the position of my learned friend. Now, that is the question which I am going to put to you very seriously; and I ask you to consider the consequences of answering that question in either way. You have it proved very distinctly, I think – to an absolute certainty almost – that on the 19th February the prisoner was not in possession of arsenic. I say proved to a certainty for this reason: because when she went to buy arsenic afterwards, on the 21st February and the 6th and the 18th March, she went about it in so open a way that it was quite impossible that it should escape observation if it came afterwards to be inquired into. I am not mentioning that at present as an element of evidence in regard to her guilt or innocence of the second or third charges. But I want you to keep the fact in view at present for this reason, that if she was so loose and open in her purchases of arsenic on these subsequent occasions, there was surely nothing to lead you to expect that she should be more secret or more cautious on the first occasion. How could that be? Why, one could imagine that a person entertaining a murderous purpose of this kind, and contriving and compassing the death of a fellow-creature, might go on increasing in caution as she proceeded, but how she should throw away all idea of caution or secrecy upon the second, and third, and fourth occasions if she went to purchase so secretly upon the first, that the whole force of the prosecutor has not been able to detect that earlier purchase, I leave it to you to explain to your own minds. It is incredible. Nay, but, gentlemen, it is more than incredible; I think it is disproved by the evidence of the prosecutor himself. He sent his emissaries throughout the whole druggists' shops in Glasgow, and examined their registers to find whether any arsenic had been sold to a person of the name of L'Angelier. I need not tell you that the name of Smith was also included in the list of persons to be searched for; and therefore, if there had been such a purchase at any period prior to the 19th February, that fact would have been proved to you just as easily, and with as full demonstration, as the purchases at a subsequent period. But, gentlemen, am I not struggling a great deal too hard to show you that the possibility of purchasing it before the 19th is absolutely disproved? That is no part of my business. It is enough for me to say that there is not a tittle or vestige of evidence on the part of the prosecutor that such a purchase was made prior to the 19th, and, therefore, on that ground, I submit to you with the most perfect confidence as regards that first charge, that it is absolutely impossible that arsenic could have been administered by the prisoner to the deceased upon the evening of the 19th of February.

Nay, gentlemen, there is one circumstance more before I have done with that which is worth attending to. Suppose it was the 19th, then it was the occasion in reference to which Mr Thuau told you that, when the deceased gave him an account of his illness and the way in which it came on, he told him that he had been taken ill in the presence of the lady – a thing totally inconsistent with the notion, in the first place, that the arsenic was administered by her, and its effects afterwards produced and seen in his lodgings, but still more inconsistent with Mrs Jenkins's account of the manner and time at which illness came on, which, if I recollect right, was at four o'clock in the morning, after he had gone to bed perfectly well. Now, gentlemen, I say, therefore, you are bound to hold not merely that there is here a failure to make out the administration on the 19th, but you are bound to give me the benefit of an absolute negative upon that point, and to allow me to assume that arsenic was not administered on the 19th by the prisoner. I think I am making no improper demand in carrying it that length.

Now, see the consequences of the position which I have thus established. Was he ill from the effects of arsenic on the morning of the 20th? I ask you to consider that question as much as the prosecutor has asked you; and if you can come to the conclusion, from the symptoms exhibited, that he was ill from the effects of arsenic on the morning of the 20th, what is the inference? That he had arsenic administered to him by other hands than the prisoner's. The conclusion is inevitable, irresistible, if these symptoms were the effect of arsenical poisoning. If, again, you are to hold that the symptoms of that morning's illness were not such as to indicate the presence of arsenic in the stomach, or to lead to the conclusion of arsenical poisoning, what is the result of that belief? The result of it is to destroy the whole theory of the prosecution's case – a theory of successive administrations, and to show how utterly impossible it is for him to bring evidence up to the point of an actual administration. I give my learned friend the option of being impaled on one or other of the horns of that dilemma, I care not which. Either L'Angelier was ill from arsenical poisoning on the morning of the 20th, or he was not. If he was, he had received arsenic from other hands than the prisoner's. If he was not, the foundation of the whole case is shaken.

I have disposed of the first charge, and in a way which I trust you won't forget in dealing with the remainder of the case, because I think it enables me to take a position from which I shall demolish every remaining atom of this case. But before I proceed to the consideration of the second charge more particularly, I want you to follow me, if you please, very precisely as to certain dates, and you will oblige me very much if you take a note of them. The first parcel of arsenic which is purchased by the prisoner was upon the 21st of February. It was bought in the shop of Murdoch the apothecary, and the arsenic there purchased was mixed with soot. Murdoch was the person who ordinarily supplied medicines to Mr Smith's family, and she left the arsenic unpaid for, and it went into her father's account; and I shall have something to say about these circumstances hereafter. I merely mention them at present. Now, on Sunday, the 22nd, it is said – and we shall see by-and-by with how much reason – that L'Angelier again had arsenic administered to him and, so far, it may be that we have, in regard to the second charge, a purchase of arsenic previous to the alleged administration. I shall not lose sight of that weighty fact but, from the 22nd February onwards, there appears to me to be no successful attempt on the part of the prosecutor to prove any meeting between these persons. He was confined to the house after that illness, as you have heard, for eight or ten days. There are letters written at that time which completely correspond with that state of matters, speak of his being confined, and of the possibility of seeing him at his window. But it is not pretended that there is any meeting during all that time, which lasted for eight or ten days after the 22nd.

Now, suppose it lasted for eight days, that brings you down to the 2nd March. On the 5th March there is said to be a letter written by L'Angelier to the prisoner, and there is a letter from the prisoner to L'Angelier which is said to have been written on the same day. But neither of these letters indicates the occurrence of a meeting upon that day, nor bears any reference to any recent meeting, nor any anticipated or expected meeting. In short, there is not, from the 22nd of February to the 6th of March, any attempt to prove a meeting between the parties. I think I am justified in stating the import of the evidence to be so. I shall be corrected if I am wrong, but I think, I am quite certain, that there is not an insinuation that there was a meeting between the parties from the 22nd February to the 6th March.

On the 6th March the prisoner goes with her family to the Bridge of Allan, and there she remains till the 17th. And on the 6th March, immediately preceding her departure to the Bridge of Allan, she buys her second parcel of arsenic, and that she buys in the company of Miss Buchanan, talks about it to two young men who were in the shop, signs her name on the register as she had done on the previous occasion. Every circumstance shows the most perfect openness in making the purchases. Well, she goes to the Bridge of Allan on the 6th, and confessedly does not return till the 17th.

Let us now trace, on the other hand, the adventures of L'Angelier. He remains in Glasgow till the 10th. He then goes to Edinburgh, and returns on the 17th at night. He comes home by the late train to Glasgow. On the 18th he remained in the house all day, and is not out at night. I thought, but was not quite sure, that I was right in thinking that the witness said so, and I am glad to find that my learned friend the Lord Advocate in his speech corroborates my recollection of this fact – that L'Angelier was in the house all the 18th. On the 19th, in the morning, he goes first to Edinburgh and then to the Bridge of Allan, from which he did not return till the night preceding his death, on the 22nd. I have missed directing your attention at the proper place to the fact that on the 18th, on her return from the Bridge of Allan, the prisoner purchases her third portion of arsenic in the same open way as before.

Observe, gentlemen, that unless you shall hold it to be true, and proved by the evidence before you, that these two persons met on the 22nd of February, which was a Sunday, or unless, in like manner, you hold it to be proved that they met again on the fatal night of the 22nd March, there never was a meeting at all after the prisoner had made any of her purchases of arsenic. I maintain that there not only was no meeting – that we have no evidence of any meeting – but that practically there was no possibility of their meeting. I say that, unless you can believe on the evidence that there was a meeting on the 22nd of February, or again on the 22nd of March, there is no possible occasion on which she either could have administered poison, or could have purposed or intended to administer it. You will now, gentlemen, see the reason why I wanted these dates well – fixed in your minds, for from the first alleged purchase of poison to the end of the tragedy, there is no possibility of contact or of administration, unless you think you have evidence that they met on one or other or both of these Sundays, the 22nd February and the 22nd March.

Let us see if they did meet on the 22nd February. What is the evidence on that point of Mrs Jenkins, L'Angelier's landlady? She says he was in his usual condition in the 21st, when he made that celebrated dinner to which I have already adverted, and when she thought he was making himself ill, and on that 21st he announced to her that he would not leave the house all the Sunday – the following day. He had therefore no appointment with the prisoner for the Sunday, else he would never have made that statement. On the 22nd, Mrs Jenkins says she has no recollection of his going out, in violation of his declared intention made the day before. Gentlemen, do you really believe that this remarkably accurate woman would not have remembered a circumstance in connection with this case of such great importance as that he had first of all said that he would not go out upon that Sunday, and that he had then changed his mind and gone out? It is too daring a draft on your imagination. She has no recollection of his going out, and I am entitled to conclude that he did not. And when he did go out of a night and came in late, what was his habit? Mrs Jenkins says he never got into the house on those occasions – that is, after she went to bed except in one or other of these two ways; either he asked for and got a check-key, or the door was opened to him by Mr Thuau. Mrs Jenkins says there was no other mode. She says he did not ask the check-key that night. If he had done so she would have recollected. Thuau says he certainly did not let him in. Now, gentlemen, I must say that to conjecture, in the face of this evidence, that L'Angelier was out of the house that night, is one of the most violent suppositions ever made in the presence of a jury, especially when that conjecture is for the purpose of rendering the second administration of poison a possible event; without that conjecture it is impossible.

L'Angelier did not come home ill. There is no evidence that he ever came home at all, or that he ever was out; all we know, as matter of fact, is that he was taken ill in the morning, about four or five o'clock. Only one attempt was made by my learned friend to escape from the inevitable results of this evidence. And it was by a strange and forced use of a particular letter, written on a Wednesday, in which letter the prisoner says she is sorry to hear he is ill; but the portion on which he particularly founded was that in which she added: 'You did look bad Sunday night and Monday morning.' My learned friend says that that letter was written on the 25th of February, and points out to you that the Sunday before that was the 22nd. And, no doubt, if that were conclusively proved, it would be a piece of evidence in conflict with the other, and a very strong conflict and contradiction it would indeed be, and one which you, gentlemen, would have great difficulty to reconcile. This, however, would not be a reason for believing the evidence of the Crown, or for convicting the prisoner, but for a very opposite result.

But, gentlemen, in point of fact, the supposed conflict and contradiction are imaginary; for the only date the letter bears is Wednesday, and it may be, so far as the letter is traced, any Wednesday in the whole course of their correspondence. There is not a bit of internal evidence in this letter, nor in the place where it was found, nor anywhere else, to fix its date, unless you take that reference to Sunday night, which is, of course, begging the whole question. Therefore, I say, again, gentlemen, that it might have been written on any Wednesday during the whole course of their correspondence and connection. But it is found in an envelope, from which its date is surmised. And, gentlemen, because a certain letter, without date, is found in a certain envelope, you are to be asked to convict, and to convict of murder, on that evidence alone! I say that if this letter had been found in an envelope bearing the most legible possible post-mark, it would have been absurd and monstrous to convict on such evidence. But, when the post-mark is absolutely illegible, how much is that difficulty and absurdity increased?

We have no evidence even as to the month, except that the Crown witness from the Post Office says that the mark of the month has an R, and that the Post Office mark for February happens to have no R. My learned friend must condemn the evidence of his own witness before he can fix the post-mark. The witness said the letter must have been posted in the year 1857; but perhaps even on that point the Crown will not take the evidence of a witness whom they themselves have discredited. The whole evidence on this point is subject to this answer: that the envelope proves absolutely nothing. Again, to take the fact that a particular letter is found in a particular envelope as evidence to fix the date of an administration of poison is, gentlemen, a demand on your patience and on your credulity which to me is absolutely unintelligible. The Lord Advocate said in the course of his argument that, without any improper proceedings on the part of the Crown officials, nothing could be so easily imagined as that a letter should get into a wrong envelope in the possession of the deceased himself. I adopt that suggestion. And if that be a likely accident, what is the value of this letter as a piece of evidence especially in opposition to the plain evidence of two witnesses for the Crown, that the Sunday referred to in the letter could not be the 22nd of February, because on that Sunday L'Angelier was never over the door.

Well, I do not think the Crown has succeeded much better in supporting the second charge. For if the instrument be indispensable to the administration of poison, it is equally evident that there must also be the opportunity of administering it. I should like to know whether my learned friend still persists in saying that, on the morning of the 23rd February, the deceased was suffering from the effects of arsenic poisoning, for, if he does, the inference recurs that the deceased was in the way of receiving arsenic from another hand than the prisoner's.

And now, gentlemen, am I not entitled to say that, as regards the first two charges, step by step – tediously, I am afraid, but with no more minuteness than was necessary for the ends of justice and the interests of the prisoner – I have pulled to pieces the web of sophistry which had been woven around the case.

Well, gentlemen, time goes on, and certainly in the interval between the 22nd February and the 22nd March we have no event in the nature of a meeting between these parties. Nothing of that kind is alleged, and on the 22nd of March, it is perfectly true that L'Angelier goes to Glasgow, and goes under peculiar circumstances. The events connected with his journey from Bridge of Allan, with the causes and consequences of it, I must beg you to bear with me while I detail at considerable length. He went to the Bridge of Allan on the morning of the 19th or, rather, he went first to Edinburgh, and then from there to the Bridge of Allan. You recollect that upon the 18th – from the night of the 17th, after his arrival from Edinburgh, and in the course of the 18th – he had expressed himself very anxious about a letter which he expected. He spoke to Mrs Jenkins about it several times; but he started for Edinburgh without receiving that letter; and I think it is pretty plain that the sole cause of his journey to Edinburgh that day was to see whether the letter had not gone there. Now, in Edinburgh again he receives no letter, but goes on to the Bridge of Allan, and at the Bridge of Allan he does receive a letter from the prisoner. That letter was written on the evening of Wednesday, the 18th – remember that there is no doubt about that; we are quite agreed about it and it was posted on the morning of Thursday. It was addressed by the prisoner to the deceased at his lodgings at Mrs Jenkins's, the prisoner being ignorant of the fact that he had left town. It reached Mrs Jenkins in the course of the forenoon, and it was posted in another envelope by Mr Thuau addressed to L'Angelier at Stirling, where he received it upon

Friday. I hope you follow this exactly, as you will find it immediately of the greatest consequence. It reached the Post Office at Stirling, I think, about ten on the morning of Friday.

Now, gentlemen, there are two or three circumstances connected with this letter of the greatest consequence. In the first place, it is written on the evening before it is posted. In that respect it stands very much in the same position as by far the greater part of the letters written by the prisoner, which were almost all written at night and posted next morning. In the second place, it undoubtedly contained an appointment to meet the deceased on the Thursday evening. That was the evening after it was written – the evening of the day on which it was posted. But L'Angelier, being out of town, and not receiving it until the Friday, it was, of course, too late for the object, and he did not come to town in answer to that letter – a very important fact too, for this reason, that it shows that if the tryst was made by appointment for one evening, he did not think it worth while to attempt to come the next evening, because he could not see the prisoner but by appointment. Remember how anxious he was about this letter before he left Glasgow; remember that he made a journey to Edinburgh for the very purpose of getting the letter that he expected. He was burning to receive the letter – in a state of the greatest anxiety – and yet, when he gets it on the Friday morning in Stirling, seeing that the hour of appointment is already past, he knows that it is in vain to go. She cannot see him except when a tryst is made.

Now, most unfortunately – I shall say no more than that of it at present – that letter was lost; and, most strangely, not merely the original envelope in which it was enclosed by the prisoner herself, but the additional envelope into which it was put by Thuau are both found, or said to be found in the deceased's travelling bag, which he had with him at Stirling and Bridge of Allan. But the letter is gone; where, no man can tell. Certainly, it cannot be imputed as a fault to the prisoner that the letter is not here, for that it was received is without doubt. On the Friday he writes a letter to Miss Perry, in which he makes use of this expression, 'I should have come to see some one last night, but the letter came too late, so we were both disappointed.' He got the letter; he knew that it contained an appointment for that night, and the mention of this letter to Miss Perry proves its contents so far. But the letter itself is gone, and I cannot help thinking – although I am not going to detain you by any details on the subject – that the Crown is responsible for the loss of that letter. If they had been in a position to prove, as they ought to have done, that these two envelopes were certainly found in the travelling bag without the letter, they might have discharged themselves of the obligation that lay upon them; but, having taken possession of the contents of that travelling bag, which are now brought to bear on the guilt or innocence of the prisoner, I say again, as the fact stands, that that letter is lost, and they are answerable for the loss.

Now, then, the next day there is another letter, which is sent to the Bridge of Allan through the same channel. It is addressed to Mrs Jenkins, and bears the post-mark of 21st March – that is to say, Saturday morning. It reached Mrs Jenkins in the course of the forenoon; it was posted to Stirling by Mr Thuau in the afternoon of the same day, and was received by the deceased at the Bridge of Allan on Sunday morning. Here is the letter, 'Why, my beloved, did you not come to me? Oh, my beloved, are you ill? Come to me. Sweet one, I waited and waited for you, but you came not. I shall wait again to-morrow night – same hour and arrangement. Oh, come, sweet love, my own dear love of a sweetheart. Come, beloved, and clasp me to your heart; come, and we shall be happy. A kiss, fond love. Adieu, with tender embraces. Ever believe me to be your own ever dear, fond Mimi.' When was it that she 'waited and waited'? It was upon Thursday evening – that was the tryst. The letter to Miss Perry proves conclusively that it was on the Thursday she waited, expecting him to come in answer to her previous invitation. When, then, do you think it was likely that she should write her next summons? I should think that, in all human probability, it was on the following evening – that is, on Friday. She almost always wrote her letters in the evening, and I think I am not going too far when I say, that when she did not write them in the evening – she almost always put the hour to them at which they were written; and when she wrote her letters in the evening they were invariably posted next morning, and not that evening, for very obvious reasons.

Now, then, is it not clear to you that this letter, this all-important letter, written upon the Friday evening, was posted on the Saturday morning, while she still believed that he was in Glasgow with Mrs Jenkins, making the appointment for Saturday evening: 'I shall wait tomorrow night, same hour and arrangement?' It is the very same amount of warning that she gave him in the previous letter written on Wednesday, and posted on the Thursday morning when she made the appointment for Thursday evening. Here, in like manner, comes this letter written, as I say, upon the Friday evening, and posted upon the Saturday morning – fixing a meeting for the Saturday evening. The two things square exactly; and it would be against all probability that it should be otherwise. She was most anxious to see him; she believed him to be in Glasgow; and she entreated him to come to her. Oh, but, says my learned friend, they were not in the way of meeting on Saturdays – Sunday was a favourite night, but not Saturday. Really, gentlemen, when my learned friend has put in evidence before you somewhere about 100 out of 200 or 300 letters, that he should then ask you to believe, because there is no appearance of a Saturday evening meeting in any of them which he has read, that there is no such appearance in any that he has not read would be a somewhat unreasonably demand.

But, unhappily for his theory or conjecture, it is negatived by the letters that he has read, as you will find. In one letter, October, 1866, she says, 'Write me for Saturday if you are to be on Saturday night.' That is, to meet her on Saturday night. Again, in letter No. 111, she says, 'I shall not be at home on Saturday, but I shall try, sweet love, to meet you, even if it be but for a word,' alluding to her return from some party. Now, these are two examples selected out of the very letters that my learned friend himself has used negativing the only kind of supposition that he has set off against what I am now advancing.

Gentlemen, I think further, with reference to the supposed meeting on the Sunday evening, that I am entitled to say to you that there is no appearance of their ever having met without previous arrangement. The very existence of that number of references in various parts of the correspondence, and at different dates, to meetings then made or that were passed – the constant reference to the aid and assistance of Christina Haggart, whenever there was anything more than a mere meeting at the window required – all go to show that in meetings between these parties there always was and always must have been, in order to their being brought about at all, previous arrangement. If indeed, as regards Blythswood Square house, the theory of the prosecutor had been correct, that the deceased had it in his power at any time to go to the window in Mains Street and call her attention by some noisy signal, the case might have been different. But I have already shown how constantly she repeated to him her warning that he was on no account to make the slightest knocking or noise of any kind, that when she wanted to see him she would watch for him and tell him when to come. But a signal at the window was to be avoided of all things, because it was sure to lead to discovery. Therefore, without previous arrangement it does not appear to me to be possible for these parties to have met on the occasion the prosecutor said they did.

And now, let us see what the condition of Blythswood Square house and its inmates was upon this all-important Sunday, the 22nd March. If I am right in my reading of the letters, she expected him on Saturday evening, and she waited for him then – waited most impatiently – waited and waited, as she had upon the Thursday, but he came not. On the Sunday evening she did not expect him. Why should she? When, he did not come on the Thursday evening, she did not expect him, and he did not come on the Friday evening. When he did not come on the Saturday evening, why should she expect him on the following evenings? Having broken his appointment of the Thursday, he did not understand he could procure an interview on the Friday. Having broken it on the Saturday, why should he expect that the meeting was transferred to the following evening?

Well, then, that is the state in which her expectations were on that occasion, and her conduct precisely squares with these expectations. She is at home in the family, with her father, mother, brother, and sisters. They are all at prayers together at nine o'clock. The servants come up to attend prayers along with the family. Duncan Mackenzie, the suitor of

Christina Haggart, remains below while the family are at worship. The servants afterwards go downstairs after prayers, and go to bed as usual, one after the other, first the boy, then Christina Haggart, and lastly the cook, who gets to bed about eleven o'clock. The family then retire to rest, and the prisoner with her youngest sister descends from the dining room to her bedroom between half-past ten and eleven. They take half an hour to undress. They both get into bed about the same time. The prisoner apparently is undressed as usual, goes to bed with her sister and, so far as human knowledge or evidence can go, that house is undisturbed and unapproached till the prisoner is lying in the morning, side by side with her sister, as she had fallen asleep at night.

Do you think it possible that, if there had been a meeting between these two parties, no shred of evidence of that meeting would have been forthcoming? The watchman was on his beat, and he knew L'Angelier well, and he saw nothing. As you must be aware, this is a very quiet part of the town; it is not a bustling thoroughfare, but a quiet west-end square of dwellings, about which the appearance of a stranger at a late hour on a Sunday evening would attract attention. The policeman, whose special charge was, on such an evening, and in such circumstances, to see every one passing there – and there is no charge against him of not having been upon his beat, and nothing in the least to detract from his evidence – sees nothing. Neither within the house, nor without the house, is there the slightest vestige of ground for suspecting that that meeting of which they had been disappointed on Saturday took place on the Sunday.

But now let me turn to L'Angelier. It is said that he came from the Bridge of Allan in answer to the invitation sent him by the prisoner in the course of Saturday. I don't think that is altogether a reasonable presumption. But even if you assume it, it won't advance the prosecutor's case one step. But I say it is not a reasonable presumption. I say it for this reason, because to say that he came into Glasgow on a Sunday, at such great inconvenience, to keep an appointment which was already past, is to suppose him to contradict on Sunday what he did, or rather omitted to do, on Friday under precisely similar circumstances. If he had wanted to have a meeting on an evening subsequent to that for which it was appointed, he could have been in on Friday, and the circumstances were the same. But yet on Sunday, when there was far less facility for putting his purpose into execution, when he required to walk a considerable part of the way, instead of going by rail, as he could have done on Friday, he is represented as having done this on purpose to keep a meeting which had been appointed for the previous night. I say that is not a reasonable supposition. We do not know what other letters he received at the Bridge of Allan on Sunday morning. There is no evidence of that. The prosecutor might have given it, but he has failed to do so. Then there is surely a great deal of mystery attending the prosecution of this journey from the Bridge of Allan to Glasgow on that Sunday.

But before I go into that, let me remind you, with reference to the correspondence between him and Mr Thuau as to the forwarding of his letters, that we have this in his letter of the 16th March. He says, 'I have received no letters from Mr Mitchell. I should like to know very much what he wants with me.' Now we don't know anything of Mr Mitchell, and the Crown has not told us, but apparently L'Angelier was expecting letters from this Mr Mitchell when he was in Edinburgh. He was anxious to receive them, and anxious to know what Mitchell wanted. And who can tell what letters he received at Bridge of Allan on Sunday morning? Who can tell whether there was not a letter from this Mitchell? And, if so, who can tell what it contained?

Well, he came to Glasgow. He is seen by Mrs Jenkins at his lodgings on his arrival at about eight o'clock. He remains there till nine, and then goes out. He is seen in different streets. He calls about half-past nine o'clock on his friend McAlester, who lives some five minutes' walk from Blythswood Square. He calls there, but finds that McAlester is not at home. Again I ask, why have we not McAlester here to tell us what he knows about him, or whether he expected him? Could McAlester have told us anything about the Mitchell of the letter? Could not McAlester have explained what was the errand on which he had come from the Bridge of Allan? Why do the Crown leave all these different things unexplained on this, the last and most important day in his history?

Now, gentlemen, from half-past nine till half-past two o'clock – at least five hours – he is absolutely lost sight of. And I was startled at the boldness of the manner in which my learned friend the Lord Advocate met this difficulty. He says it is no doubt a matter of conjecture and inference that in the interval he was in the presence of the prisoner. Good heavens! Inference and conjecture! A matter of inference and conjecture whether, on the night he was poisoned, he was in the presence of the person who is charged with his murder! I never heard such an expression from the mouth of a Crown prosecutor in a capital charge before, as indicating or describing a link in the chain of the prosecutor's case. It is absolutely new to me. I have heard it many a time in the mouth of a prisoner's counsel, and I daresay you will hear it many a time in mine yet before I have done, but for the prosecutor himself to describe one part of his evidence as a piece of conjecture and hypothesis is to me an entire and most startling novelty and yet my learned friend could not help it. It was honest and fair that he should so express himself if he intended to ask for a verdict at all. For he can ask for this verdict on nothing but a set of unfounded and incredible suspicions and hypotheses.

Let us now look at this third charge in the light of probabilities, since we must descend to conjecture, and let us see whether there is anything to aid the conjecture, which the Crown has chosen to consider as the most probable one. If you believe the evidence of the Crown, L'Angelier suspected the prisoner of having tried to poison him before. But then, says my learned friend, his suspicions were lulled; she had become more kind to him before he had left the town, and his suspicions were lulled. But I think my learned friend said in another place that he was brooding over it when he was in Edinburgh, and spoke of it in a very serious tone to Mr and Mrs Towers at Portobello. That was the 16th of March, after which he had nothing to change his mind in the shape of kindness or confidence from the prisoner; and, therefore, if he did once entertain the suspicion, however unfounded, there was nothing, so far as the prisoner was concerned, to remove it from his mind anterior to the evening of Sunday, the 22nd of March.

A man whose suspicions are excited against a particular person in not very likely to take poison at that person's hand. I am merely uttering a very commonplace observation when I say this, but the circumstance of its being a commonplace observation makes it all the stronger here. It is a thing so plain and obvious on the face of it, that nobody can fail to see it, and yet what are we asked to believe that he did that night? We are asked to believe that he took, from her hand, a poisoned cup in which there lurked such a quantity of arsenic as was sufficient to leave in his stomach, after his death, 88 grains – such a dose, indicating the administration of at least double – aye, I think, as Dr Christison said, indicating the administration of at least half an ounce, 240 grains – and this he took, that evening, from the hand of the prisoner, with all his previous suspicion that she was practising on his life. It is a dose which, as far as experience goes, never was successfully administered by a murderer. There is not a case on record in which it has ever been shown that a person administering poison to another ever succeeded in persuading him to swallow such a quantity. There is the greatest improbability of such a thing being ever done. It is a most difficult thing to conceive a vehicle in which it could be given. Yet with all these extraordinary circumstances attending the character and quantity of the dose, this gentleman swallowed it, having had his suspicions previously excited that the prisoner was practising on his life.

Nay, more, even supposing he did swallow all this arsenic in a cup of cocoa, as is suggested, it is at least next to impossible, that with all the gritty undissolved powder passing over his throat, he should not become aware that he had swallowed something unusual. And yet, instead of immediately seeking medical aid, or communicating his alarm or his suspicions to anybody, he staggers home in great pain, and through the long dreary hours of that fatal morning, amidst all his frightful sufferings, neither to the landlady nor to the doctor does he ever suggest that he, may have been poisoned or breathes a suspicion against her whom he had previously suspected of an attempt to poison him.

But, gentlemen, here comes again another point in which the evidence for the Crown is very defective, to say the least of it. They knew very well when they were examining and analysing the contents of this poor man's stomach, and the condition of his intestines generally, what was the arsenic that the prisoner had bought. They knew perfectly well, from her own candid statement, disclosed the moment she was asked, that the arsenic that she bought was got partly at Murdoch's and partly at Currie's. Murdoch's arsenic was mixed with soot; Currie's arsenic was mixed with waste indigo. If that arsenic had been swallowed by the deceased, the colouring matter should have been detected in the stomach. I confess I did not expect to have it so clearly proved, when the witnesses for the Crown were originally in the box, but you recollect what Dr Penny said when he was recalled by my learned friend on the other side, and I think a more clear or precise piece of evidence I never listened to. He said he tried the experiment with animals. He gave one dog a dose of Murdoch's arsenic, and found the soot in its stomach after its death, notwithstanding constant vomiting. He gave another dog Currie's arsenic, and, said Professor Penny, after the dog had vomited, and died, 'I found particles that might correspond with the colouring matter in Currie's arsenic.' But I asked him whether they did precisely correspond, and he said yes.

Now, gentlemen, there was one means of connecting the prisoner with this poison which was found in the stomach of L'Angelier, and a very obvious means. It may be very well for Professor Penny and Professor Christison to say now that their attention was not directed to this matter. Whose fault is that? The Crown, with the full knowledge of what was the arsenic which the prisoner had in her possession, could have directed their attention to it; they must have seen the importance of the inquiry, or, if they did not see that, they must suffer for their omission. Plainly, there can be no fault on the part of the prisoner for, observe, she had no means of being present, or of being represented, at these post-mortem examinations or chemical analyses. The whole thing was in the hands of the authorities. They kept them to themselves. They dealt with them secretly. And they present to you this lame and impotent conclusion.

Such is the state of the evidence on this third and last charge upon the 22nd of March; and I do venture to submit to you that if the case for the Crown is a failure, as it unquestionably is upon the first and second charges, it is a far more signal and radical failure as regards the third. The one fact which is absolutely indispensable to bring guilt home to the prisoner remains not only not proved – I mean the act of administration

– but the whole evidence connected with the proceedings of that day seems to me to go to negative such an assumption.

I might stop there, for nothing could be more fallacious than the suggestion which was made to you by the Lord Advocate, that it was necessary for the prisoner to explain how the deceased came by his death. I have no such duty imposed upon me. His lordship will tell you that a defender in this Court has no further duty than to repel the charge and to stand upon the defensive, and to maintain that the case of the prosecutor is not proved. No man probably will or can ever tell – certainly at the present moment, I believe no man on earth can tell how L'Angelier met his death. Nor am I under the slightest obligation even to suggest to you a possible mode in which that death may have been brought about without the intervention of the prisoner. Yet it is but fair that, when we are dealing with so many matters of mere conjecture and suspicion on the part of the Crown, we should, for a moment, consider whether that supposition upon which the charge is founded is in itself preferable, in respect to its higher probability, to other suppositions that may be very fairly made.

The character of this man – his origin, his previous history, the nature of his conversation, the numerous occasions upon which he spoke of suicide – naturally suggest that as one mode by which he may have departed this life. I say, gentlemen – understand me – that I am not undertaking to prove that he died by his own hand. If I were doing anything so rash I should be imitating the rashness of the prosecutor – but I should not be stepping a hair's breadth further out of the beaten track of evidence and proof and demonstration. For I think there is much more to be said for suicide than for the prisoners guilt. But I entreat you again to remember that that is no necessary part of my defence. But, of course, I should have been using you very ill – I should have been doing less than my duty to the prisoner – if I had not brought before you the whole of that evidence which suggests the extreme probability of the deceased dying by his own hand at one time or another.

From the very first time at which we see him, even as a lad, in the year 1843, he talks in a manner to impress people with the notion that he has no moral principle to guide him. He speaks over and over again in Edinburgh, Dundee, and elsewhere of suicide. Aye, and the prisoner's letters show that he had made the same threat to her, that he would put himself out of existence. The passages were read to you, and I need not now repeat them. And is it half as violent a supposition as the supposition of this foul murder, that upon this evening – the 22nd of March – in a fit of that kind of madness which he himself described came over him when he met with a disappointment – finding, it may be, that he could not procure access to an interview which he desired – assuming that he came to Glasgow for the purpose, assuming, even, that he mistook the evening of the meeting, and expected to see her on the Sunday – can anything be more probable than that in such a case, in the excited state in which he then was, he should have committed the rash act which put an end to his existence. I can see no great improbability in that.

It is said, no doubt, that his deathbed scene is inconsistent with the supposition of his having taken poison for the purpose of self-destruction, because he willingly received the services of Dr Steven. What is the evidence as to that? He refused most of the remedies suggested. He rejected the blister as useless. And he also rejected laudanum, and assigned a false reason for doing so. And, finally, he told his landlady after Dr Steven's departure, 'the doctor does not know how ill I am' which seems to indicate his own knowledge of a cause for his illness, which was unknown to others.

But even supposing that he had taken the treatment of the medical man with more appearance of a reliance on its efficacy, this would not be at all inconsistent with suicide. The cases mentioned by Dr Paterson, and the still more remarkable case of which Dr Lawrie gave so interesting an account, establish, as matter of medical experience, that persons who take arsenic for the purpose of self-destruction may and do conceal the fact, during the intense sufferings which precede death, and submit to medical treatment as if they expected and hoped that it might save their lives. This is the fair result of experience. But what experience is there to support the wild hypothesis that one who has drunk poison in such quantities as to ensure detection, and that poison administered by a suspected hand, should yet die after hours of bodily torture without suggesting poison as the cause, or hinting a suspicion against the administrator of the dose?

But whether he met his death by suicide, or whether he met his death by accident, or in what way so ever he met his death, the question for you is: is this murder proved? You are not bound to account for his death. You are not, in the least degree, bound to account for his death. The question you have got to try is whether the poison was administered by the hands of the prisoner. I have shown you, from the indictment, that that is the fact which you are asked to affirm. I pray you to remember that you are asked to affirm that on your oaths, to affirm on your oaths, as a fact, that the arsenic which was found in that man's stomach was presented to him by the hands of the prisoner.

Gentlemen, I have spoken of the improbabilities which belong to this story, to this charge. But surely you cannot have omitted to observe how very unnatural and extraordinary a crime it is to impute to a person in the prisoner's situation. I stated to you before, and I state to you again, as a piece of undoubted experience, that no one sinks to such a depth of depravity all at once. And now I ask you to remember at what period we left this correspondence. At a period when she desired to break off with L'Angelier no doubt – at a period when she desired to obtain possession of her letters. The return of them was refused. I am most unwilling to intersperse my address with severe remarks upon the character of a man who is now no more. But picture to yourselves the moral temperament; paint the feelings of a human being who, having received such letters from a girl as you have heard read in this Court, would even preserve them. He must have been dead to all feelings of humanity or he would never have refrained from burning those letters. But he not only preserves them, he retains them as an engine of power and oppression in his hands. He keeps them that he can carry out his cold-blooded original design not merely of possessing himself of her person, but of raising himself in the social scale by a marriage with her. It was his object from the first, and that object he pursues constantly, unflinchingly, to the end. He will expose her to her friends and to the world – he will drive her to destruction, or to suicide itself, rather than let her out of his power.

It may be said that I am only describing the great provocation which she received, and therefore enhancing the probability of her taking this fearful mode of extricating herself from her embarrassment. I don't fear that, gentlemen.

I want you to look now at the picture which I have under her own hand of her state of mind at this time, not for the purpose of palliating her conduct, not for the purpose of vindicating her against the charge either of unchasteness, or inconstancy, or of impropriety as regards Mr Minnoch, but for the purpose of showing you in what frame of mind that poor girl was at the time, the very time at which she is said to have conceived and contrived this foul murder. There are two or three letters, but I select one for the purpose of illustrating what I now say. It is written on the 10th February, and it is written after she has asked for the return of her letters and been refused: 'Tuesday evening, 12 o'clock. Emile, I have this night received your note. Oh, it is kind of you to write me. Emile, no one can know the intense agony of mind I have suffered last night and today. Emile, my father's wrath would kill me; you little know his temper. Emile, for the love you once had for me do not denounce me to my P. Emile, if he should read my letters to you, he will put me from him, he will hate me as a guilty wretch.' [The Dean of Faculty read the letter, entire.]

Is that the state of mind of a murderess, or can any one affect that frame of mind? Will you for one moment listen to the suggestion that the letter covers a piece of deceit? No! The finest actress that ever lived could not have written that letter unless she had felt it. And is that the condition in which a woman goes about to compass the death of him whom she has loved? Is shame for past sin, burning shame, the dread of exposure, what leads a woman not to advance another step on the road to destruction, but to plunge at once into the deepest depths of human wickedness? The thing is preposterously incredible; and yet it is because of her despair, as my learned friend called it, exhibited in that and similar letters, that he says she had a motive to commit this murder. A motive! What motive? A motive to destroy L'Angelier? What does that mean? It may mean, in a certain improper sense of the term, that it would have been an advantage to her that he should cease to live. That cannot be a motive, else how few of us are there that live who have not a motive to murder some one or other of our fellow-creatures. If some advantage, resulting from the death of another, be a motive to the commission of a murder, a man's eldest son must always have a motive to murder him that he may succeed to his estate; and I suppose the youngest officer in any regiment of Her Majesty's line has a motive to murder all the officers in his regiment; the younger he is, the further he has to ascend the scale, the more murders he has a motive to commit. Away with such nonsense. A motive to commit a crime must be something a great deal more than the mere fact that the result of that crime might be advantageous to the person committing it. You must see the motive in action – you must see it influencing the conduct before you can deal with it as a motive; for then, and then only, is it a motive in the proper sense of the term; that is to say, it is moving to the perpetration of the deed. But, gentlemen, even in this most improper and illegitimate sense of the term, let me ask you what possible motive there could be? I mean what possible advantage could she expect from L'Angelier ceasing to live, so long as the letters remained? Without the return of his letters she gained nothing. Her object, her greatest desire, that for which she was yearning with her whole soul, was to avoid the exposure of her shame. But the death of L'Angelier, with these letters in his possession, instead of ensuring that object, would have been perfectly certain to lead to the immediate exposure of everything that had passed between them. Shall I be told that she did not foresee that? I think my learned friend has been giving the prisoner too much credit for talent in the course of his observations upon her conduct. But I should conceive her to be infinitely stupid if she could not foresee that the death of L'Angelier, with these documents in his possession, was the true and best means of frustrating the then great object of her life.

So much for the motive. And if there is no assignable or intelligible motive in any sense of the word, see what another startling defect that is in the case for the prosecution. Shall I be told that the motive might be revenge? Listen to the letter which I have just read. Tell me if it is possible that, in the same breast with these sentiments, there could lurk one feeling of revenge? No, the condition of mind in which that poor girl was, throughout the months of February and March, is entirely inconsistent with any of the hypotheses that have been made on the other side, utterly incredible in connection with the perpetration of such a crime as is here laid to her charge. It is of importance, too, that we should keep in mind the way in which her spirit was thus broken and bowed down with the expectation of an exposure of her unchastity for, when the death of L'Angelier was made known to her, can you for a single moment doubt that her apprehensions were keenly awakened, that she foresaw what must be the consequences of that event; and, dreading to meet her father or her mother, feeling that, in the condition of the family, it was impossible she could remain among them, she left her father's house on the Thursday morning?

I really don't know whether my learned friend meant seriously to say that this was an absconding from justice from a consciousness of guilt. An absconding from justice by going to her father's house at Rhu? Oh, he said, all we know is that she left Glasgow early in the morning, and that she was found at three in the afternoon on board a steam-packet going from Greenock to Helensburgh; the interval is unaccounted for. If my learned friend were only half as ingenious on behalf of the prisoner as he is in supporting the prosecution, he could have very little difficulty in knowing that one who starts by water to Helensburgh in the morning may be easily overtaken by others travelling by railway to Greenock in the afternoon. She was on board a steam-packet, but its destination was no further than Helensburgh and its neighbourhood. And that he calls absconding from justice. Gentlemen, it is no fleeing from justice, but it is fleeing from that which she could as little bear – the wrath of her father and the averted countenance of her mother.

But she came back again without the slightest hesitation and, upon the Monday morning, there occurred a scene as remarkable in the history of criminal jurisprudence as anything I ever heard of, by which that broken spirit was altogether changed. The moment she was met by a charge of being implicated in causing the death of L'Angelier, she at once assumed the courage of a heroine. She was bowed down and she fled, while the true charge of her own unchastity and shame was all that was brought against her. But she stood erect, and proudly conscious of her innocence, when she was met with this astounding and monstrous charge of murder. You heard the account that Mr de Mean gave of the interview that he had with her, in her father's house, on the Monday. That was a most striking statement, given with a degree of minute and accurate truthfulness that could not be surpassed. And what was the import of that conversation? He advised her as a friend – and that was the very best advice that any friend could have given her – if L'Angelier was with her on that Sunday night, for God's sake, not to deny it. And why? Because, said Mr de Mean, it is certain to be proved. A servant, a policeman, a casual passer-by, is certain to know the fact, and if you falsely deny his having met you that evening, what a fact that will be against you.

Gentlemen, the advice was not only good, but most irresistible in the circumstances, if that meeting had taken place. But what was her answer? To five or six suggestions she gave the same constant answer, and at length she said, 'I swear to you, Mr de Mean, I have not seen L'Angelier for three weeks.' Is this not proved to be true? If it is true that she did not see him on the 22nd March, then she did not see him at all for three weeks. Mr de Mean was in doubt whether she said three weeks or six weeks, either of which would have been practically quite true. Immediately afterwards, she was brought before the magistrate and interrogated on the circumstances implicating her in the suspicion which had come upon her. What does she say? She tells the truth again with a degree of candour and openness which very much surprised the magistrate, and which you too must be struck with. Listen to the words of her declaration; for though these must lose much of their effect from the want of being listened to as spoken by her, I must ask you to look at two or three particular passages there stated which it is of the utmost importance that you should mark:

'I learned about his death on the afternoon of Monday, the 23rd March current, from mamma, to whom it had been mentioned by a lady named Miss Perry, a friend of Mr L'Angelier. I had not seen Mr L'Angelier for about three weeks before his death; and the last time I saw him was on a night about half-past ten o'clock. He was in the habit of writing notes to me, and I was in the habit of replying to him by notes. The last note I wrote to him was on the Friday before his death, viz., Friday, the 20th March current. I now see and identify that note and the relative envelope, and they are each marked No. 1. In consequence of that note I expected him to visit me on Saturday night, the 21st current, at my bedroom window in the same way as formerly mentioned; but he did not come, and sent no notice. There was no tapping at my window on said Saturday night or on the following night, being Sunday. I went to bed on Sunday night about eleven o'clock, and remained in bed till the usual time of getting up next morning, being eight or nine o'clock. In the course of my meetings with Mr L'Angelier, he and I had arranged to get married, and we had, at one time, proposed September last as the time the marriage was to take place, and subsequently the present month of March was spoken of. It was proposed that we should reside in furnished lodgings, but we had not made any definite arrangement as to time or otherwise. He was very unwell for some time, and had gone to the Bridge of Allan for his health; and he complained of sickness, but I have no idea what was the cause of it.'

My learned friend, the Lord Advocate, said that this showed that she knew he had gone to the Bridge of Allan. Certainly it showed she knew it then, for she had been told it by Mr de Mean. But it does not show – it does not in the least degree tend to show – against the real evidence of her own letter, which was addressed to Mrs Jenkins – that she knew at the time. She says, 'I remember giving him some cocoa from my window one night some time ago, but I cannot specify the time particularly. He took the cup in his hand and barely tasted the contents, and I gave him no bread to it. I was taking some cocoa myself at the time, and had prepared it myself. It was between ten and eleven pm. when I gave it to him. I am now shown a note or letter and envelope, which are marked respectively No. 2, and I recognize them as the note and envelope which I wrote to Mr L'Angelier and sent to the post. As I had attributed his sickness to want of food, I proposed, as stated in the note, to give him a loaf of bread; but I said that merely in a joke, and, in point of fact, I never gave him any bread.'

And it is perfectly plain from her letters that it was merely a joke.'I have bought arsenic on various occasions.' No hesitation about the buying of the arsenic. 'The last I bought was a sixpence worth, which I bought in Currie, the apothecary's in Sauchiehall Street, and, prior to that, I bought other two quantities of arsenic, for which I paid sixpence each, one of these in Currie's, and the other in Murdoch, the apothecary's shop in Sauchiehall Street.'

And then she goes on to specify the use she intended to make of it, and did actually make of it, after she got it. She is also asked about who was present when she purchased the arsenic; and she states this with perfect precision and accuracy, as has been proved, and she says that she entered her name in the book when she was asked to do it; and gives a particular account of everything that took place when she made these purchases, so far as she recollected, all which is precisely in accordance with the evidence now before us. Then, she admits her engagement with Mr Minnoch, and makes various other statements, with regard to which my learned friend was not able to say that any one has been contradicted by the evidence. Such openness and candour of statement, under such circumstances, first to Mr de Mean, a friend, and next the magistrate interrogating her on the charge, and who had, as was his duty, informed her that whatever she said might be used to her prejudice, but could not possibly be used to her advantage – I leave to speak for themselves.

But I have now to request your attention to one particular point in connection with this declaration – the different purchases of arsenic. With regard to the purchase from Murdoch I shall not trouble you with any further observations after what I have already said on this subject; but the occasion of the second purchase is too remarkable to be passed over without some further observations. It was made on the 6th of March, the day the prisoner went to the Bridge of Allan. For what purpose, for what murderous purpose could that purchase have been made? She had been doing everything in her power, as you see from one of her letters, to dissuade and prevent the deceased from going to the Bridge of Allan at the same time as herself, and she had succeeded in persuading him to abstain from going; and, yet, when going away to the Bridge of Allan, she buys this arsenic – when going away from the supposed object of her murderous attack – when therefore she could have no possible use for it. She carries it with her, it is to be presumed – it could not have been bought for the purpose of leaving behind her – she carries it with her, and my learned friend says that whenever she found, either that she had some left over after the administration of a dose, or that she had got arsenic which for the time was of no use to her, she put it away. And it is in this way my learned friend accounts for none of the arsenic being left or found in her possession.

But what is this she does on the 6th as connected with what she does on the 18th? She bought arsenic when she was going away from the man she wanted to murder, and when she could have no opportunity of administering it to him. And then, I suppose, we must take it for granted, on the Lord Advocate's theory, that, finding she could not administer it to him, she threw it away. What on earth could she mean by that? He says – that is his theory – she kept it at the Bridge of Allan in case he should come there. Well, then, she kept it down to the 17th. Why did she throw it away on the 17th and buy more on the 18th? Can anybody explain that? Why did she throw away the arsenic when she was coming back from the Bridge of Allan to be in the immediate neighbourhood of her victim? And why, above all, having thrown it away, did she forthwith purchase more the very day after she came back, with those circumstances of openness and exposure and observation that are perfectly inconsistent with the existence of an illegitimate purpose? Why expose herself to the necessity of a repeated purchase, when she could get or had got enough at once to poison twenty or a hundred men? Her conduct is utterly unintelligible on any such supposition as has been made by the prosecutor.

Let us now look at what was her object at this time in another view. She wanted L'Angelier to go away; she was most anxious that he should go to the south of England – to the Isle of Wight – for ten days. Oh, says my learned friend, her object was to marry Mr Minnoch in the meantime. Why? There was no arrangement, up to that time, of the day of her marriage with Mr Minnoch. She was going away herself for ten days on a casual visit to the Bridge of Allan. If L'Angelier had followed her advice and gone to the south of England for ten days, while he would, in the meantime, have been absent and beyond her reach, he would have returned only to find matters where they were – nothing more definite than in the month of January – Mr Minnoch still her suitor, but not her husband. Then, again, L'Angelier's absence could surely be of no advantage to her if she wanted to give him poison. All the facts, gentlemen, relating to this part of the case go to show this, that she had no object but perhaps to get rid of him for the time, to keep him from going to the Bridge of Allan and to get him to go elsewhere, out of regard for his health, as expressed in her letter.

But the possession of this arsenic is said to be unaccounted for, as far as the prisoner herself is concerned. It might be so – it may be so – and yet that would not make a case for the prosecution. She says she used it as a cosmetic. This might be startling at first sight to many of us here, but after the evidence we have heard it will not in the least amaze you. Her statement, which has been so far borne out by evidence, was that at school she had read of the Styrian peasants using arsenic for the strengthening of their wind and the improvement of their complexions. No doubt they used it internally and not externally as she did, but in the imperfect state of her knowledge that fact is of no significance. L'Angelier, too, was well aware of the same fact. He stated to more than one witness – and, if he stated falsely, it is only one of a multitude of lies proved against him – that he used it himself. It is not surprising, if L'Angelier knew of this custom, that he should have communicated it to the prisoner. It is not surprising that, under these circumstances, the prisoner should have used the arsenic externally, for an internal use is apparently a greater danger, which might have suggested to her to try it externally; and there is no reason to suppose that, if used externally, as the prisoner says she did use it, it would be productive of any injurious effects; so that there is no reason to suspect on that ground the truth of the statement that the prisoner had made.

No doubt we have had medical gentlemen coming here and shaking their heads and looking wise, and saying that such a use of arsenic would be a dangerous practice. Well, so should we all say, that it is both a dangerous and foolish practice. But that is not the question. The question is, whether the prisoner could actually so use it without injurious effects; and that she could do so is demonstrated by the experiment of Dr Lawrie, fortified by the opinion of Dr Maclagan. The publication in *Chambers Journal, Blackwood's Magazine*, and Johnston's *Chemistry of Common Life*, of information on such uses of arsenic had reached not the prisoner alone, but a multitude of other ladies, and had incited them to the same kind of experiments. The two druggists, Robertson and Guthrie spoke to the fact of ladies having come to their shops seeking arsenic for such purposes on the suggestion of these publications. It cannot, therefore, be surprising to you, gentlemen, to learn that, when the prisoner bought this arsenic, she intended to use it, and did afterwards actually use it, for this very purpose.

My learned friend, the Lord Advocate, said that, great as was the courage the prisoner displayed when charged with this serious crime, such a demeanour was not inconsistent with the theory of her guilt. He said that a woman who had the nerve to commit the murder would have the nerve calmly to meet the accusation. I doubt that very much. Gentlemen, I know of no case in which such undaunted courage has been displayed, from first to last, by a young girl, confronted with such a charge, where that girl was guilty. But, gentlemen, our experience does furnish us with examples of as brave a bearing in as young a girl when innocent. Do you know the story of Eliza Fenning? She was a servant girl in the city of London, and she was tried on the charge of poisoning her master and family by putting arsenic into dumpling. When the charge was first made against her, she met it with a calm but, indignant denial. She maintained the same demeanour and self-possession throughout a long trial; and she received a sentence of death without moving a muscle. According to the statement of an intelligent bystander, when brought upon the scaffold, she seemed serene as an angel, and she died as she had borne herself throughout the previous stages of the sad tragedy. It was an execution which attracted much attention at the time. Opinion was much divided as to the propriety of the verdict, and the angry disputants wrangled even over the poor girl's grave. But time brought the truth to light: the perpetrator of the murder confessed it on his deathbed, too late to avoid the enacting of a most bloody tragedy. That case, gentlemen, is now matter of history. It happened at a time beyond the recollection of most of those whom I now address; but it remains on record, a flaming beacon to warn us against the sunken rocks of presumptuous arrogance and opinionative self-reliance, imbedded and hid in the cold and proud heart; it teaches us, by terrible example, to avoid confounding suspicion with proof, and to reject conjectures and hypotheses when they are tendered to us as demonstrations. I fear, gentlemen, that this is not a solitary case – either the recollection or the reading of any of us may recall other occasions – when, after execution, Judgement hath repented o'er his doom. But I pray God that neither you nor I may be implicated in the guilt of adding another name to that black and bloody catalogue.

I have thus laid before you, as clearly as I could, what I conceive to be all the important branches of this inquiry, separately, and as calmly and deliberately as I could, and I now ask you to bring your judgement, to bring the whole powers with which God has endowed you, to the performance of your most solemn duty. I have heard it said that juries have nothing to do with the consequences of their verdicts, and that all questions of evidence must be weighed in the same scale, whether the crime be a capital one or merely penal in a lower degree. I cannot agree to that proposition. I cannot too indignantly repudiate such a doctrine. It may suit well enough the cramped mind of the legal pedant, or the leaden rules of a heartless philosophy, but he who maintains such a doctrine is entirely ignorant of what materials a jury is, and ought to be, composed.

Gentlemen, you are brought here for the performance of this great duty, not because you have any particular skill in the sifting or weighing of evidence, not because your intellects have been highly cultivated for that or similar purpose, not because you are a class or caste set apart for the work, but you are here because, as the law expresses it, you are indifferent men, because you are like, not because you are unlike other men, not merely because you have clear heads, but because you have warm and tender hearts, because you have bosoms filled with the same feelings and emotions, and because you entertain the same sympathies and sentiments as those whose lives, characters, and fortunes are placed in your hands.

To rely, therefore, upon your reason only, is nothing less than impiously to refuse to call to your aid, in the performance of a momentous duty, the noblest gifts that God has implanted in your breasts. Bring with you then to this service, I beseech you, not only your clear heads, but your warm hearts, your fine moral instincts, and your guiding and regulating consciences, for thus, and thus only, will you satisfy the oath which you have taken. To determine guilt or innocence by the light of intellect alone is the exclusive prerogative of infallibility; and when man's presumptuous arrogance tempts him to usurp the attribute of Omniscience, he only exposes the weakness and frailty of his own nature. Then, indeed,

Man, proud man,

Dressed in a little brief authority,

Most ignorant of what he is most assured,

Plays such fantastic tricks, before high Heaven,

As make the angels weep.

Raise not, then, your rash and impotent hands to rend aside the veil in which Providence has been pleased to shroud the circumstances of this mysterious story. Such an attempt is not within your province, nor the province of any human being. The time may come – it certainly will come – perhaps not before the Great Day in which the secrets of all hearts shall be revealed – and yet it may be that in this world, and during our own lifetime, the secret of this extraordinary story may be brought to light. It may even be that the true perpetrator of this murder, if there was a murder, may be brought before the bar of this very Court. I ask you to reflect for a moment what the feelings of any of us would then be. It may be our lot to sit in judgement on the guilty man. It may be the lot of any one of you to be empanelled to try the charge against him. Would not your souls recoil with horror from the demand for more blood? Would not you be driven to refuse to discharge your duty in condemning the guilty, because you had already doomed the innocent to die?

I say, therefore, ponder well before you permit anything short of the clearest evidence to induce or mislead you into giving such an awful verdict as is demanded of you. Dare any man hearing me, dare any man here or elsewhere say that he has formed a clear opinion against the prisoner? Will any man venture, for one moment, to make that assertion? And yet, if on anything short of clear opinion you convict the prisoner, reflect – I beseech you, reflect – what the consequences may be.

Never did I feel so unwilling to part with a jury. Never did I feel as if I had said so little as I feel now after this long address. I cannot explain it to myself, except by a strong and overwhelming conviction of what your verdict ought to be. I am deeply conscious of a personal interest in your verdict, for if there should be any failure of justice, I could attribute it to no other cause than my own inability to conduct the defence; and I feel persuaded that, if it were so, the recollection of this day and this prisoner would haunt me as a dismal and blighting spectre to the end of life. May the Spirit of all Truth guide you to an honest, a just, and a true verdict! But no verdict will be either honest, or just, or true, unless it at once satisfies the reasonable scruples of the severest judgement, and yet leaves undisturbed and unvexed the tenderest conscience among you.

Chapter Six

The Dean of Faculty had spoken upwards of four hours. It was an address that would go down in legal history as one of the most eloquent and powerful speeches ever delivered. After a short interval, the Lord Justice-Clerk proceeded to sum up. (The following is a very brief excerpt of his charge to the jury).

Gentlemen of the Jury – The contest of evidence and of argument is now closed, and the time has now come for deliberation and decision; and to enable you to discharge that duty aright and justly, it is necessary that you remember that the case is to be tried and decided solely on the evidence. You are not to give the slightest weight to the personal opinion of the guilt of the prisoner, which I regret my learned friend the Lord Advocate allowed himself to express. Nor are you, on the other hand, to be weighed in the prisoner's favour by the more moving and earnest declaration made by her counsel of his own conviction of her innocence. I think on both sides such expressions of opinion by the counsel ought never to be brought before a jury. Neither of them are so good judges of the truth as all of you are.

Gentlemen, poisoning is a crime which must generally be proved by circumstantial evidence; and may be most satisfactorily proved by circumstantial evidence alone. But, on the other hand, great care must be taken that the circumstantial evidence is such as to exclude the conclusion either of innocence on the one hand, or of an unexplained and mysterious occurrence on the other. It is one great misfortune attending the administration of poison that, if the party is not immediately detected in some way such as to leave no doubt of actual guilt, suspicions arise, often most unjustly, and obtain great weight and great hold over the public mind, just because it is a crime committed in secret. The person who last gave the deceased a cup of coffee, or a glass of water, or a glass of wine – the person who made the last appointment with him – is thus exposed to strong and apparently well-founded suspicions, and may be subjected even to false and groundless charges. You must, therefore, keep in view that, while on the one hand, the crime has been perpetrated secretly, and no eye has seen the parties at the time, or what passed, on the other hand you must not allow positive evidence to be supplied by suspicion, and still less admit of loose presumptions. You must be satisfied by proper evidence that the parties were together when the poison was said to have been administered, satisfied that there was the purpose to administer poison upon the occasion referred to, that the accused had the poison in her possession, and that it was given and administered upon that particular occasion, and in the circumstances set forth in the indictment.

The duty I have to do in aiding you, as far as I possibly can, to come to a decision is very different from what fell to the lot of either counsel. I have simply to go over the evidence in detail, in case it may not be sufficiently in your recollection, and to make such observations as the evidence suggests as proper and fitting for your assistance; but what I want to impress upon your minds is, that whatever doubt you may have of the matters set forth in her defence, you must have evidence against her, satisfactory and convincing to your minds, in which you find no conjectures, but only irresistible and just inferences. I wish you to keep in view that, although you may not be satisfied with any of the theories that had been propounded on behalf of the prisoner, though all these matters may fail in her defence, the case for the prosecution may be radically defective in evidence.

The Lord Justice-Clerk spoke from about 2 p.m. until 5.30 p.m. on this, the eighth day of the trial. He continued his charge to jury, for the best part of another three hours of the following morning, concluding,

> I am quite satisfied that whatever verdict you may give, after the attention which you have bestowed upon this case, will be the best approximation to truth at which we could arrive. But let me say also, on the other hand, as I said at the outset, that, of the evidence, you are the best judges, not only in point of law, but in point of fact; and you may be perfectly confident that, if you return a verdict satisfactory to yourselves against the prisoner, you need not fear any consequences from any future, or imagined, or fancied discovery, which may take place. You have done your duty under your oaths, under God, and to your country, and may feel satisfied that remorse you never can have.

At 1.05 p.m., the jury retired to consider their verdict. The courtroom was instantly filled with the buzz and hum of voices. Madeleine, quiet and composed, was one of only a few who remained seated. Her Edinburgh solicitor, Mr Rankin, came and sat beside her. Just under half an hour had passed when the tinkle of a bell announced the jury's return. The judges immediately resumed their places while a complete silence fell on the Court. The Lord Justice-Clerk warned the audience against an exhibition of any sort when the verdict was returned. As the jurors filed in, every eye studied them, looking for some sign of Madeleine's fate in their expressions, and when they were seated, one juror in the front row turned to his neighbour, said something and smiled. That, for all who saw it, seemed to rule out the gallows.

The silence was broken when the Clerk of Court got to his feet and asked, 'Gentlemen, have you agreed your verdict?' The foreman replied, 'we have.' Madeleine looked steadily at the man; she showed no obvious sign of anxiety. 'How say you, gentlemen; do you find the prisoner guilty or not guilty?' Mr Rankin took Madeleine's hand; the female warder, sitting on her right, took the other. The foreman answered,

My Lords, in respect of the first count, the jury, by a majority, find the panel Not Guilty. In respect of the second count, the jury, by a majority, find the charge against the prisoner Not Proven; and, in respect of the third count, the jury find, by a majority, the charge against the prisoner Not Proven.

Madeleine's head fell slightly, as loud applause and then cheers erupted all around. She then looked up and smiled at Mr Rankin and the female warder. In the public gallery, inevitably, one enthusiastic voice was heard above the rest and the Lord Justice-Clerk ordered the man's apprehension. It was some time before the macers and other officers of the Court succeeded in restoring order but, throughout, the Dean of Faculty had had his head in his hands. His reactiob to the verdict would soon be misinterpreted by a succession of commentators who had never heard or properly read his address to the jury nor had any notion of the work he had done towards achieving the verdict of Not Guilty that he had demanded, and expected.

The Lord Justice-Clerk thanked the jury for the patient and deliberate attention they had given, adding, 'I may say that the inclination of my own opinion went along with the majority, and I am not, therefore, surprised at your verdict.' He concluded by complimenting them on their patience and intelligence and then, turning to the macers, he said, 'macers, have you got that young man in custody?' The macer replied, 'yes my Lord.' The Lord Justice-Clerk said, 'then bring him into the Court.' The Clerk of Court announced that the prisoner was dismissed from the bar. Madeleine, to yet another round of cheering and applause, was taken downstairs. The young man who had caused the disturbance was then brought in. The Lord Justice-Clerk said, 'the court certainly intended to commit you to prison, but we think you so foolish that we do not think you worthy of being so treated. It is a privilege that we will not, at present, accord to you.' There was loud laughter from the body of the Court and from the bench. The court then adjourned.

As the audience, still smiling, spilled out into Parliament Square, they were met with the multitude that had gathered there for the last few hours. Animated and elated, they were now determined to wait for a glimpse of Madeleine as she left the Court. It was not to be. Madeleine's solicitor, Mr Forbes, had planned a quieter exit. He had previously asked the police sergeant in attendance if he could find a girl about Madeleine's size to impersonate her, and go through the ordeal of the cab journey down the High Street to the jail. The sergeant believed he had the very girl for the job. For several days, a girl had been begging the police to get her a sight of the prisoner, saying she would give anything for the privilege. They found her and brought her to the Court, telling her that not only would she get to meet Miss Smith, but she would have the dress Madeleine had been wearing, if she would help them lead the crowds away from the Square. A rumour was then circulated that Miss Smith was going to drive to the jail to change her dress before going home. When the officers moved in to clear a space about the courtroom doors, it seemed obvious that Madeleine's exit from the Court was imminent. Police held back the excited onlookers as the girl, nearly passing out with nervousness, came out by the front door and, accompanied by two police officers, was helped into the carriage. It drove off at speed, followed by most of the spectators, leaving Parliament Square and the surrounding area all but deserted in a few moments.

Madeleine, meanwhile, had put on a different dress and veil. Accompanied by her brother Jack, she was taken through the adjoining Advocates Library and quietly walked out into the daylight to a cab waiting in front of St Giles Church. They were driven to Slateford, where they met the Glasgow train. Her father's carriage was waiting for them at a station before Glasgow, and they were taken straight on to Rowaleyn.

The spectacle was over but the press weren't ready to let the story go just yet. There was an appetite still for more information, more commentary and, if possible, more revelations. One outraged individual, a Glaswegian by the name of Pringle, took it upon himself to restore the reputation of the much-maligned deceased and wrote to, amongst others, L'Angelier's mother. Her reply to Pringle, published in the *Scotsman* newspaper, helps shed some light on the story in a way which was certainly not intended. It is worth bearing in mind that Melanie L'Angelier had the opportunity to read this over before she posted it.

Sir, the harrowing feelings under which I have been labouring, in consequence of the bereavement of my poor boy, ever since he came to his untimely death, have been most painfully aggravated by the cruel and wanton malice of those who have made it their business to slander his memory. Such persons, supposing they are gifted with any feeling, must have been aware that their envenomed shafts should recoil with double force on his distressed mother and sisters, whose tears have scarcely dried up since the news reached them of their irreparable loss. Had they been able to conceive the agony of mind of a widowed mother, suddenly bereft of her main hope and support, would they have added a fresh sting to the first shock sustained by the loss of a good and affectionate child? Would they have thus wantonly added to a mother's grief?

Far from the scene where both the sad tragedy and the revelation of the horrid deed was publicly rehearsed, without a single friend to condole with at the time, who will, who can properly conceive the anguish of his more than distressed mother, left to devour her tears in silence and, in the midst of all this, to be apprised that there were beings, bereft of all the feelings of human nature, malicious enough to assail her dead, her murdered child's reputation? This, Sir, was too bad, too much to endure, and yet what could she do but weep in silence; what could she say but deplore the malignity of the world? Yet, in the midst of her deep affliction, it was a great consolation to hear that there are still noble-hearted minds in whose breast the sacred flame of truth and justice is not extinguished, and who, like the champions of old, are ready to come forward in the defence of the weak, the unprotected, the deeply injured. Among these, Sir, you stand most prominent. Permit me to thank you most cordially for your very kind interference, and to express the hope that your generous efforts may be crowned with success.

In compliance with your request, I have applied to a few friends to whom my son was personally known, and who have readily come forward to testify to his moral conduct. Allow me, in turn, to say on behalf of my poor Emile, that he was not only a dutiful and affectionate son, but that he did all in his power to assist his mother and sisters by remitting to them occasionally a part of his earnings and contributing, with his limited resources, to defray a part of his sister's scholastic expenses. Upon him, we fondly cherished the hope that the time would come when he should be the main support of us all. How this hope has been crushed; how his demise has annihilated our future prospects in life, I leave you to judge.

Meanwhile, Sir, receive, I pray you, our warm-hearted thanks for your kindness, and beg you to believe me, with much regard, your most grateful and most humble servant, Melanie L'Angelier.

This brings us back to the mind of the man himself. So many of his acquaintances spoke highly of him. Bernard Saunders in Jersey said he was, '… kind-hearted and dutiful … always easy and obliging in his manners, sober, honest and industrious.' Thomas Kennedy of Huggins described Emile in very similar terms, '… he conducted himself with great propriety … attentive to business, industrious, honest, sober, and of an obliging and agreeable manner … highly moral young man.' It seems inconceivable that someone of such apparently exemplary character could have contemplated, let alone enacted, such a terrible revenge but, to anyone involved in the business of forensic psychology, it would come as no surprise to learn that the perpetrator of some monstrous crime was highly thought of by almost all who knew him.

The key to the mystery of L'Angelier's death lies not in the evidence that the jury had to weigh. The dates and times, the proofs and the inferences, are all-important to the machinery of justice, but there is a simple underlying fact that, whether by instinct or by erudite understanding, tells us in which direction to look. Put aside the suspicions surrounding L'Angelier's death, and the personality of

Madeleine Smith could be that of a thousand young girls of her age in any town.

If we list her crimes we find that, at the age of nineteen, she was in a relationship that her parents did not approve of; she was told to put an end to it but she didn't; she lied to her parents; she lost her virginity before marriage; she met another man and then started seeing both at the same time; she lied to both; when the new boyfriend proposed, she tried to get rid of the old one. If that's the most shocking story in your neighbourhood, it must be a very small parish. Underneath it all, there is a caring and loving nature that was abused and exploited but still shows through when her family is under threat. She had thought she was finishing a relationship that had worn itself out; she had no idea that she was in the coils of a reptile. When she is threatened with exposure, and comes face to face with the magnitude of what she has done by putting her every thought on paper, her true nature surfaces. Her concern is not only for herself but for her family, for 'the shame it would bring on them all.' If we dissect and delineate her personality, it adds little to our understanding of the story. She is, effectively, interchangeable with any number of young girls of her age and social status. This could, for example, just as easily have been the story of a girl from a Fifeshire family whose name was not mentioned.

In contrast, L'Angelier's personality is far from normal. The clues are legion. In 1852 he was distraught over his broken engagement to the girl in Fife. At the Rainbow Tavern, he would get up at night and walk up and down the room in an excited state. He threatened, on one occasion, to throw himself out of the window and on another, from Leith pier. He was found crying in the public walkway of Princes Street Gardens. In Dundee, he threatened to stab himself with the counter-knife and spoke frequently of suicide. In Glasgow, he told De Mean that he had once been jilted by a wealthy English girl and was 'almost mad for a fortnight.' As De Mean said, 'when he had any cause of grief, he was affected very much.' That was gross understatement but it summed up an important and highly relevant aspect of L'Angelier's character. He remarked to William Anderson in Dundee that if he was jilted he would have revenge in some shape or other. His reaction to disappointment was significantly abnormal; he was utterly consumed by self-pity and anger, and virtually devoid of self-control. Even so, he could, when it suited him, modify his behaviour radically. He knew how to behave in the company of Miss Perry and how to play the part of the sober, highly-principled young man in front of his employers and acquaintances in Huggins.

He collected ferns, and he collected acquaintances. Each new acquaintance was a stepping stone to another, and then another. He was almost a visitor, by profession. His rightful position in society was, he thought, amongst the wealthy, the aristocratic and the influential. The notion that any importance should be attached to what he actually did in the world was completely alien. His position in society was rather a matter of a natural entitlement, by reason of his imagined essential superiority.

From the start and all through the correspondence, he is manipulative and calculating. In her first letter she writes, 'I am trying to break myself off all my very bad habits. It is you I have to thank for this.' He adopts the role of her mentor and guide in all things. He criticises her dress, her mannerisms and her behaviour, establishing himself as a figure of archetypal Victorian authority in a way which her own father had never done – 'I have given you warning long enough to improve yourself.' While pretending to be in a position to better her morals and conduct, he encourages, steadily and insidiously, ever more explicit expression of her most personal thoughts and feelings, and every line strengthening his hold on her.

He absolves himself, always, of responsibility. When they have broken the taboo of pre-marital sex, it is her fault – 'Why, Mimi, did you give way after your promises? ... I was not angry at your allowing me, Mimi, but I am sad it happened. You had no resolution.'

It is, however, his lack of compassion that so completely sets him apart from more ordinary men. He courted sympathy and yet had none to give. Emile was almost incapable of empathy. The two letters Madeleine writes, after he has threatened to expose her, would have filled the hardest man with a lasting shame for having brought a girl to such depths of despair. L'Angelier is no more moved than the spider sensing the tremble of the web.

For the purposes of understanding the man, it would have been convenient to find that there was a psychological classification that fits these characteristics. The Hare checklist[1] for psychopathic tendencies certainly includes many of L'Angelier's traits but he is some way from satisfying a sufficiency of the criteria to qualify. The genuine psychopath, however, is a very peculiar case.

In spite of recent studies suggesting both genetic and psychological factors underlying psychopathic behaviour, the psychopath is still primarily defined and understood only in terms of his behaviour, hence the 'checklist' method of identifying the psychopathic personality. Different approaches exist but, broadly speaking, to 'qualify' as a psychopath, the individual must score above, for example, thirty out of a possible forty where scores are allocated according to the absence of a trait (0), the partial presence of the trait (1), or the clear and substantial presence (2). These traits generally include the likes of: superficial charm; grandiose sense of self-worth; pathological lying; manipulative behaviour; lack of remorse or guilt; shallow feelings; callous behaviour or lack of empathy; failure to accept responsibility for actions, etc.

The important thing to remember about this evaluation is that it provides an indicator of the degree of psychopathy, degree being the operative word. The terminology is somewhat misleading since there is an arbitrary breakpoint at which an individual may or may not be classified as a psychopath. In fact, to achieve a score on the Hare checklist means nothing of any significance; it is only a high score that indicates a problem. It is a matter of degree and degree only. With only a slight modification of the test criteria, the Hare checklist could accommodate the entire population, each of us having a score lying somewhere

1 Hare, R.D. *The Hare Psychopathy Checklist-Revised (PCL-R)*. (Toronto, Ontario: Multi-Health Systems, 1991)

between the saint and the psychopath, between great strength and great weakness. It might seem a bizarre statement, but the psychopath is not suffering from any form of mental illness; there is nothing clinically wrong with his mind; he is a statistical phenomenon. The condition of the mind of the psychopath is simply that of extreme character weakness. It is, it can be demonstrated, a very peculiar form of immaturity – immaturity of the libido. The true psychopath has the characteristic thoroughly passive libido of an infant – but it is no more than that. As alluded to earlier, there may be accompanying physiological indicators and, in many cases, it may be possible to identify genetic factors. It would, however, be a mistake to lose sight of the fact that psychopathy is a matter of degree and degree only.

Emile L'Angelier was not a psychopath but his characteristics place him closer to the psychopathic personality than anyone we would wish to know. He shared so many of the psychopath's traits that, had the case occurred in the twenty-first century where his behaviour might have come under the scrutiny of a forensic psychologist, the investigation would have taken a very different course.

Approaching the case with an understanding of the two principle characters radically changes our interpretation and even our reasoned inferences. The first charge of attempted murder on 19 February was rightly dismissed by the jury as being without foundation and it deserves no more discussion now. As to the second charge, on Sunday 22 February, we find that there is no evidence that he left his lodgings at all, except that there is a letter, written by Madeleine, in which she says, '... You did look bad Sunday night and Monday morning.' This letter was undated, headed only 'Wednesday.' It was found amongst letters that appeared to belong to the week beginning Monday 23 February. The Dean of Faculty did not miss the fact that it could have been written on any Wednesday throughout the whole correspondence. He did not, and could not, however, suspect that the letter had been placed there deliberately.

L'Angelier hadn't asked for the pass-key that night nor had Thuau let him back in to the house. As the Dean of Faculty pointed out, this, the only reliable evidence, strongly suggested that he had remained at home on Sunday 22 February, and the only proof that L'Angelier had seen Madeleine, that he had left the house at all, was in that letter. By looking on L'Angelier as the victim, our tendency is to assume that the letter was in its proper envelope and in its proper place in the sequence. When we know the personality of the man, the balance of probability swings in entirely the other direction. On such evidence, the second charge should have been rejected unanimously.

As to the charge of murder, it is all too clear now, that the introduction of L'Angelier's diary in evidence could have been welcomed by the Defence. As soon as we begin to doubt L'Angelier's word, the whole circumstantial evidence that was intended to bring Madeleine to the gallows falls apart. We consider the missing letter to have appointed Friday and his failure to return until Sunday as being compatible only with deliberate intent. Knowing his response to disappointment, however, there is something else that is startlingly conspicuous by its absence. On 10 February, he finds that his dreams have, once again, been utterly destroyed. On the 11th he starts a new diary, writing simply, 'Dined with Mr Mitchell.' From that day onwards, his conduct was calm, reasonable, sober and, apart from his 'illnesses', he appears to be in a thoroughly mild and contented frame of mind. We see immediately that there is an immense quantity of emotional energy entirely unaccounted for. The self-pity and the anger that we should expect to find is entirely absent. There is only one solution to that equation and it explains the events that ensued over the next few weeks. That self-pity and fury and hatred had found an outlet.

With an understanding of the two personalities and with either the most cursory, or the most detailed and rigorous examination of the evidence, we are faced with one remaining mystery: how could it happen that, for 150 years, the most obvious villain has been believed to be the victim and the most obvious victim, the villain?

Soon after the trial, the Smith family sold their homes in Glasgow and in Rhu. They found no more anonymity, however, in their new home in Polmont, Stirlingshire. Mrs Smith, Bessie and Janet had to sit in the church there, on one occasion, and listen to a sermon based on Madeleine's story, warning the flock to pay close attention to the lessons to be learnt from her descent into depravity. Mr Smith kept his office in Glasgow but his health never fully recovered.

Madeleine moved to London, living at 72 Sloane Street, Chelsea and, on 4 July 1861, she married artist, draftsman and designer George Young Wardle. Mr Smith was one of the witnesses at the wedding and he placed £2,000 in trust for them, providing an annual income of £100. Their first child, Mary, was born on 27 May 1862. They then spent some time in Southwold, Suffolk, and their second child, Thomas Edmund, was born there on 30 November 1863. Exactly a month later, Mr Smith died, aged fifty-seven.

Madeleine, George and their children continued to make regular visits to Scotland to see Mrs Smith and the family but her life now revolved around George's work. Some of his drawings recording the medieval decoration in Saint Edmund's Church, Southwold were purchased in 1864 by the Victoria & Albert Museum. According to the V&A, it was on the strength of these that William Morris commissioned George Wardle to tour other East Anglian churches, recording their decoration. A copy of this work was subsequently made for the museum in 1868. By that time, George Wardle was employed by Morris as a draftsman and bookkeeper but before long he was to become William Morris's factory manager.

Their life in London was active and absorbing, and that simply because they were both talented, outgoing people who by nature took an interest in the world around them and didn't wait for life to entertain them. Their friends included the architect Philip Webb, designer of Red House, and the Pre-Raphaelite artists Ford Madox Brown, Dante Gabriel Rossetti and Edward Burne-Jones.

Morris, Webb and George Wardle were founder members of the Society for the Protection of Ancient Buildings. George's love of art, past and present, was complemented by an abhorrence of the wanton destruction of old architecture that often accompanied so-called renovation and redevelopment, obviously a subject close, also, to Madeleine's heart. In response to a request that Morris & Co alter one of the panels in the window in the south transept of Jesus College Chapel so that it could be used as a ventilator, George wrote: 'Mr. Morris is horrified. He says it would be fatal to the window & you must really give it up ... What a monster the stove must be to demand such a sacrifice. If it is to be done pray do not ask our connivance. That Mr. Morris will never give.'[2]

In the artistic and politically-conscious set to which they belonged, Madeleine's past was well-known and, occasionally, the butt of humour. The British Library holds Rossetti's copy of a mock play, penned by him and sent to Jane Morris – *The Murder of Topsy* – featuring the 'Young' Wardles (Tom, Mary and George Young Wardle) in which Topsy (Rossetti's nickname for William Morris on account of his unruly curls, not because he just growed) was being poisoned by Mrs Wardle's coffee. There was a subtitle: 'A Drama of the Future in One Unjustifiable Act.'

George's sister Elizabeth Wardle was married to Thomas Wardle (later Sir Thomas) of Leek in Staffordshire. Thomas Wardle was a successful silk dyer and printer and it was through George that his work was brought to William Morris's attention. The two formed a close and lasting business association. Madeleine was always made very welcome by her in-laws in Leek and she stayed with the family often. In 1879, Elizabeth Wardle founded the Leek Embroidery Society and when, some time later, she decided that England should have at least a replica of the Bayeux Tapestry, Madeleine – Lena Wardle, as she was now known – was one of the thirty-five women who set to work on it.

Like her father, Lena also took a passionate interest in politics. She shared William Morris's socialist views and as a council member of the Socialist League she was known to many of the well-known figures of the early days of the labour movement. One of these, George Bernard Shaw, was quizzed about his impressions of the notorious Madeleine Smith. In typically dismissive fashion, he curtly replied

2 Nick Salmon's 'William Morris Chronology' – *Thoemmes Continuum*

that she was an ordinary, good-humoured woman with absolutely nothing sinister about her.

The first of several trips to the USA came in 1880 to expand Morris's market there and the next in 1883 when William Morris took a stand at the Boston Exhibition. On 1 Sept 1888, George and Lena attended their son Tom's marriage to Annita Bied Charreton. It's known, in the family, that Annita's marriage, if not actually arranged, was something in which both Madeleine and George took a hand. Annita was a good Catholic girl with a convent schooling. On the marriage certificate, both have professional names: Annita was a singer, Anna di Fiori, and Tom, at that time, was a dramatic agent, Thomas Edmunds. The witnesses were Lena Wardle and Pasquale Novissimo. Mary was married the following year to artist John Scarratt Rigby and by 1891 Lena and George had two grand-children: Violet Wardle and Stephen Rigby. By the time Tom's first child Violet was born, he was working as journalist. A second daughter, May, was born around 1893 but by 1896 Tom and his family had settled in the USA where their son Jack was born.

After George's death in 1910 in a Plymouth nursing home, Madeleine moved permanently to the USA. Her son Tom, who was later to buy a farm in up-state New York, had, at this time, a bar in New York City. No-one was really sure whether he owned it or just managed it but Madeleine frequently helped out in the bar. She was well-liked and got on well with the customers. She was then seventy-six years old but always looked much younger than her age and in her latter years she was never seen without a wig – she had two wigs, one always at the hairdresser's. It is said that she married again in her late seventies to New Yorker William Sheehy, some twenty years her junior, and it may yet prove to be true but all that is remembered with certainty is that they lived together, they were happy together, and that they were known as Mr and Mrs Sheehy.

After William Sheehy's death in 1926, to the surprise and dismay of the family, on the morning of the funeral Madeleine announced she would not be going. Sheehy and Madeleine had got on so well together – 'he thought the world of her … there was nothing he wouldn't have done for her' – but no amount of persuading would change her mind. Now we can understand that there was the possibility of a reporter turning up in the hope of a story. It was better that her family thought the worst of her than risk a confrontation at the graveside. Sheehy was buried in the Catholic cemetery and, as Annita and Tom's children had been brought up as Catholics, one of them was later buried with Sheehy.

Unbeknown to her family, the trial had haunted Madeleine almost to the last. She did her best to make sure that none of Tom's family would have to bear the stigma of being descended from the notorious Madeleine Smith or suffer the prurient interest as she had done. Accordingly, as far as the family knew, Madeleine was English. Neither Madeleine nor Tom ever mentioned Scotland, only London. They had no idea that she had been that young girl who had been admired as one of the belles of Glasgow and had danced at society balls in Edinburgh Castle. They entirely lost their Scottish heritage and had absolutely no knowledge of their descent from a fascinating family of Scottish architects and masons. George Wardle's history, likewise, had to be played down rather than risk inspiring family curiosity. They knew he was an artist and draftsman, and no more than that. Even as an old woman in the USA, there had been attempts to revive the story. One film company is famously reported to have asked her to feature in a film based on her life and, on her refusal, it is said that they tried to have her deported.

The last member of the family who, as a young boy, had actually known Madeleine, died only a few years ago. When asked about his great-grandmother, he told me, 'she was just a grandma. I can't imagine her even having a boyfriend, let alone being accused of murdering one.'

Madeleine died on 12 April 1928, in the care of her granddaughter, at the age of ninety-three. In Mount Hope Cemetery, outside New York, there stands a small gravestone. It is inscribed simply, 'Lena Sheehy'.

Appendix One

L'Angelier's Diary

FEBRUARY 1857

[no previous entries]

Wed 11	Dined at Mr Mitchell's;
	Saw M. at 12pm in CH Room.
Thu 12	Spent the Even at Pat Kennedy's.
	Major Stuart and his wife – D. Jameson & family.
Fri 13	Saw Mr Phillpot, saw Mimi, dined at 144 Renfrew St.
Sat 14	A letter from M.
Sun 15	St Judes.
Mon 16	Wrote M. – Saw Mr Phillpots.
Tue 17	Dined at 144 Renfrew St.
Wed 18	
Thu 19	Saw Mimi a few moments – was very ill during the night.
Fri 20	Passed two pleasant hours with M. in the Drawing Room.
Sat 21	Don't feel well – went to T.F. Kennedy's.
Sun 22	Saw Mimi in Drawing Room. Promised me French Bible.
	Taken very ill.
Mon 23	Rec'd a letter from Mrs L.
Tue 24	Wrote M.
Wed 25	M. wrote me.

Thu 26

Fri 27

Sat 28   Mimi wrote me.

MARCH 1857

Sun 01

Mon 02   Wrote M L – miss R Brown.

Tue 03   Mimi wrote – wrote Mimi – Saw her in S.S.

Wed 04   rec a letter from Brown.

             Saw Mimi – gave her a note and got one from her.

Thu 05   a letter from Brown.

             saw Mimi – gave her a note and got one from her.

Fri 6   Mimi goes to B of A.

Sat 7   went to the gardens.

Sun 8

Mon 9   Tea at 144 Renfrew St.

Tue 10   Went to Edin.

Wed 11   Mrs White 5 Buccleugh St – Mrs Jones – McCall.

Fri 13   Diner.

Sat 14   Saw the gallery of paintings – Dine with McCall.

[no subsequent entries]

[Written on the fly-leaf at the end of the diary:]

I insist to have an explicite answer
to the questions you evaded
Who gave you the trinket
And is it true you are directly or
indirectly engaged to Mr M or anyone else but me.
I must insist on this answer

Appendix Two
Selected letters not introduced in evidence

POSTMARK: 13TH MAY 1856

To: Emile L'Angelier Esq., W.B. Huggins, 10 Bothwell Street, Glasgow.

Monday night

Beloved husband darling Emile. Something tells me you would not be pleased with my note this morning. I fear you would think it cold. I hope and trust to God your cold is better my husband dear. To think that you have got more cold coming to see me – me, your own Mimi, to have been the cause of your being worse, perhaps very much worse. I have blamed myself for bringing you – tell me how you are, dearest of my soul. I feel sad tonight, sorry – and yet I can not give a reason – but I have felt sad and dull all day. I have thought much of you my pet. When I review my past conduct, I hate myself. I have made many good resolutions but you will think I cannot keep them. You have no trust in me. This makes me sad – I pray that the day may come when Emile shall love and trust his wife. It shall be my endeavour to regain your lost love, to try and merit your love.

If you were to cease to love me, I know not what I should do. I would be miserable and unhappy for life. You think another would fill your place in my heart. You think I have no feelings. You think I am cold and indifferent. But Emile, never never could I love another as I do you. I love you my dearest with all the ardour of a woman's love. You are my life, my all.

I have promised to myself to behave well for your sake. Yes, Emile, for you my own true husband's sake. You have a right to order me to leave off all foolish practices – and I as your dear wife ought – and must obey you – I shall, for the future, do what I can to merit your esteem, your love. If you are angry with me, you will, I know, have reason – but I shall try to prevent your anger.

The very wind this night makes me weep. Oh, if only you were beside me tonight, I could talk to you. I was stupid the last night. Forgive me. I feel much love for you tonight. If my mother could only feel the love I have for you this night, she would give in – but I shall never make her to feel that – she is too cold, too worldly to feel that love. If she would only recall her youthful days but when I told her so, she minded not. I shall get no compassion from her. She will not give consent to our union, my poor dear Emile – I know it. I look at her often but I only get a cold look in return. She knows when I am thinking of you, my own my beloved my ever dear Emile.

I did not get anything from Jack – I was not five minutes with him. All the time I look forward to your dear and kind letter of Thursday. You cannot think what pleasure it gives me to hear from you my pet. Can you read this writing, it is as small as yours. I shall write you again this week – so I shall say Farewell with much love. I am thy own beloved thy very fond and ever devoted wife, Mimi.

P.S. I have read 'Meteors' and like it very much. I like to read articles on astronomy. I shall read 'Family on the Wing' – 'Blackwoods' for this month is very good. I have read it with pleasure – but I always like Blackwoods. Adieu, my love to you my husband dear – a kiss, a fond embrace from thine own Mimi. Excuse this very bad paper – there is no better thin paper to be had in Helensburgh.

POSTMARK: 3RD JULY 1856

To: M. L'Angelier, W.B. Huggins, 10 Bothwell Street, Glasgow.

Wednesday night

My own, my ever beloved Emile, I trust you got home safe. I was not heard by anyone, so I am safe. Were you, my dearest, any the worse for being out in the night air? Emile, perhaps I did wrong in taking you into my room – but are you not my husband? It can be no sin, dearest – but I won't do it again. I was so glad to see you darling. Would I could be ever with you to keep you company. You stayed so short, I got nothing said to you. I had thought of so many things to ask you about. But I hope, love, your next visit will be longer.

Emile, my husband, I have been thinking of all you said to me last night. Now, in the first place, I promise you I shall save as much of pin money as I can. I shall put it to many useful things. I shall spend the money I save in things I shall require when I am your wife. Will this please you? In the second place, I shall not go about as of old with Bessie. I shall go out before the afternoon. And in the next place, I shall not go to any public balls without your consent. Will this please you, my dear little husband? I shall try and do all I can to please you and keep your mind free – and do be happy – and, darling, if you continue to love me, I shall please you in many things.

Emile, if you go into the French Army, you know you will never return to Scotland – and, of course, I am your wife, and I can never be the wife of any other one. So my mind is made up. If you go, I shall go where no-one shall see me more. I shall be dead to the World. But dearest love, I trust we shall get on so that you won't go. I shall behave well for your dear sake. Yes, my own sweet Emile, I shall make you happy. You shall, some day I hope, say you have a faithful and loving wife. And my prayer shall be that you shall never regret taking me for your wife.

Emile, I often think we do not know each other much, that is, we do not know the temper and character of each other – we have never seen each other but under peculiar circumstances, so we shall have all that to study after our marriage. But I don't think dear love it shall be difficult to do. What do you say pet?

Papa is not down tonight. Only fancy, when I came in from a walk at luncheon, I found no less than ten strangers here this forenoon. The fine day brought a host of friends from Strome and Greenock. They all left with the last boat, so we are all alone tonight. Aunt goes home tomorrow. Bessie and I had an invitation this morning to join a picnic which is to be given to the officers of the 42nd at Stirling – but Mama said at once, No, which is a comfort for I would not have gone – I have a very great dislike of picnics. They are so stupid.

I am going to Perth the end of August or beginning of September. What a nice letter that is of Mrs L. How kind of you to send such nice plants. I can not get our gardener to get me the ferns. He always says he has some other thing to do, and tells me to wait until the winter. I have got a large glass shade and all but the ferns. But I expect them in time. I am beginning to know about flowers a little. I go with William (the gardener) every day and see how things are getting on. I have a pit of melons under my care just now. They are getting on very well. William's is a nice letter. When you write, give him my kindest love and send him a kiss from me. You won't object to that love dearest. I should so like to see him. I think, from his letters, he must be a very good young man. Serious, is he not? You are fortunate in having him for a friend. Was he in Glasgow?

I am now quite well – my cold is gone. I did as you told me – took medicine this morning – but I am quite well. I shall now say goodnight. It is later than when you left me last night. Adieu, my love, my good dear husband. I adore you more and more each time I see you. You were looking in my eyes very well last night. I forgot to tell you last night that I have had great pain in getting my first Wisdom tooth. So after I get them all, you will expect something like wisdom from me. Adieu sweet love, my fond embrace – a dear sweet kiss from your devoted and your truly loving your affectionate wife, your own dearest true Mimi.

POSTMARK: 4TH JULY 1856

To: Mr L'Angelier, at Mr Clark's, Royal Botanical Gardens, Glasgow

Thursday evening 12 o'clock, July 3rd '56

My own very much loved Emile, I have been thinking since I parted from you that I was cool to you on Tuesday. Did you think so, my sweet one? You stayed so short a time with me and the time did pass so quick – but it always does when I'm with you. Papa came home tonight. Only fancy, MacKenzie is to be with us on Saturday morning. What has brought him here again, I don't know. The house is to be full on Saturday – there is Captain Browne (from London) to be here I think. I hope, darling, you won't think that, because there are three military men with us, I shall flirt. Indeed, Emile, I shall not – this I promise you. So don't be annoyed about me. I shall be quite civil but I won't flirt. But you will say, 'ah Mimi, you make fine promises, promises which you break.' But really do believe me for once.

How are you, my own fond, my ever dearest Emile? Is your cold better? Do take care of yourself, for my sake. I feel quite happy that you are not going away to a far country. I shall do all that is in my power to prevent you going. I shall do what I promised in my last note (Wednesday night). I shall do all I can to please you – so that you may have more trust in me ere we are married. You have been kind and good to me. Not one in a thousand would have stood what you have done. I ought to do double for you. Oh, I shall try and please you – yes dearest, I shall. I am serious only don't be angry with me – but yet you can not help being angry when you see me thoughtless and cool to you. Mama thinks the best way to manage my temper is not to be angry at me, but just to speak to me.

How can you get away from Huggins to take De Mean's place? It is a pity about Madame De Mean. I hope she will soon be well. When is Mary to be home? Give her my love and say I hope she is not very much displeased with me. You do try and make some excuse for me to her, love. Oh Emile, how much I do love you – how happy I was with you the other night. But we must not so indulge again. What if anything was to occur. What would they say? But, darling, it is hard to resist the temptations of Love. My heart burns this night with love for you. I grow excited while I write you.

I long to be your wife then there shall be no danger. We may love each other. My love for you, sweet one, increases daily, ah hourly, Emile. You are my constant thought. Your name is ever on my lips. Many a time I feel inclined to call other people by your name, then I recollect and correct myself.

I told Papa tonight nothing would ever make me like Mr Minnoch. He said he did not want me to like him – but I know better. He has been with papa those last days in Town. He will be here tomorrow. You are my only love, the only one I can ever marry. I am your wife. You will not leave me, darling. I shall write you for Monday. Adieu, love, sweet kisses and fond embraces from thy own true and ever dear wife. Thy ever loving and ever devoted Mimi.

A kiss my pet, Adieu.

Appendix Three

George Wardle's will

Be It Known that George Young Wardle of Cliff Lawn Fowey in the County of Cornwall formerly of 8 Gordon Place, Campden Hill in the County of Middlesex died on the 11th day of September 1910 at Plymouth in the County of Devon

And Be It Further Known that at the date hereunder written the last Will and Testament with a Codicil thereto of the said deceased was proved and registered in the Principal Probate Registry of His Majesty's High Court of Justice, and that administration of all the estate which by law devolves to and vests in the personal representative of the said deceased was granted by the aforesaid Court to Frederick Darlington Wardle of 15 Bathwick Hill in the City of Bath, solicitor, nephew of the deceased, the sole executor named in the said Codicil.

Dated 21st day of December 1910
Gross value of the Estate £3674-1-0
Net value of Personal Estate £3623-5-3

(10 August 1904)
I George Young Wardle at present residing at 8 Gordon Place, Campden Hill in the County of London Esquire in order to settle the succession to my means and estate after my death Do hereby give grant assign dispone devise legate and bequeath to and in favour of George Gilbert Treherne

Treherneand Henry William Strickland both of No 28 Bedford Row London Gentlemen and to the acceptor or survivor of them and their or his successors in Office as Trustees or Trustee for the ends uses and purposes hereinafter specified (the persons or person acting for the time as Trustees or Trustee under these presents being hereinafter referred to as 'my Trustees') and to the assignees of my Trustees the whole means estate and effects heritable and moveable real and personal of every kind and wherever situated that shall belong or be addebted to me at the time of my death together with the whole writs titles vouchers and instructions thereof and I nominate and appoint my Trustees to be my Executors But it is hereby declared that these presents are granted in trust always for the ends uses and purposes following vidilicet

(First) I direct my Trustees to pay all my just and lawful debts deathbed and funeral charges and the expenses of executing this trust and also an immediate legacy of Fifty pounds to my Wife to defray the expense of her ante-nuptial Contract of marriage hereinafter mentioned

(Secondly) I direct my Trustees in the event of my said wife surviving me to hold the residue of my estate and to pay the free annual income or produce thereof to my said Wife during all the days of her life and that at such times and in such proportions as my Trustees may find most suitable and convenient

(Thirdly) Upon the death of my said Wife if she shall survive me or on my own death if she shall predecease me I direct my Trustees to divide and pay over the capital of said residue in equal shares to and between my son Thomas Edmund Wardle and my daughter Mrs Mary Rigby Wife of John Scarratt Rigby of No 75 Woodstock Road Bedford Park in the County of Middlesex Gentleman declaring (1) that if either of my said children shall predecease the survivor of my said Wife and me leaving issue such issue shall be entitled equally amongst them (if more than one) to the share whether original or accrescing as after mentioned to which their parent would have been entitled if alive (2) that if either of my said children shall predecease the survivor of my said Wife and me without leaving issue the share which would have fallen to such predeceaser shall accresce and be payable to the survivor or to his or her issue and (3) that the interests of my children and their issue shall not become vested in them until the death of the survivor of my said Wife and me

(Fourthly) In the event of my children and their issue all dying prior to the death of the survivor of my said Wife and me then I direct my Trustees to divide and pay over the capital of said residue and the accruing income to my nephew Frederick Darlington Wardle at present residing at 18 Cleveland Road Manningham in the County of York Esquire in acknowledgement of his services in the administration of the Trusts created by the Will of my Mother and by my Ante-nuptial Contract of Marriage next hereinafter referred to

(Fifthly) Whereas by Ante-nuptial Contract of Marriage dated fourth July One thousand eight hundred and sixty one between me and my said Wife therein named Miss Madeline Hamilton Smith I inter alia bound and obliged myself to effect an Insurance Policy or Policies of Insurance to be take in the names of the Trustees nominated by the said Contract namely John Hamilton Smith and Thomas Wardle which sum of One thousand pounds to be contained in the Policy or Policies so effected together with the whole additional sums of money that might accrue under the same by way of bonus accumulations or otherwise it was provided by the said Contract should be held by the Trustees under the Contract in trust for the purposes therein mentioned and inter alia after the decease of my said Wife in trust for behoof of the child or children to be born of the marriage thereby contracted and to be paid and made over to the said child or children (if more than one) and the issue of any who might have predeceased their Mother in such shares and proportions at such times and subject to such conditions restrictions and limitations as I which failing as my said Wife should appoint by any deed or writing under my or her hand

And whereas by the said Contract James Smith Esquire of Polmont Bank Architect in Glasgow father of my said Wife as a provision for her and her issue as therein mentioned bound and obliged himself and his heirs executors successors and representatives whomsoever within six months from the date of the Contract to pay to the Trustees named in the Contract the sum of Two thousand pounds with interest at five per centum per annum from the date of the solemnisation of the marriage thereby contracted to be held by the said Trustees for my said Wife and me in liferent as therein mentioned and after the decease of the survivor of her and me in trust for behoof of the issue of our marriage and also the issue of my said wife by any subsequent marriage as therein mentioned and with regard to the said principal sum of Two thousand pounds or the share thereof falling to the child or children of the marriage thereby contracted it was provided and agreed to that the same should be divided among the said children (if more than one) and the issue of such of then as might have predeceased in such shares and proportions at such times and subject to such conditions restrictions and limitations as I which failing as my said Wife should appoint by any deed or writing under my or her hand all as the said Contract which contains sundry other clauses in itself more fully bears

And whereas I duly insured my life for the said sum of One thousand ponds by effecting a Policy in the names of the Trustees under the said Contract with the North British and Mercantile Insurance Company which is dated fourth March One thousand eight hundred and sixty two and the said James Smith has also made payment to the said Trustees of the said sum of Two thousand pounds

And whereas there are two children of the marriage between my said Wife and me namely my said son and daughter And whereas I have lately spent and have undertaken further to spend various sums of money for the maintenance of my said daughter and have made no similar expenditure on account of my said Son I am therefore desirous of exercising the powers of appointment reserved to me by the said Contract with regard to the proceeds of the said Policy on my life and also with regard to the capital of the said sum of Two thousand pounds settled by the said James Smith subject to the life interest conferred upon my said Wife by the said Contract. Therefore I do hereby appoint the proceeds of the said Policy as follows namely

The trustees shall subject as aforesaid in the first place set aside and appropriate the sum of Five hundred pounds part of the proceeds of the said Policy and pay the same to my said son and in the next place shall pay and divide the residue of such proceeds unto and equally between my said son and daughter And I hereby also appoint the capital of the said sum of

Two thousand pounds to be divided between my said son and daughter in equal shares

And I declare that (1) that if either of my said children shall predecease the period of payment of their respective shares of the said Policy monies and the said sum of Two thousand pounds leaving issue such issue shall be entitled equally amongst them (if more than one) to the share whether original or accruing as aftermentioned to which their parent would have been entitled if alive and (2) that if either of my said children shall predecease the period of payment of their respective shares without leaving issue the share which would have fallen to such predeceaser shall accresce and be payable to the survivor of his or her issue

And I hereby declare that if after my death and that of my Wife in the event of her surviving me both my said son and daughter shall have died without leaving any issue then I hereby direct and appoint that the proceeds of the said Policy and the said sum of Two thousand pounds shall be paid and belong to the said Frederick Darlington Wardle

Provided nevertheless that if either or both of the sisters of my said Wife namely Bessie Smith and Janet Hamilton Smith should be then alive and in such case I direct and declare that the whole means estate and effects which shall have been derived or come to me through my said Wife shall go and belong to the said Bessie Smith and Janet Hamilton Smith or the survivor of them, the said Frederick Darlington Wardle in that case being only entitled to the proceeds of the Policy moneys

And I empower my Trustees to pay any sum falling by virtue of these presents to anyone who may not have attained majority when the same becomes payable to any person or persons who may be acting or willing to act Guardian or Guardians to such beneficiary although not legally appointed And I hereby expressly declare that the whole provisions herein contained in so far as in favour of or descending upon females shall be for their separate use and exclusive of the jus mariti right of administration and curatorial powers of their respective husbands

And I hereby provide and declare that the provisions herein contained in favour of my said Wife and children are and shall be accepted by them as in full of all that they respectively could ask or claim by virtue of the said

Contract of Marriage or otherwise by or through my decease And to enable my Trustees to carry out the purposes of this settlement and of any Codicil which I may make hereto I confer on them all requisite powers and particularly (but without prejudice to such generality) I empower them to retain the property and securities in which my means and estate may be invested at the time of my death and also whenever they think fit to sell realise and convert into money the whole estate or any part thereof (whether as left at my death or at any time invested) and to execute and deliver all deeds and writings necessary for divesting themselves of the premises as also from time to time to lend out or invest the trust funds or any part thereof upon good heritable security or in the purchase of stocks or shares in any Railway or other incorporated company where the liability of the shareholders is not unlimited or in the Mortgages or Debenture Bonds of such Companies or in the purchase of heritable property (such investments however being always made upon securities or Property within Great Britain) with power also to my Trustees to alter and vary the Trust investments from time to time

And I also empower my trustees to compromise or settle by arbitration or by the advise of Counsel all disputed claims competent to or against the Trust Estate and also to submit any question or difficulty which may arise out of these presents or in connection with the affairs of the Trust to one or more Counsel and to settle any such question or difficulty in accordance with the opinion which may be obtained without being liable to be called in question for so doing

And I declare that my Trustees shall be entitled to the fullest powers privileges and immunities usually conferred in such cases and according to the most liberal interpretation and particularly (without prejudice to said generality) I declare that they shall not be liable for omissions or singuli in solidum but each for his own actual intromissions only nor shall they be liable for the intromissions of any Factor or Law Agent Banker Broker or other person employed by them or for the securities upon which they may lend out or invest the trust funds or for any loss which may arise from the depreciation or failure of such securities

And I reserve my own liferent and full power to alter or revoke these presents in whole or in part And I consent to registration hereof for preservation And I declare that my Trustees and Executors may employ and pay a Solicitor or any other Agent to transact all the business of the Trust and that they shall be entitled to receive all usual professional charges and emoluments notwithstanding their acting as my Trustees and Executors.

In Witness whereof I have hereunto set my hand this tenth day of August One thousand nine hundred and four – George Young Wardle – SIGNED by the above named Testator George Young Wardle as and for his last Will and Testament in the presence of us both being present at the same time who at his request in his presence and in the presence of each other have hereunto subscribed our names as Witnesses – George D. Horton – Alf. J. Newell Clerks to Messrs Gadsden & Treherne 28 Bedford Row London WC

(4th September 1910)

I the before named George Young Wardle hereby revoke the appointment made in the foregoing of George Gilbert Treherne Treherne and Henry William Strickland as Trustees and Executors and I also revoke all the grants devises and bequests made to them and in their stead I appoint my said nephew Frederick Darlington Wardle now residing at 18 Bathwick Hill Bath to be my Trustee and Executor and I give grant assign dispone devise legate and bequeath to him and to his successors in office and to the assignees of my Trustee the whole means estate and effects heritable and moveable real and personal of every kind and wheresoever situated that shall belong or be addebted to me at the time of my death to be held by him as my Trustee and Executor in all respects as if he had been originally named in the foregoing in the place of the said George Gilbert Treherne Treherne and Henry William Strickland

And at his own request I hereby revoke all the dispositions in favour of the said Frederick Darlington Wardle contained in the foregoing so that on failure of the trusts hereinbefore contained my next of kin shall take Signed by me as a Codicil this fourth day of September One thousand nine hundred and ten – George Young Wardle – SIGNED by the Testator George Young Wardle as a Codicil to his Will in the presence of us both being present at the same time who at his request in his presence and in the presence of each other hereunto subscribe our names as Witnesses – Marion E.

Tabb, Sister-in-Charge, Friary Nursing Home Plymouth – Winnie Morris, Nurse, Friary Nursing Home Plymouth.

On the 21st day of December 1910 Probate of this will and Codicil was granted to Frederick Darlington Wardle the sole Executor.

Appendix Four

Janet's will

Trust Disposition and Settlement of Miss Janet Hamilton Smith

At Edinburgh the thirteenth day of June One thousand nine hundred and twenty two the Deed hereinafter Engrossed was presented for registration in the Books of the Lords of Council and Session for preservation and is registered in the said Books as follows:-

I, Miss JANET HAMILTON SMITH, residing at Belmont Falkirk for the settlement of my affairs, Do hereby Assign and Dispone to and in favour of James Dykes Black, Thomas Walter Donald and James MacGregor Reid, all Writers in Glasgow and such other person or persons as may hereafter be nominated by me or assumed into the Trust hereby created and the acceptors and acceptor, survivors and survivor of them the major number of them accepting and surviving and resident in Great Britain from time to time being a quorum and the heir of the survivor as Trustees and Trustee for the ends uses and purposes aftermentioned (the said Trustees and their foresaids and their quorum being hereafter referred to as 'my Trustees') All and Sundry the whole estate heritable and moveable real and personal which may belong to me or of which I may have the power of disposal by mortis causa deed or otherwise at the time of my decease with the Writs, Titles and Vouchers thereof And I nominate and appoint my Trustees to be my Executors and Executor But these presents are granted in trust always for the ends, uses and purposes following vizt:-

In the First Place for payment of all my just and lawful debts sickbed and funeral expenses and also of the expenses of every kind connected with the Execution of the Trust hereby created:

In the Second Place for payment and fulfilment of all such Legacies or Bequests Instructions or Directions as I my leave bequeath or give by any Codicil hereto or by any Writing under my hand (however informally executed or defective) showing my wishes and intentions

In the Third Place for payment and fulfilment at the first term of Whitsunday or Martinmas that shall occur six months after my death or as soon thereafter as my Trustees may find convenient of the following legacies free of legacy duty vizt:-

(First) the sum of three hundred pounds to the Rector for the time at the date of my death of Christ Church Episcopal Church, Falkirk to be used by him for such purposes in connection with the said Church, as he in his sole discretion may think proper,

(Second) the sum of two hundred pounds to Miss Margaret Evelyn Paterson, residing at twenty five Bryanston Street, Portman Square, London,

(Third) the sum of One hundred pounds to Katherine Henery, Domestic Servant in my service and that whether or not she may be in my employment at the time of my death,

(Fourth) the sum of fifty pounds to Miss Elsie Aitken, residing at Gartcows House, Falkirk,

(Fifth) the sum of fifty pounds to each of Misses Harriet Elsie Fraser and Agnes Fraser both daughters of Dr. Alexander Duncan Fraser residing at Stratheric, Falkirk,

(Sixth) the sum of fifty pounds to Miss Janet Sinclair residing at Ardlea, Kersland Drive, Milngavie,

(Seventh) the sum of fifty pounds to Agnes Sutherland formerly domestic servant in my employment now residing at five Bowling Green Place, Bonnybridge,

(Eighth) the sum of Ten pounds to Margaret Jeffrey, domestic servant in my service and that whether or not she maybe in my employment at the time of my death

(Ninth) the sum of three hundred pounds to the Glasgow and West of Scotland Society for the Prevention of Cruelty to Animals, and

(Tenth) the sum of One hundred pounds to the Falkirk District Nursing Association it being declared that the receipts of the said Rector and of the Treasurers for the time of the said Society and Association shall be a sufficient discharge to my Trustees for the said Legacies paid to them respectively

In the Fourth Place, I direct my Trustees to hold, apply, pay and convey the whole residue and remainder of the means and estate hereinbefore conveyed for behoof of my sister, Mrs Madeline Hamilton Smith or Wardle, Widow, presently resident in the United States of America, in liferent for her liferent alimentary use allenarly and for her children jointly with the issue per stirpes of such of them as may die leaving issue, equally in fee, declaring that the provisions hereinbefore conceived in favour of the children and remoter issue of the said Mrs Madeline Hamilton Smith or Wardle shall not vest in or be payable to them until the death of the said Mrs Madeline Hamilton Smith or Wardle, and as regards her children until they respectively attain the age of twenty one years in the case of sons or attain that age or be married whichever event shall first happen in the case of daughters declaring further that in the event of any of the children of the said Mrs Madeline Hamilton Smith or Wardle predeceasing me or surviving me but dying before acquiring a vested interest in my estate leaving lawful issue such issue shall be entitled equally among them per stirpes to the share or shares original and accrescing to which their parent would have been entitled if in life, and in the event of any of said children predeceasing me or surviving me but dying before acquiring a vested interest as aforesaid, without leaving lawful issue the share or shares original and accrescing which would have fallen to such predeceaser on survivance shall fall to the surviving children jointly with the issue per stirpes of any of them who may have died leaving issuer such issue taking always equally among them per stirpes the share to which their parent would have boon entitled if in life declaring further that my Trustees shall have full power in their own absolute discretion notwithstanding what is before written to pay to the said Mrs Madeline Hamilton Smith or Wardle the whole or any part of the Capital or fee of the residue liferented by her and that for any purpose which my Trustees may think proper:

And In the Last Place in the event of the children and remoter issue of the said Mrs Madeline Hamilton Smith or Wardle predeceasing me or all failing to take the said residue, in terms of these presents hereby direct my Trustees to apply, pay and convey the said residue among such charitable Institutions in Glasgow as they may in their own absolute discretion select: And Whereas under the Trust Disposition and Deed of Settlement of my father the late James Smith, Senior, of Polmont Bank, Architect in Glasgow, dated twenty seventh July Eighteen hundred and sixty two and registered in the Books of Council and Session on twenty second January Eighteen hundred and sixty four I have an absolute power of disposal of the sum of three thousand pounds which by the said Trust Disposition and Deed of Settlement he directed to be laid aside and invested for my use and behoof in liferent I hereby expressly declare that these presents are subject to the declaration underwritten, intended to operate as an exercise by me of the said power of disposal:

And whereas the said sum of Three thousand pounds was in the year Eighteen hundred and seventy six invested in a Bond and Disposition in Security over subjects in Blackburn Street, Glasgow: And Whereas the Trustees of my said father of whom I am one have been unable to obtain repayment of the said loan and have been in informal possession of the said property for many years I hereby specially declare that the investment representing the said provision of three thousand pounds or the proceeds thereof as and when it shall be realised shall be taken as it stands as at my death and as at the period of vesting of the fee of the residue of my estate and shall be accepted in full of the said provision of three thousand pounds: And I further provide and declare that in the event of any person who may be interested in my Estate whether as liferenter or fiar repudiating this declaration and condition he or she shall ipso facto forfeit him or her whole right and interest under these presents and shall not be entitled to succeed to any share of the said sum of three thousand pounds or the proceeds thereof or of my own personal means and estate, and the share destined to any person or persons so repudiating shall thereupon fall into and form part of the residue of my means and estate:

Declaring also that the provisions hereinbefore conceived or which may be conceived in any Codicil or other writing by me in favour of or which may devolve upon females shall be exclusive of the jus mariti and right of administration of any husbands they may have married or may marry and shall not be affectable for such husbands debts or deeds or attachable by the diligence and execution of such husbands Creditors And I do hereby nominate and appoint my Trustees to be Tutors and Curators or Tutor and Curator to all persons taking benefit under these presents who may be in pupillarity or minority and who may not have any Tutors or Curators quoad such benefit during their respective pupillarities and minorities:

And without prejudice to the powers privileges and immunities conferred upon Trustees by any Act of Parliament applicable to Scotland or to which Trustees may be entitled at common law all of which in so far as not inconsistent herewith are hereby conferred upon the said Trustees, Executors, Tutors and Curators I hereby authorise my Trustees to sue and defend all actions connected with the Trust Estate in any Court of Law:

To sell feu and dispose of the whole or any part of the Trust Estate either by public roup or private bargain with or without advertisement and at such price or prices and for such feu duties or ground annuals as they may determine:

To excamb any portion of my Heritable Estate if they find it necessary or expedient to do so: To grant leases of any duration they my think proper of the said Heritable Estate or any portion thereof:

To borrow money on the security of the Trust Estate and grant in favour of the Creditors Bonds and Dispositions in Security containing powers of Sale ex facie absolute Dispositions and such other Deeds Writings and

Securities affecting the Trust Estate as they may think proper and to invest the Trust funds in the purchase or on the security of lands houses feu duties or ground annuals or other heritable property or in the shares or stock ordinary. preference or guaranteed or on bonds or mortgages or debentures or debenture Stock of any Incorporated or Joint Stock Companies or Public Trusts whether British Colonial foreign and to realise and change the said Investments from time to time:

Declaring that my Trustees shall be entitled to continue undisturbed in their own names all such investments as I my have made notwithstanding that these investments may not be such as they are hereby empowered to make and to accept and pay for new or additional shares or stock or debentures to which they may become entitled as holders of any of said investments: Declaring that purchasers lenders and all other parties paying money to my Trustees shall have no concern with the application thereof or with the purposes of this Trust:

Further I empower my Trustees to appoint any one or more of their own number to be Factor or Factors under them or to be Law Agent or Law Agents for the Trust and to allow such Factor or Factors a reasonable remuneration for their trouble and such Law Agent or Law Agents their professional charges:

And in general I empower my Trustees to do everything which in their discretion they may conceive to be for the interest of my Estate: And I declare that my Trustees Executors Tutors and Curators shall not be liable for the intromissions of any Factors or Agents whom they may appoint or employ if habit and repute responsible at the time of appointment nor for any Banks or Bankers in which or in whose hands they may deposit the Trust funds nor for the sufficiency of any security or investment which they may take or make in connection with the Trust in terms of the powers hereby conferred upon them: And I reserve my own liferent use and enjoyment of my said Estate: And I reserve power at any time to alter, innovate or revoke these presents: And I dispense with the delivery hereof:

And I consent to Registration hereof for preservation IN WITNESS WHEREOF these presents written on this and the three preceding pages by Lawrence Gillespie, Clerk to McGrigor, Donald and Company,

Writers in Glasgow are (under the declaration that the word 'Margaret' in the thirty-first line of page first is written on erasure) subscribed by me at Belmont aforesaid on the tenth day of January Nineteen hundred and fourteen before these witnesses the Reverend Francis Ellington Wright, Rector of Christchurch Episcopal Church, Falkirk, and Ada MacKenzie, Housekeeper at Christchurch Rectory there.

(Signed)

Hamilton Janet Hamilton Smith

Francis Ellington Wright

Witness Ada Mackenzie Witness.

I Miss Janet Hamilton Smith the granter of the foregoing Trust Disposition & Settlement do hereby make the following alterations thereupon vizt: I cancel and revoke the Legacies provided by the third trust purpose of my said Trust Disposition & Settlement excepting only those provided (fifth) to the Misses Fraser and those immediately hereinafter referred to: And I increase the Legacy provided to Katherine Henery to Three Hundred Pounds Sterling and I reduce the Legacy provided to Miss Margaret Evelyn Paterson to One Hundred Pounds; Further I bequeath a Legacy of Ten Pounds to Michael McGowan presently occupying the Lodge at Belmont on the terms & conditions stated in the said third trust purpose: And with this Codicil & subject to the alterations thereby effected I confirm my said Trust Disposition & Settlement IN WITNESS WHEREOF I have subscribed these presents written on this & part of the preceding page, at Falkirk on the Twenty third day of May Nineteen hundred & seventeen before these witnesses James MacGregor Reid, Writer in Glasgow, and Mrs. Margaret Henery, Widow, presently residing with me at Belmont, Falkirk. Declaring that the word First in the second line of this page is deleted

(Signed)

Janet H. Smith

James M. Reid

Witness Margaret Henery Witness

Belmont 10th June 1919

Dear Mr. Reid

I wish you and Mr. Donald to have the Silver and Black Bowl. I don't
wish it sold. Please accept it with Kindest regards from
Yours sincerely and gratefully
(Signed) J.H. Smith

I MISS JANET HAMILTON SMITH, the granter of the foregoing Trust
Disposition and Settlement and Codicil Do hereby make the following
alterations thereupon namely

(first) I increase the Legacy provided to Katherine Henery to Five hundred
Pounds sterling and with reference to that Legacy I empower my Trustees
in their sole discretion at any time before actual payment notwithstanding anything provided in my said Trust Disposition and Settlement and
Codicil

(a) to postpone payment of the whole or any part of the said Legacy
for such period or periods as they may from time to time think proper on
paying to the said Katherine Henery the revenue thereof or

(b) to restrict the interest of the said Katherine Henery therein in
whole or in part either temporarily or permanently to a liferent alimentary interest not assignable by her or affectable by her debts or deeds or
attachable by the diligence or execution of her creditors and to hold the
fee for behoof of such person or persons in such shares and proportions
as the said Katherine Henery may appoint by any testamentary writing
under her hand and failing any such appointment for behoof of her heirs
in mobilibus or

(c) to end the whole or any part of the said Legacy in the purchase from
an Insurance Company of good repute of an annuity for behoof of the
said Katherine Henery either payable to themselves as Trustees foresaid
in which case such annuity shall be strictly alimentary and not assignable by the said Katherine Henery or affectable by her debts or deeds or
attachable by the diligence or execution of her creditors, or payable to the
said Katherine Henery herself as my Trustees in their sole discretion may

consider desirable: And I declare that in the event of my Trustees purchasing an annuity for behoof of the said Katherine Henery her claim in respect of the said Legacy or such part thereof as may have been expended in the purchase shall be limited to her remedy against the Insurance Company and she shall have no further claim in respect of the said Legacy or the part thereof so expended as the case may be against my Trustees or the remainder of my estate

(second) I increase the Legacy provided to Michael McGowan to Fifty Pounds

(third) I bequeath a Legacy of Two Hundred Pounds to my friend Miss Ada Mackenzie residing at Twenty-eight Chalmers Street, Edinburgh, in recognition of her many kindnesses to me and that on the terms and conditions stated in the third purpose of my said Trust Disposition and Settlement;

(fourth) I leave and bequeath the sum of Five Hundred Pounds to the Glasgow and West of Scotland Society for the Prevention of Cruelty to Animals; Declaring that the receipt of the Treasurer for the time of the said Society shall be a sufficient discharge to my Trustees for the said Legacy: And with these alterations I confirm my said Trust Disposition and Settlement and Codicil: IN WITNESSS WHEREOF this Codicil is subscribed by me at Falkirk on the Fourth day of March Nineteen Hundred and Twenty two before these Witnesses Miss Margaret Grant, Saint Francis Rectory, Hope Street, Falkirk, and Edward Gregory Henery, Sectional Foreman with the Anglo American Oil Company Limited Grangemouth and residing at
Belmont, Callander Road, Falkirk.
(Signed) Janet H. Smith
Margaret Grant Witness
Edward Gregory Henery Witness ...
Belmont 30th March 1922

Dear Mr. Reid

I hope this will be all right. I will like to know you and Mr Donald have the silver. I enclose my sisters address; same will always find her son. Mrs. Rigby's can always be got from Mr. Fred. Wardle; his address I also enclose.

With Kindest regards
Yours very sincerely
(Signed) J.H. Smith.

Silver
23 Large Silver spoons
17 Small Silver spoons
30 Large Silver Forks
11 Small Silver Forks
12 Fish-Knives & Forks
8 Fruit 'white handle' Knives & Forks
12 Tea Spoons
6 Small tea Spoons
Entree Dish with extra dish cover & handle
Vegetable Dish
Breakfast Dish
Egg Stand with six Cups & five spoons
Small cruet
Toast rack
Cream Jug
Silver Sugar Box & tongs
1 Pair Sugar Tongs
1 Butter Knife with white handle
1 Tea Pot
2 Silver Butter Dishes with plates lids & handles & Glass fittings
2 Silver Butter Knives
2 Silver Salt cellars with spoons
1 Pepper pot

1 Mustard pot with china fitting & spoon

4 Silver Trays

1 Silver Lamp

1 Wine cooler

1 Port wine Strainer

1 Fish Slice

1 Cream Ladle

1 Crumb Spoon

1 Pair nut crackers

1 Reading Lamp

… [Written on envelope]

James M. Reid Esq.

172 St. Vincent Street

Glasgow

At Glasgow the twelfth day of June Nineteen hundred and twenty two In Presence of Walter Nelson Esquire One of His Majesty's Justices of the Peace for the County of the City of Glasgow Compeared Peter McMurdo of 172 St. Vincent Street, Glasgow, Cashier and James Thomas Steven of 172 St. Vincent Street, Glasgow Assistant Cashier, who being solemnly sworn and examined depone That they are well acquainted with the hand writing of the deceased Miss Janet Hamilton Smith who resided at Belmont, Falkirk , and have seen and examined the foregoing list of Silver, and that to the best of their knowledge and belief the same is entirely in the handwriting of the said Miss Janet Hamilton Smith

   (Signed) P. McMurdo Jas. T. Steven Sworn by the above named Peter McMurdo & James Thomas Steven at Glasgow in the County of Lanark this twelfth day of June Nineteen hundred and twenty two Before me (Signed) Walter Nelson Justice of Peace for County of City of Glasgow.

Typewritten by:- Jessie Allan Stevenson

Collated by:- Geo. A. N. Ironside

Appendix Five

Births, Deaths and Marriages

18 Sep 1757   Christening, in Alloa, of (Madeleine's paternal great-grandmother) Janet Dempster. Parents: John Dempster and Janet Laky

22 May 1763   Marriage, in Glasgow, of (Madeleine's maternal great-grandparents) William Hamilton, mason, and Helen Liddel

11 May 1768   Birth of (Madeleine's maternal grandfather) David Hamilton. Parents: William Hamilton, mason, and Helen Liddell

01 Mar 1772   Marriage, in Alloa, of (Madeleine's paternal great-grand-parents) Thomas Thomson, maltster, and Isabel Morrison

02 Apr 1778   Birth of (Madeleine's maternal grandmother) Magdalene Marshall. Parents: John Marshall, residenter (vintner), and Mary Miller

03 Nov 1780   Marriage, in Alloa, of (Madeleine's paternal great-grandparents) James Smith, mason, and Janet Dempster

08 Nov 1781   Birth, in Alloa, of (Madeleine's paternal grandfather) John Smith. Parents: James Smith, mason, and Janet Dempster

06 Feb 1785   Christening, Alloa, of (Madeleine's paternal grand-mother) Elizabeth (Betty) Thomson. Parents: Thomas Thomson and Isabel Morrison

05 May 1794	Marriage of (Madeleine's maternal grandparents) David Hamilton (mason) and Magdaline Marshall
04 Jan 1806	Marriage of (Madeleine's paternal grandparents) John Smith (mason) and Elizabeth Thomson
12 Aug 1806	Birth, in Alloa, of (Madeleine's father) James Smith, (baptised on 19th). Parents: John Smith (mason) and Elizabeth Thomson
10 Mar 1812	Birth of (Madeleine's mother) Janet Hamilton. Parents: David Hamilton, architect, and Magdalene Marshall
01 May 1817	Birth of Mary Arthur Perry. Parents: William Perry and Helen Todd
25 Nov 1820	Birth, in Wigtown, of William Harper Minnoch. Parents: Alexander Minnoch and Susan Harper
09 Oct 1821	Death, at age eighteen, of David, son of David Hamilton, architect
11 Oct 1821	Death, at age twenty-four, of William, son of David Hamilton, Architect
17 Jul 1822	Marriage, in St Helier, Jersey, of Pierre Francoise L'Angelier and Victoire Melanie de la Croix
24 Dec 1822	Death, in Alloa, of (Madeleine's great-grandfather) James Smith, builder, father of John Smith, builder
30 Apr 1823	Birth, in St Helier, Jersey, of Pierre Emile L'Angelier. Parents: Pierre Francoise L'Angelier and Victoire Melanie de la Croix. Baptised 1 May, St Thomas R.C. Church
01 Aug 1830	Pierre Emile L'Angelier, second baptism, as Anglican, in St Helier's Church
24 Mar 1833	Marriage, Glasgow parish, of James Smith, timber merchant, and Janet Hamilton. (Madeleine's parents)
26 Mar 1833	Marriage (second ceremony) of James Smith and Janet Hamilton, at Buchanan Street, Barony parish. (Madeleine's parents)
29 Mar 1835	Birth, at 167 Regent Street, Glasgow, of Magdalene (Madeleine) Hamilton Smith. Parents: James Smith and Janet Hamilton

09 Apr 1835   Birth, at Cardross, of Mary Buchanan (Madeleine's best friend). Parents: Robert Buchanan, surgeon, and Mary Knox Dixon

23 Mar 1836   Birth, at Leek, Staffordshire, of George Young Wardle. Parents: Hugh and Elizabeth Wardle

25 Jan 1837   Birth, at 167 Regent Street, of Betsy Smith (Madeleine's sister)

07 Feb 1839   Birth, at Bedford Place (Renfrew Street), of John Smith (Madeleine's brother)

02 Oct 1840   Birth of David Hamilton Smith

12 Nov 1840   Death, at Bedford Place, of David Hamilton Smith (aged one month)

– Feb 1842˙   Birth, at Birkenshaw, Eastwood, Renfrewshire, of James Smith (Madeleine's brother)

01 Mar 1842   Burial, at St Helier, of Pierre Francoise L'Angelier (aged fifty-two years, ten months)

– Jun 1843   Birth, at Birkenshaw, Eastwood, Renfrewshire, of Janet Smith (Madeleine's sister)

05 Dec 1843   Death of David Hamilton, architect (age seventy-five)

23 Nov 1849   Death, at Columbia Place, of Magdalene Marshall Hamilton (Madeleine's grandmother)

23 Mar 1857   Death of Pierre Emile L'Angelier

31 Mar 1857   Madeleine charged with murder

29 Apr 1858   Marriage, in Glasgow, of William Harper Minnoch and Mary Aitken

04 Jul 1861   Marriage of Madeleine Hamilton Smith of 72 Sloane Street, Chelsea, to George Wardle, artist, of 5 Bloomfield Terrace, London. Witnesses: H. Haverlock and James Smith

22 Nov 1861   Death, at 71 Grove Street of James Hamilton, architect, son of David Hamilton, architect, and Magdalene Marshall

27 May 1862   Birth of Mary Wardle. Parents: George Wardle and Madeleine Smith

30 Nov 1863   Birth, at Southwold, Suffolk, of Tom Edmund Wardle. Parents: George Young Wardle, artist, and Madeleine Smith

30 Dec 1863   Death of James Smith, architect

09 May 1887   Death of James Smith (Madeleine's brother)

01 Sep 1888   Marriage of Thomas Edmund Wardle, (dramatic agent – professional name: Thomas Edmunds), of 9 Charlotte Street, Bedford Square, and Annita Bied Charreton, (singer – professional name: Anna di Fiori) of 7 St Anne's Gardens, Queens Crescent, London. Annita's father's name: Alfonso Charreton

13 May 1889   Marriage of Mary Wardle (parents: George Wardle and Madeleine Smith) and John Scarratt Rigby, artist, both residing at 9 Charlotte Street, Bedford Square, London

13 Oct 1889   Birth, at 9 Charlotte Street, of Stephen Rigby, parents: John Scarratt Rigby and Mary Rigby, nee Wardle

08 May 1891   Birth, at 47 Hunter Street, Bloomsbury, of Violet Wardle. Parents: Thomas Edmund Wardle, journalist, and Annita Christina Wardle née Charreton

09 Dec 1894   Death, at Belmont, Falkirk, of Mrs Janet Smith (Madeleine's mother), at age eighty-two

01 May 1899   Death, at Belmont, Falkirk, of John Smith (Madeleine's brother, Jack), wine merchant

08 Mar 1910   Death, at Belmont, Falkirk, of Elizabeth (Bessie) Smith, accountant, aged sixty-eight

11 Sept 1910   Death, at North Friary Nursing Home, Plymouth, of George Wardle aged seventy-four – of Cliff Lawn, Fowey, Cornwall

20 May 1922   Death, at Belmont, Falkirk, of Janet Smith, (Madeleine's sister) aged seventy-two

12 Apr 1928   Death, in New York, of Lena Sheehy

Index

If you are interested in purchasing other books published by Tempus, or in case you have difficulty finding any Tempus books in your local bookshop, you can also place orders directly through our website

www.tempus-publishing.com